A Folk Carved Nativity

Donna Hefty

Photography by Marc Hefty

Step-by-step to a beautiful Christmas heirloom, with 11 detailed patterns

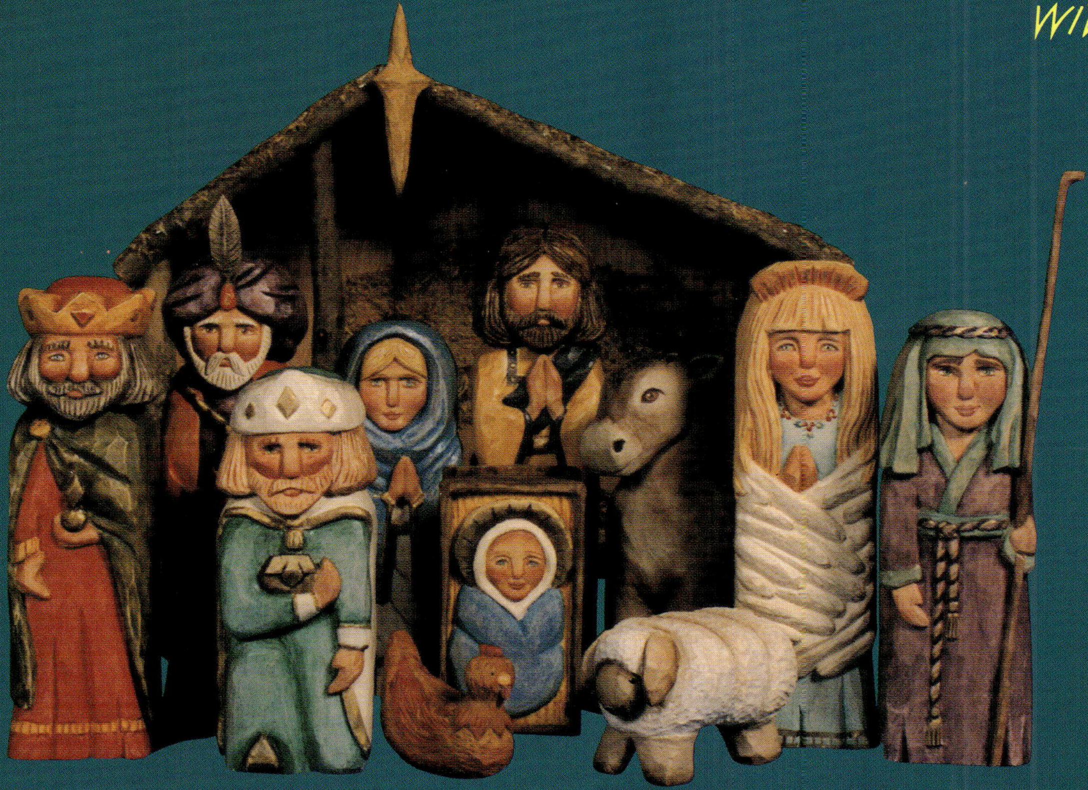

Schiffer Publishing Ltd

77 Lower Valley Road, Atglen, PA 19310

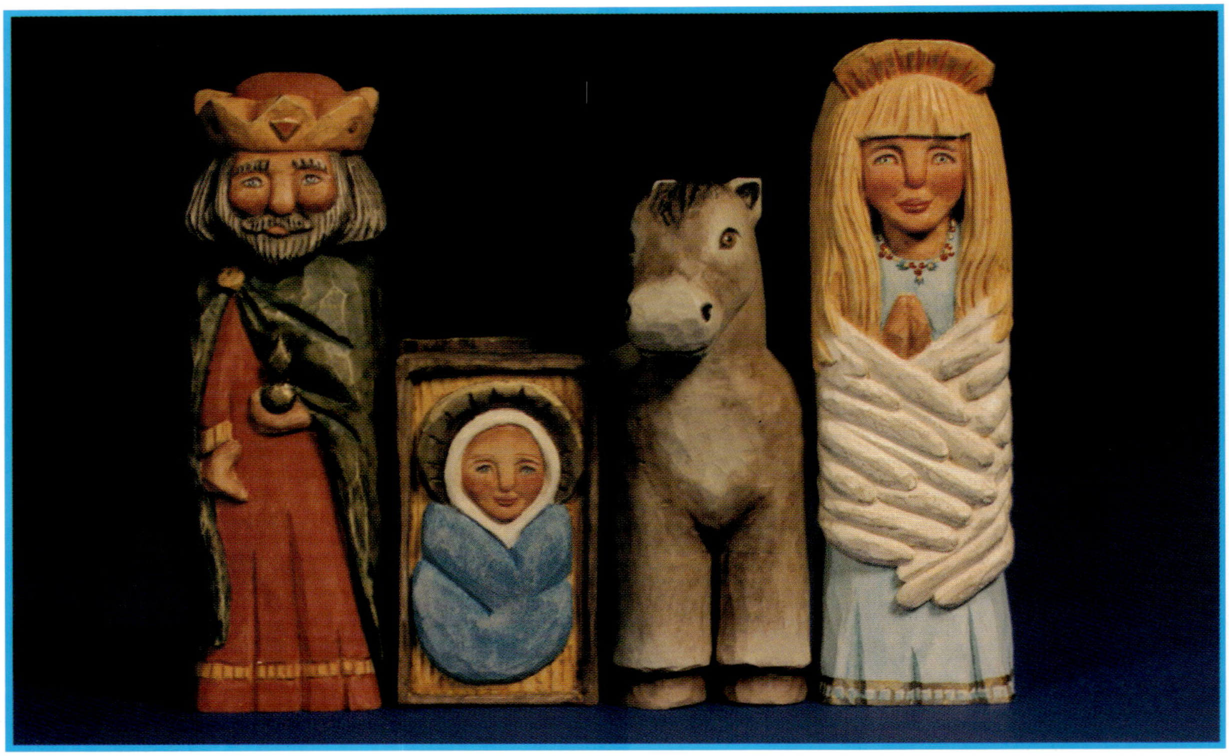

Printed in China

ISBN: 0-88740-881-8

Book Design by Audrey L. Whiteside.

Published by Schiffer Publishing, Ltd.
77 Lower Valley Road
Atglen, PA 19310
Please write for a free catalog.
This book may be purchased from the publisher.
Please include $2.95 postage.
Try your bookstore first.

We are interested in hearing from authors
with book ideas on related subjects.

Library of Congress Cataloging-in-Publication Data

Hefty, Donna.
A folk carved nativity: carved with simplicity and charm/Donna Hefty; photography by Marc Hefty.
p. cm. -- (A Schiffer book for woodcarvers)
ISBN 0-88740-881-8
1. Wood-carving. 2. Wood-carved figurines.
3. Crèches (Nativity scenes) in art. I. Title II. Series.
TT199.7.H44 1995
731'.8853--dc20 95-24047
CIP

CONTENTS

INTRODUCTION

It is a thrill to share with you a small corner of the wonderful world of wood carving. I would like to take you step by step through a carving, just as I would if you were attending one of my classes. I chose four pieces to carve for you: King I, Donkey, Angel, and Jesus. Though all of them are fairly simple, these four will pose the greatest challenge. If you can carve these, you can easily carve the rest. We will start with wood and pattern transfers, then take you from carving through the very important painting process.

The Nativity set has been very popular. It is simple, fun and well liked by both children and adults. I think you will enjoy this folk style of carving. Good luck and remember, just sit back, relax and enjoy. You will be amazed at the results, while creating a family heirloom to hand down for generations.

I would like to hear from you. If you have any questions or inquiries, please write to me at: 2021 South Higgins Avenue, Missoula, MT 59801 or phone at (406)543-5075.

Basic Tool Instruction

-The chip carving knife has a short blade which makes it easy and safe to score your lines creating stop cuts.

-The straight edge carving knife is used to round off heads, shoulders, edges, etc.

-The large gouge is used to create carve marks for a folk carved look.

-The small gouge is used to texture the sheep.

-The skew is used for narrow angled areas.

-The chisel is used to round and remove wood to your score lines or stop cuts.

-The small chisel is used for detail.

-The V-parting tool is used for hair texture.

Each person will hold these tools a bit differently. If you are a new carver, you will find the most comfortable position for yourself. Learning all your tools seems impossible, but, as I tell my students "You will learn your tools as the need arises. The more you carve, the more familiar you will become."

The Importance of Sharp Tools

Sharp tools are a pleasure to carve with. They are safer because they slice through the wood easily. If tools are not sharp, you will find yourself struggling to cut through the wood and can easily slip and cut your hand instead.

Learning to sharpen your tools takes time, patience, and skill. If you have trouble, there are many professional sharpeners who will sharpen them for you. There are also books which will show you how.

Once your tools are sharp, you can maintain that edge by stropping often during carving. You can purchase a strop and honing compound at your local hobby or craft store. You can also make your own using an old leather belt glued to a piece of wood. Stropping is the same theory as the corner barber sharpening his razor on a razor strop.

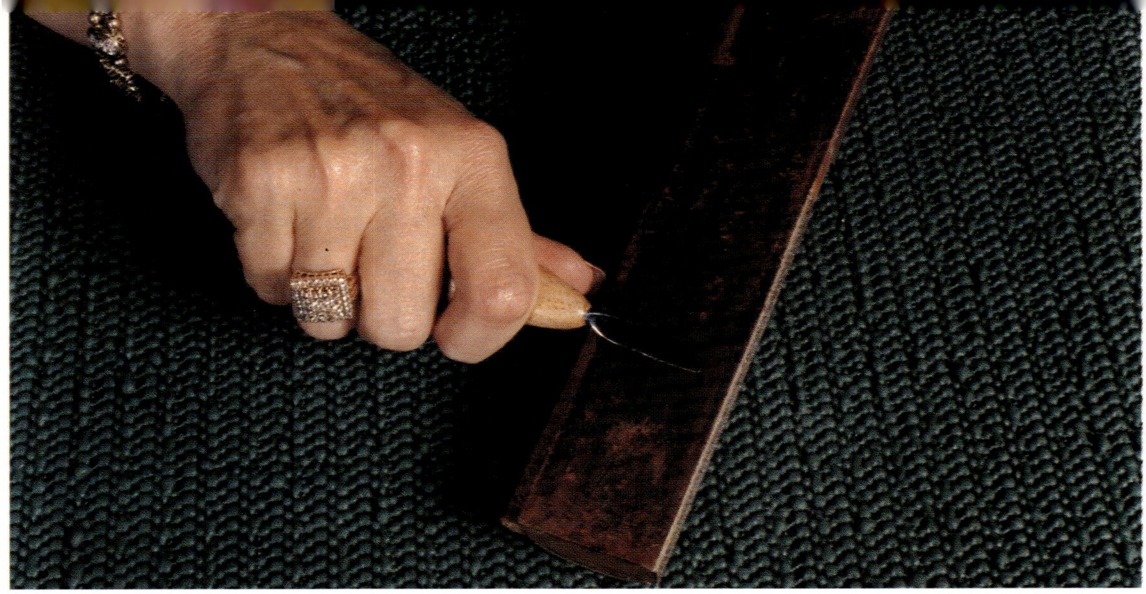

By stropping often, you will maintain the edge.

The Wood

I have used bass wood to carve this set. The reason I chose bass wood was that it is easily detailed and has a fine grain which finishes smooth for painting. You can also purchase bass wood at your local hobby or craft store. The entire Nativity Set is carved from 5 - 2″ x 2″ x 12″ pieces which are a standard size. You need a piece of 1.2″ x 1/2″ x 12″ bass for the shepherd's staff, donkey's tail, and King III's hat feather.

Tools

Chip carving knife
Straight edged carving knife
3/4″ Gouge
3/8″ Gouge
3/8″ Skew
3/8″ Chisel
3/16″ Chisel
1/8″ V-Parting Tool

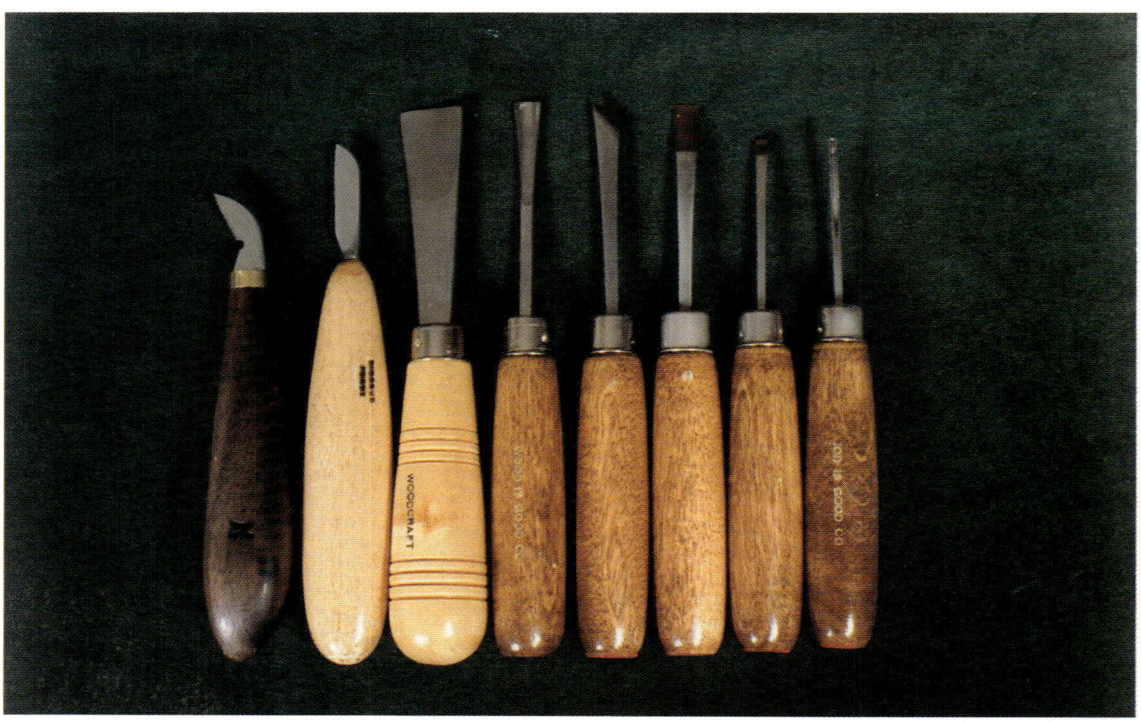

Supplies

5 pieces of 2″ x 2″ x 12″ bass wood
1 piece of 1/2″ x 1/2″ x 12″ bass wood
Hand Saw
Tracing Paper
Graphite Paper
Wood Glue
Wood Putty
Fine Sandpaper
1/2″ Flat Brush
#1 Liner
Wood Sealer
Paper Palette
Acrylic Paint according to pattern
Matte Finish Spray

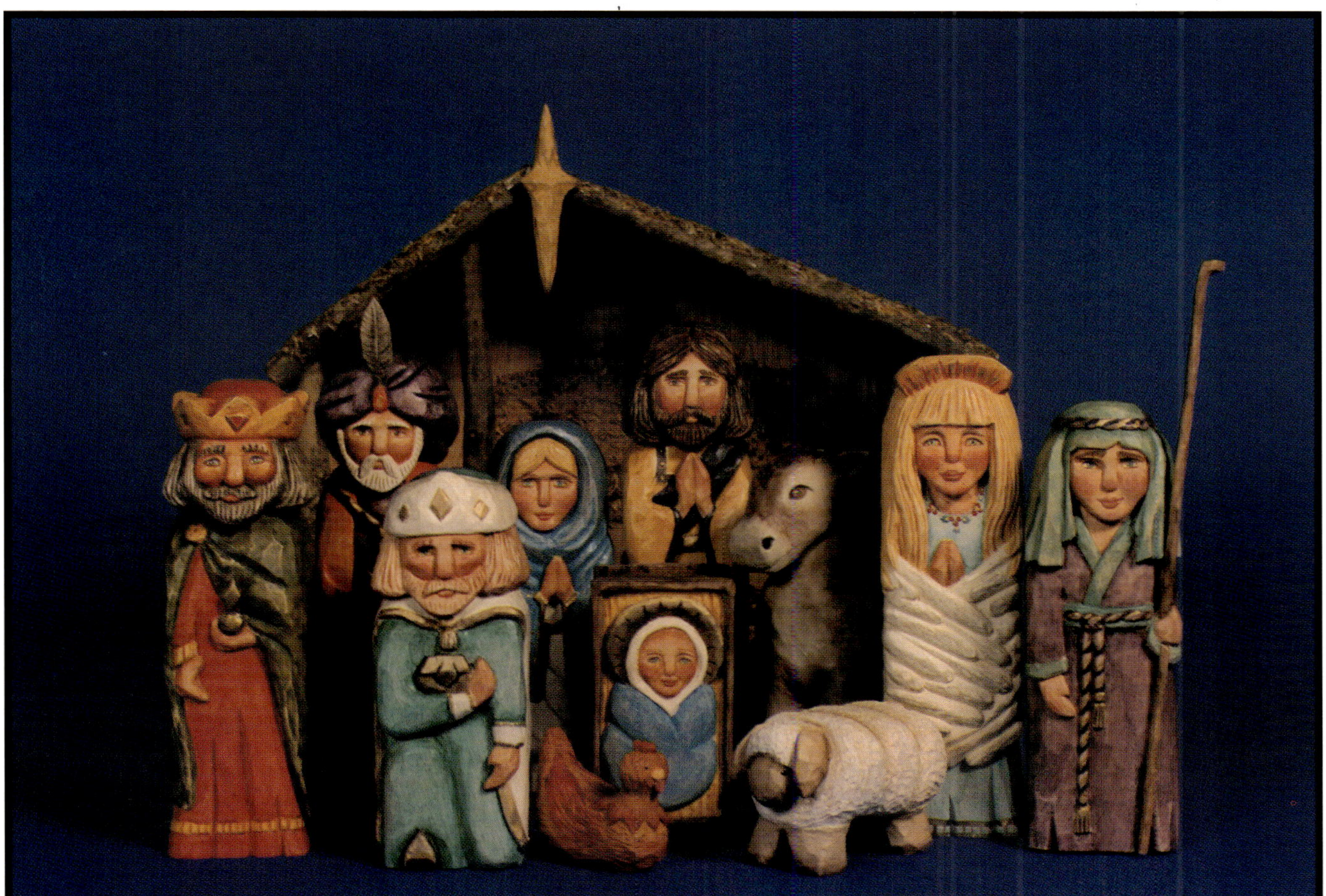

The complete Nativity Set.

CARVING KING I

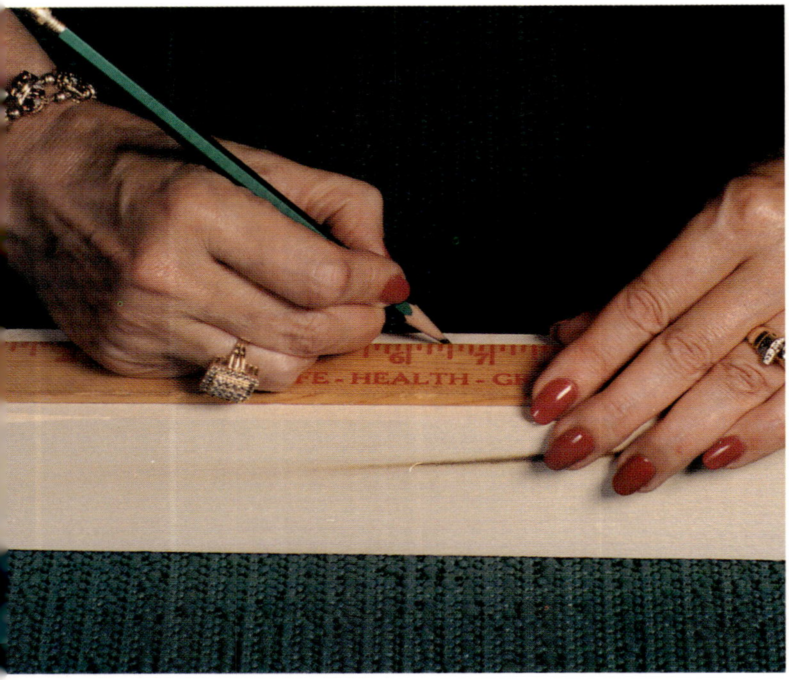

Cut from 2″ x 2″ x 12″ bass wood, King I is 6.5″. Measure and mark the wood for cutting.

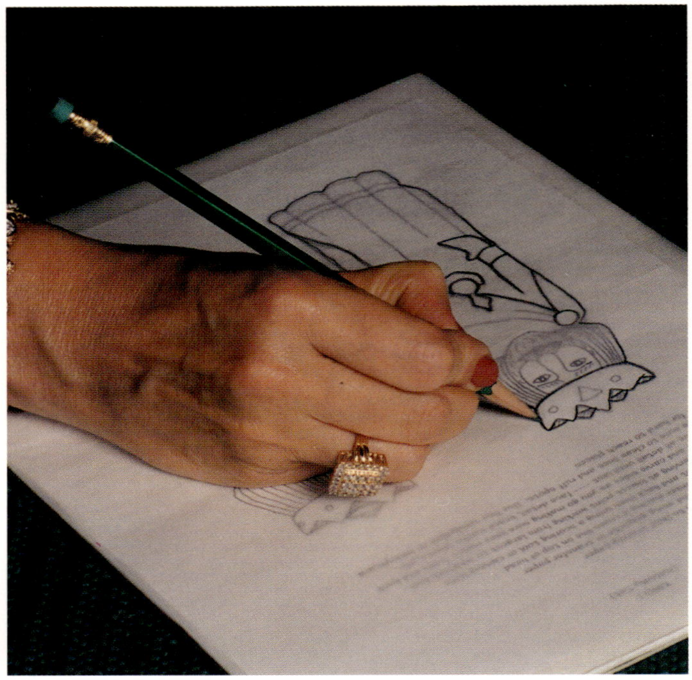

Trace the pattern onto tracing paper.

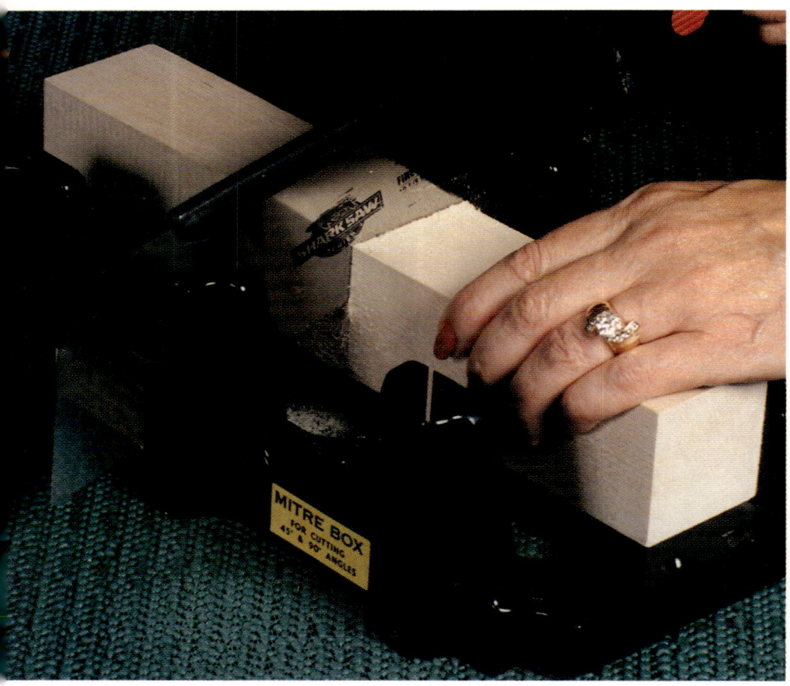

I use this simple miter box and hand saw to cut with ease and accuracy.

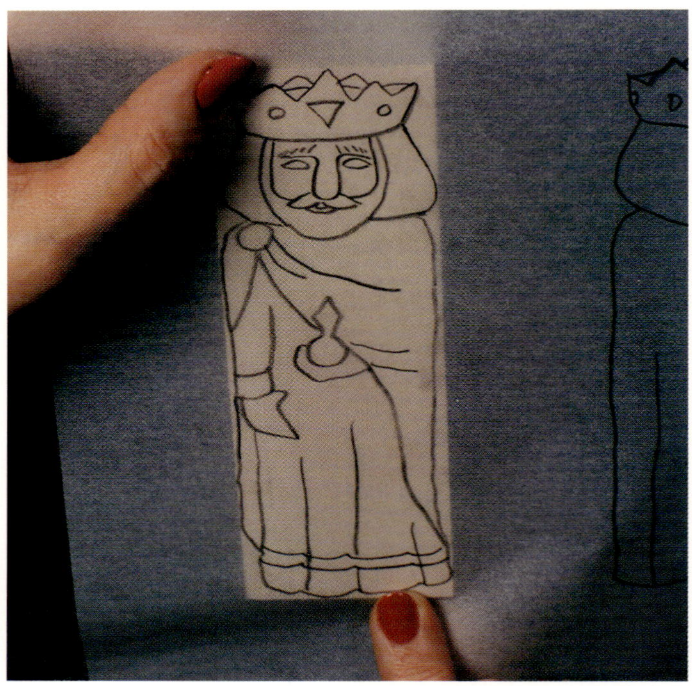

Line up the pattern on the pre-cut wood. Make sure to use the hand cut end as top of head, leaving the squarer end for the base so the king will stand straight.

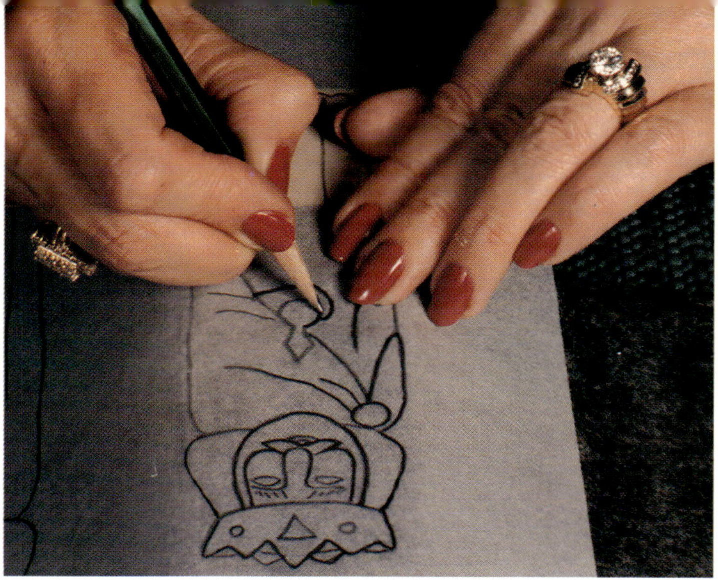

Slip a piece of graphite paper between tracing paper and wood to transfer the pattern.

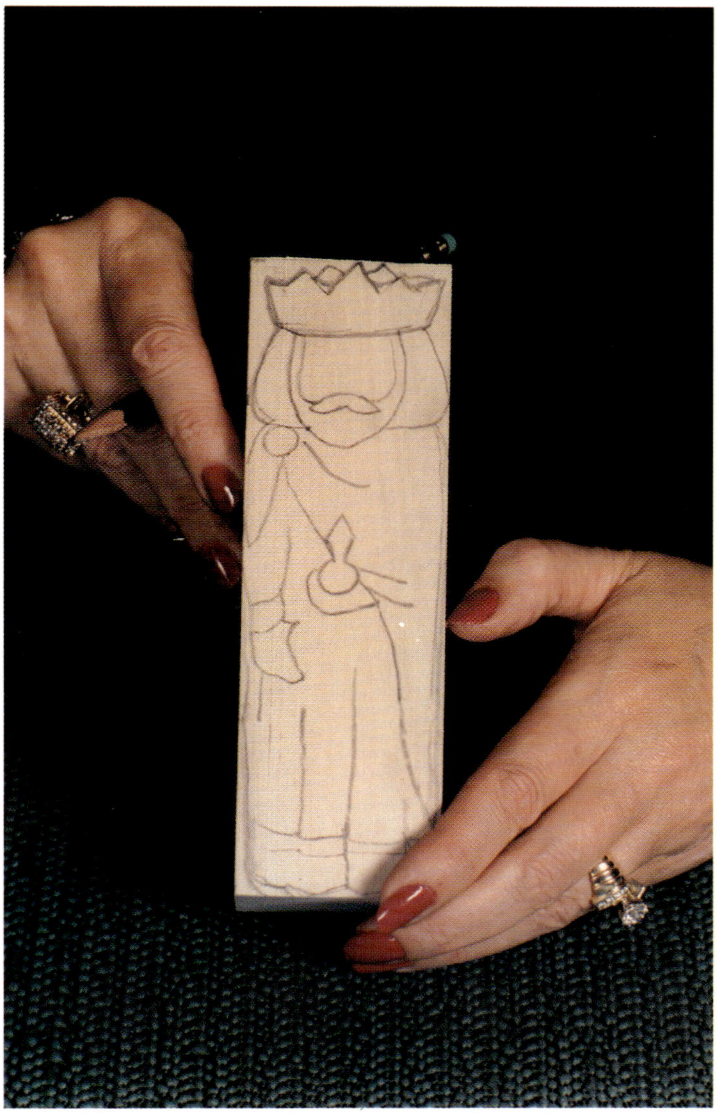

You don't need to include hair texture or eyes as they will be carved off.

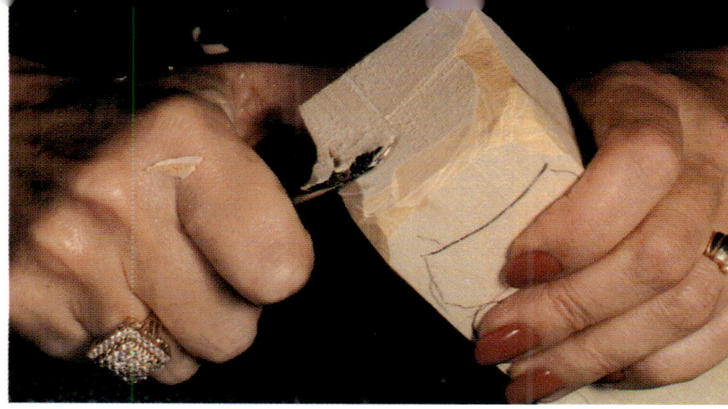

With your carving knife, start rounding at top of head. Draw the knife toward your thumb (I think of it like peeling potatoes). I am working on a non-slip rubber mat for safety.

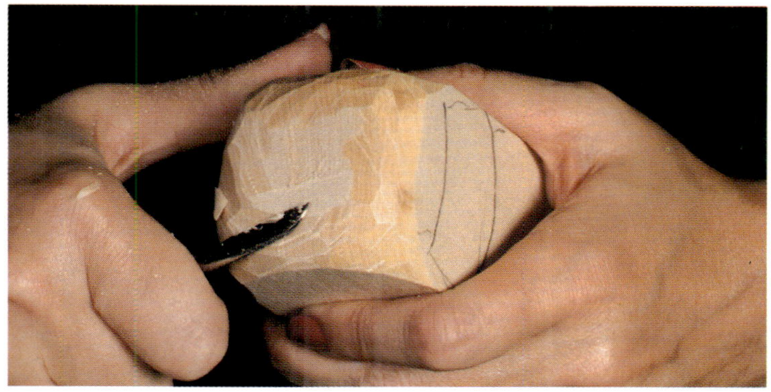

Keep rounding, taking small slices at a time.

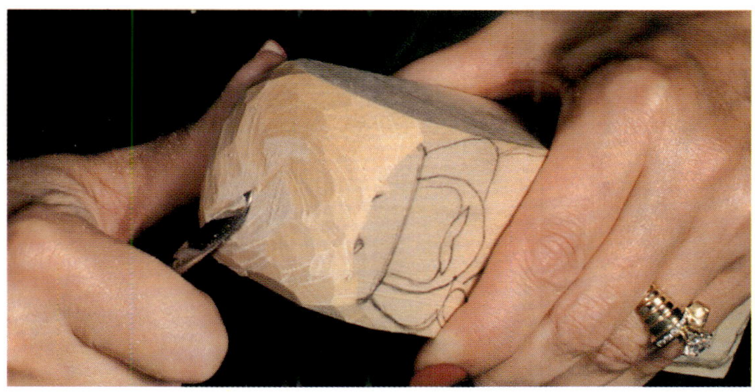

Continue until a slight dome is formed.

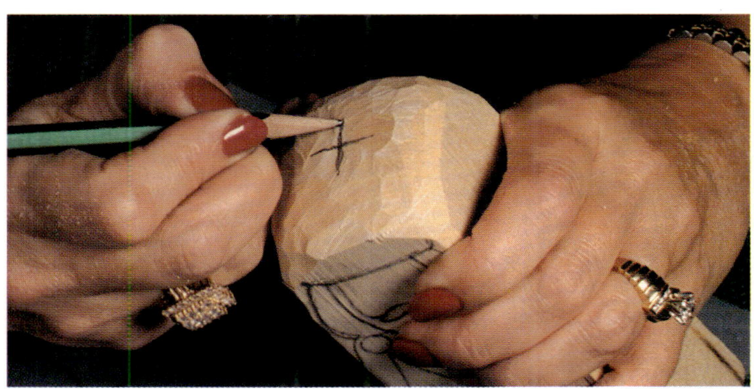

Mark the center with a cross line.

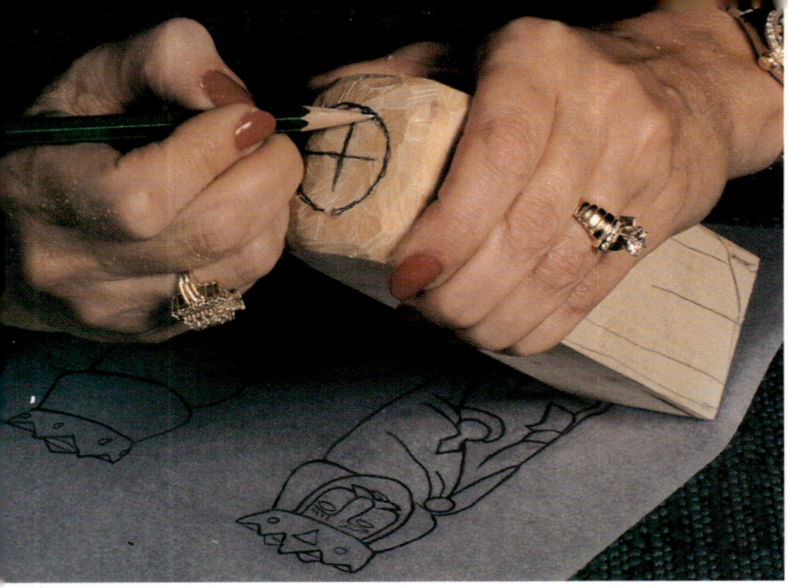

Refer to the pattern, then draw the circle of the crown.

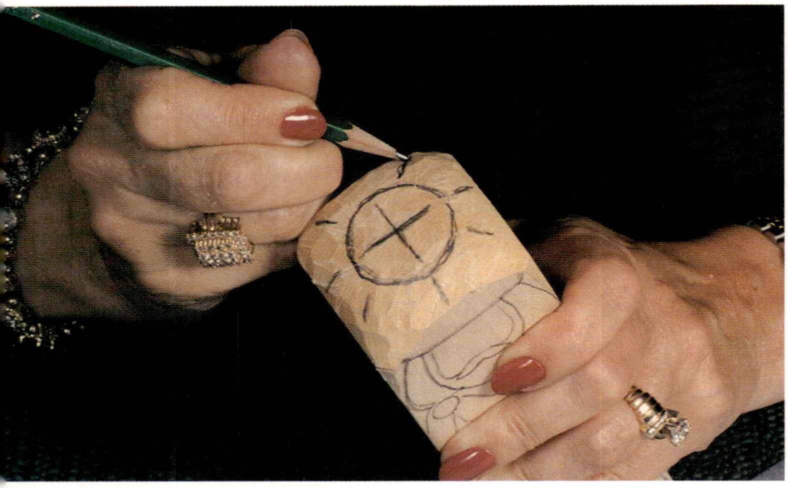

Again refer to the pattern and mark the peaks of the crown.

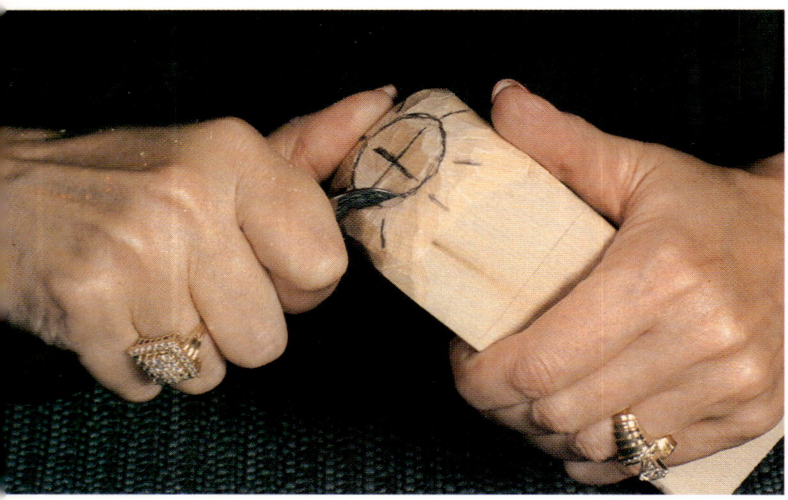

The next step is to score the circle line with your scoring tool (a chip carving knife) creating a stop cut. This is one of the most important things you will be doing. Each time you score, you are separating the wood you want to remove from the wood you want to remain.

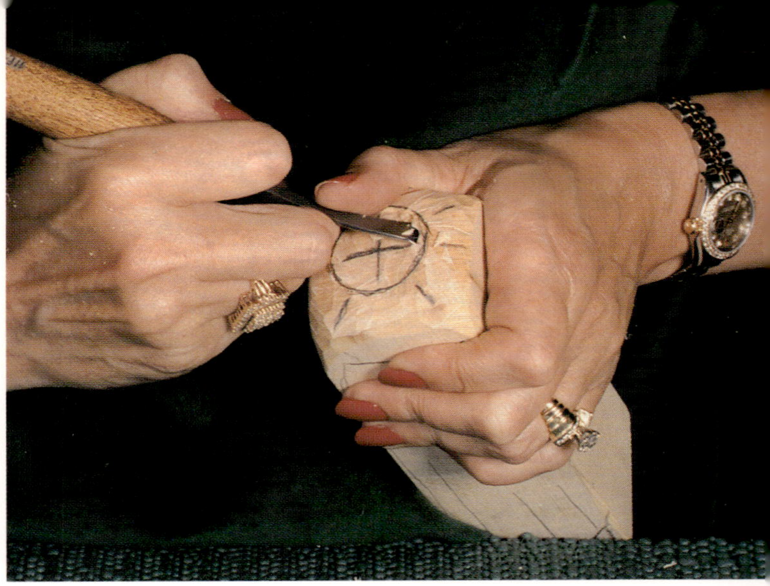

With your chisel, start rounding into the stop cut.

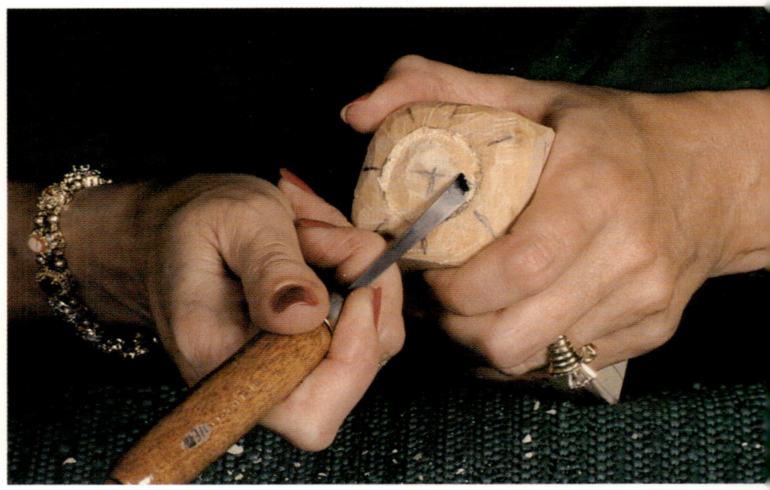

Rescore and keep rounding until another small dome is formed.

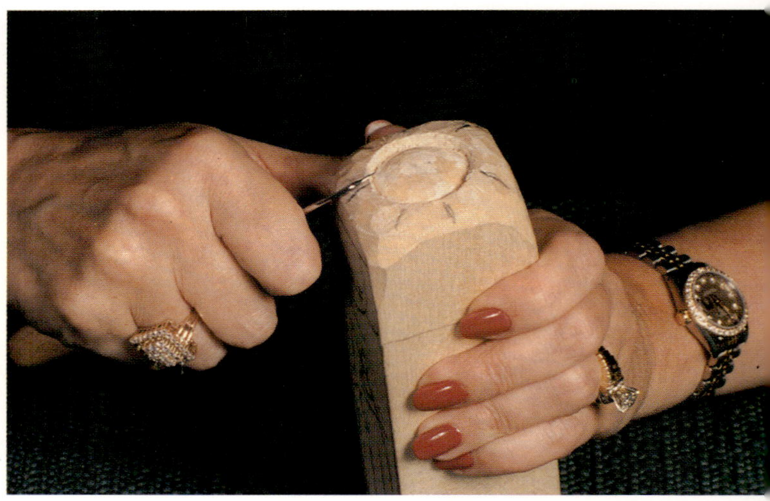

With your carving knife, start cutting down from the crown peak mark to the the next mark with an angle cut, creating a trough. Take small amounts at a time, slowly working down.

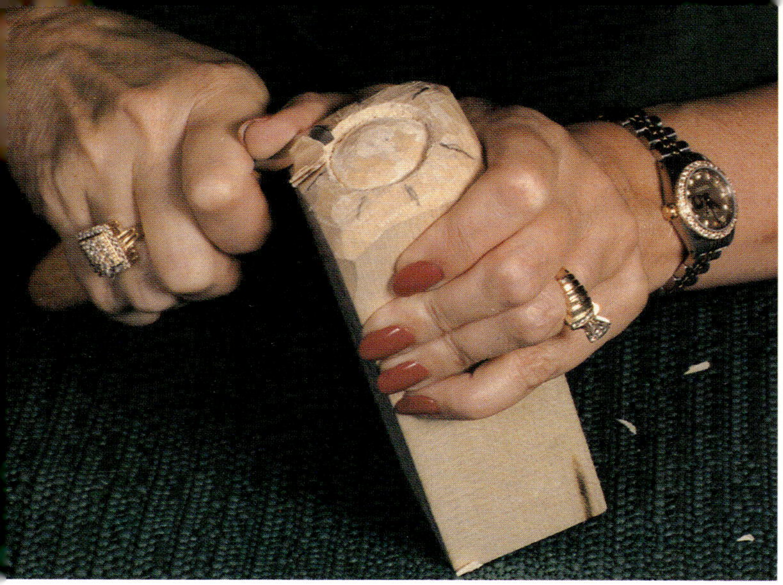

Move to the next crown peak, and slice back to trough in the same way.

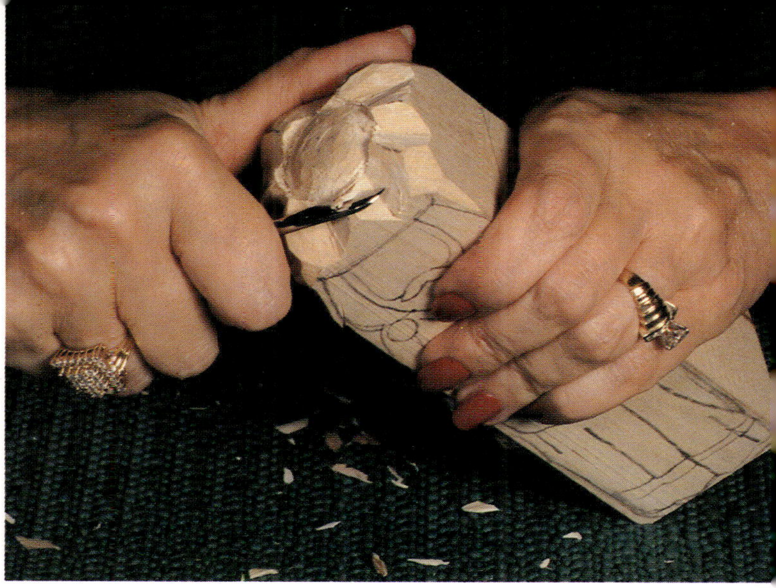

By using an angle cut, from the front of the peak to circle line, you will further define the peaks of crown.

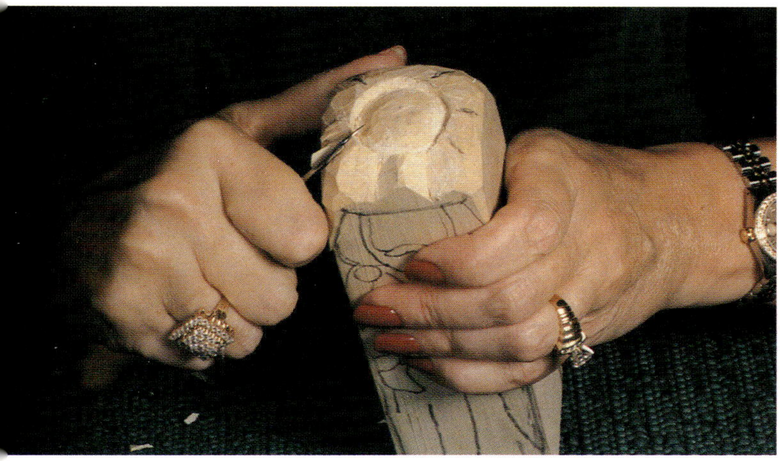

Slowly work your way around. I say "slowly" often because you will be much safer if you work slowly, and, if you are a new carver, you will be less likely to become frustrated.

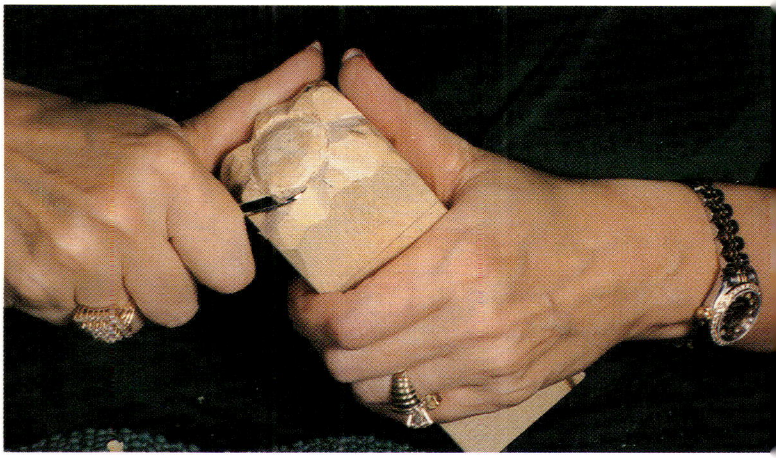

Move on around the entire crown.

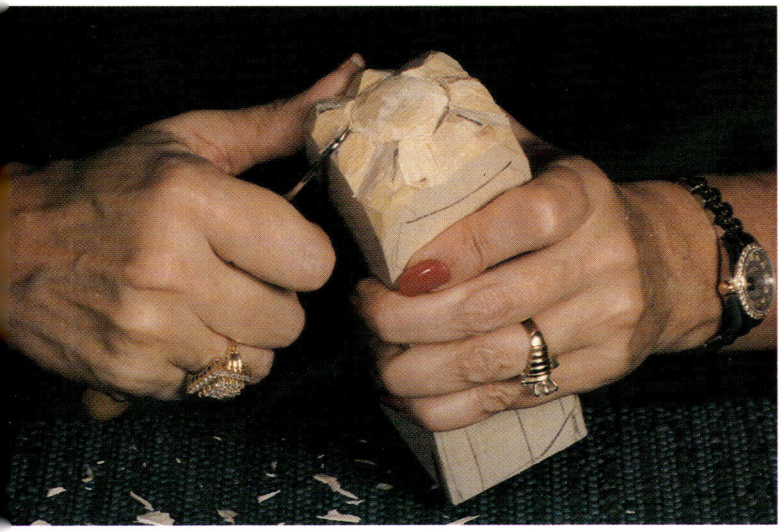

Complete all of the crown peaks.

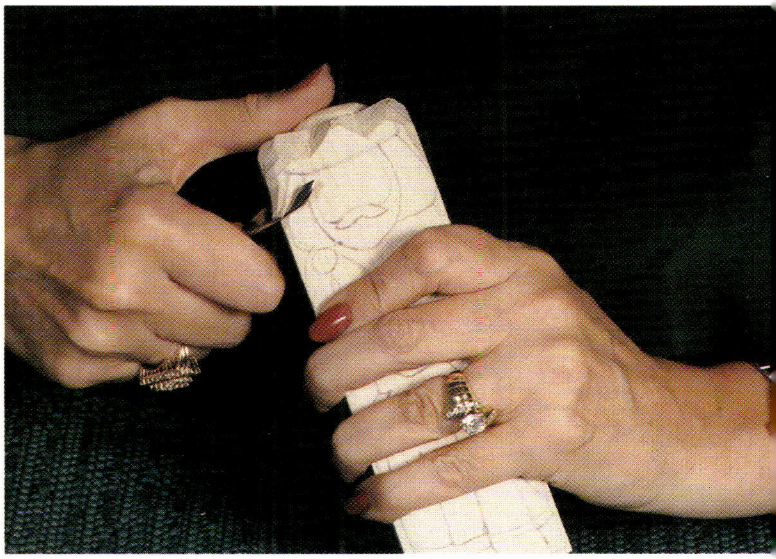

On the corner of the head, use another angle cut to come up to bottom of crown.

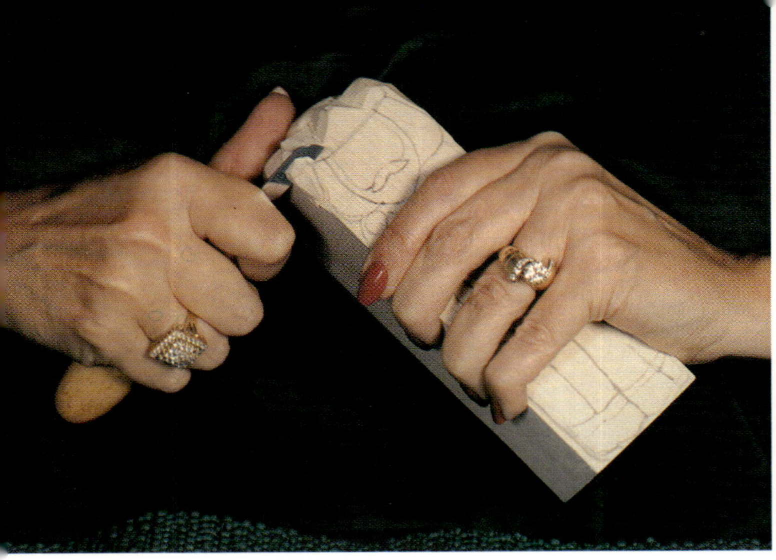

Cut down to line from the top of the crown.

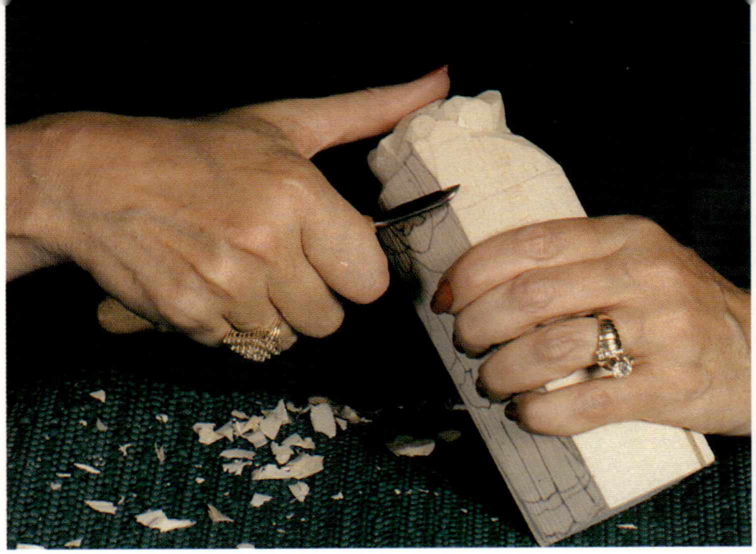

Finish carving the crown.

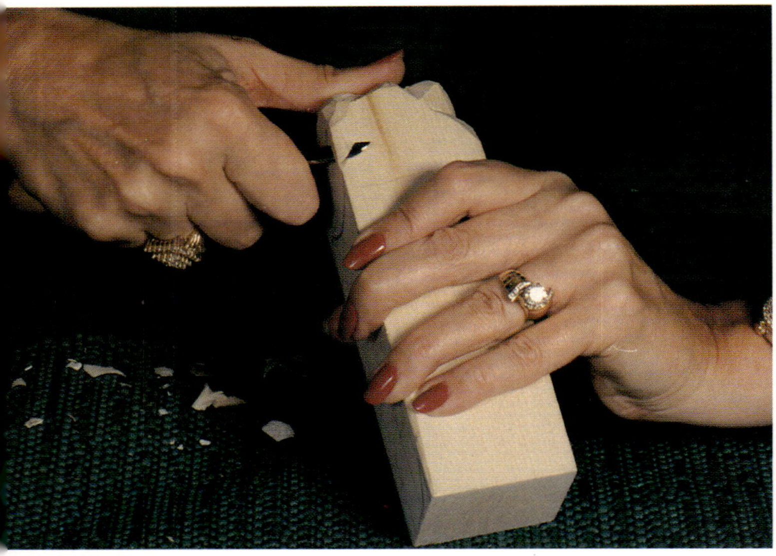

Continue on around the head, repeating this process.

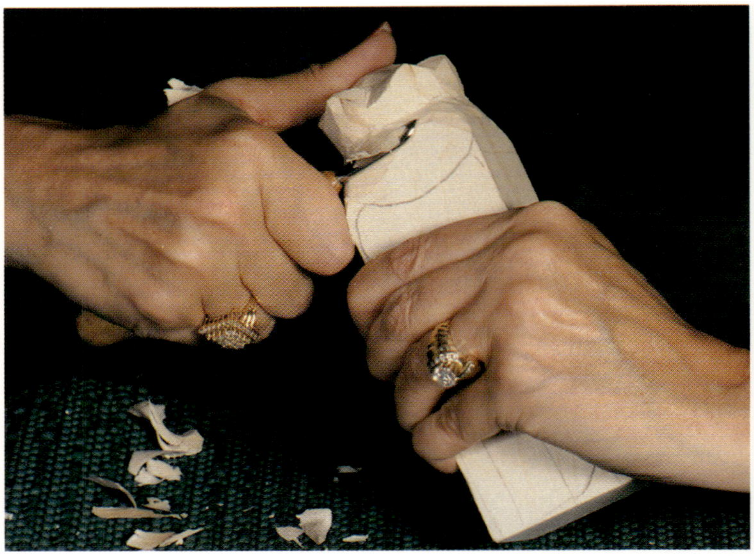

The next step is to start forming the hair. Draw your knife up from the bottom of his hair, to the bottom of the crown.

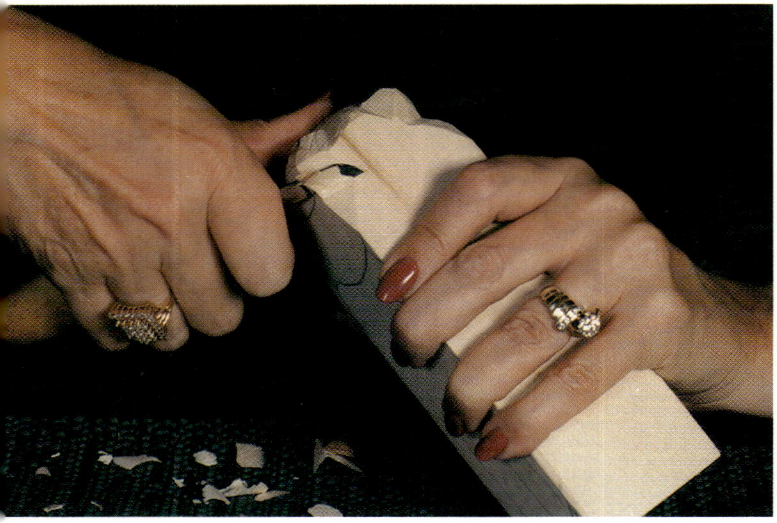

Cutting from the top to the bottom line.

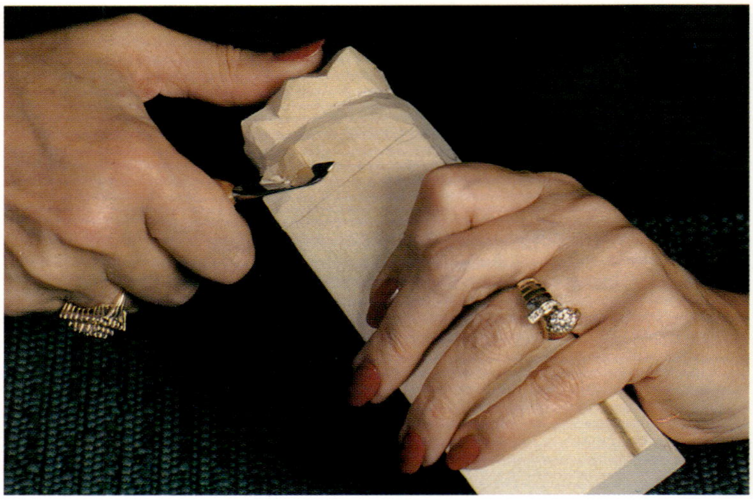

Work your way around.

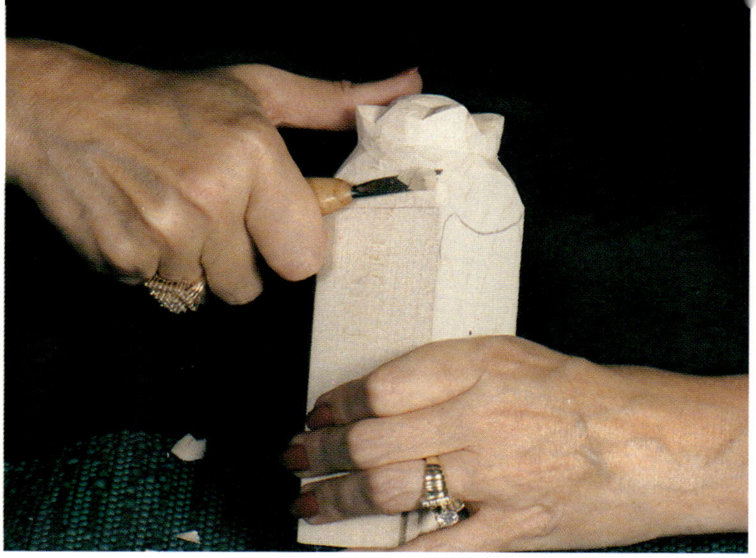

Complete the shaping of the hair.

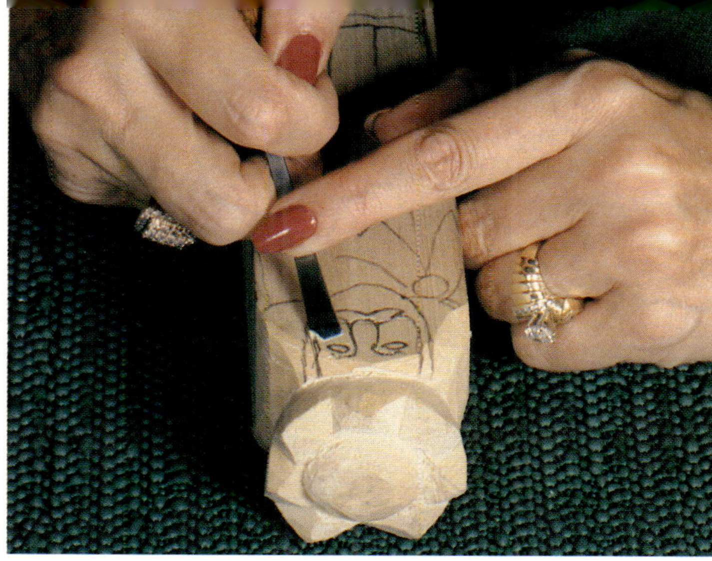

Tuck his face under the crown. Use your chisel to round the forehead back. Remember, re-score often.

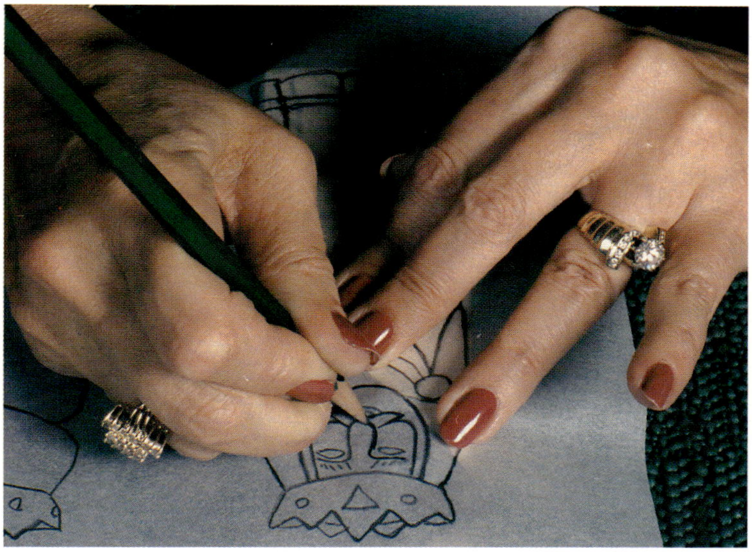

With the pattern and graphite paper, transfer eyes and nose.

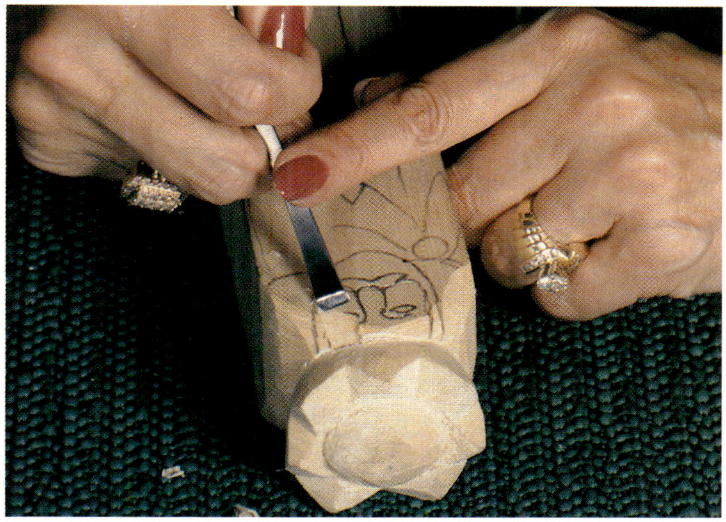

As you see, the lines are cut away, so it is important to keep your pencil handy.

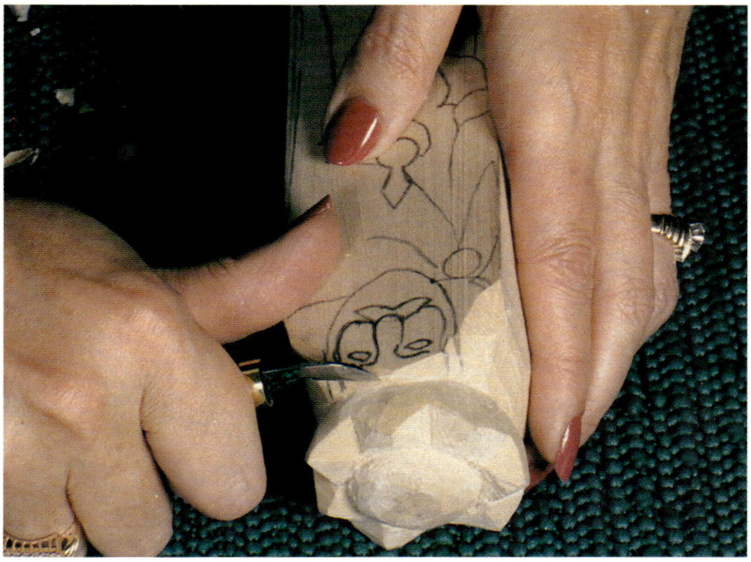

With your scoring tool, make a stop cut at base of crown.

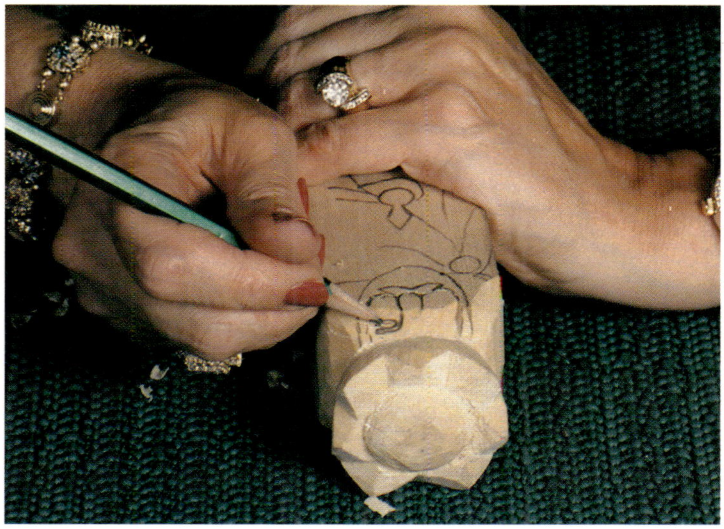

Draw the eyes once again.

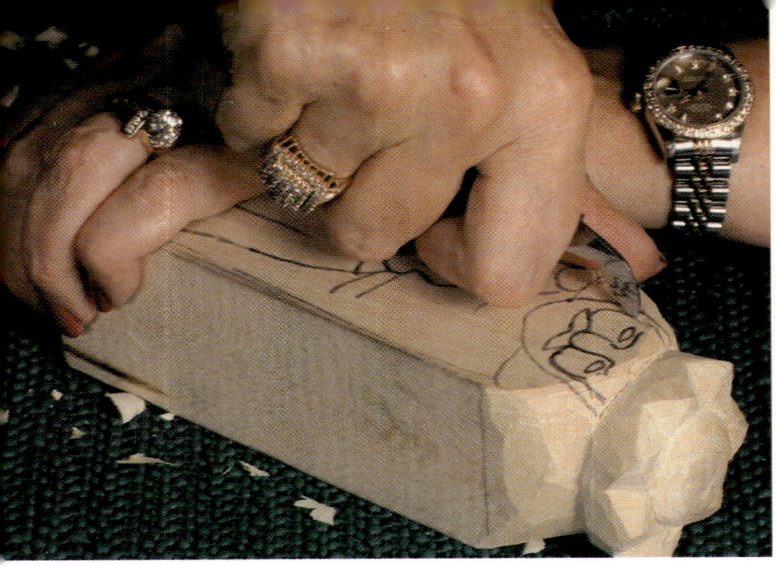

Score the face and beard lines.

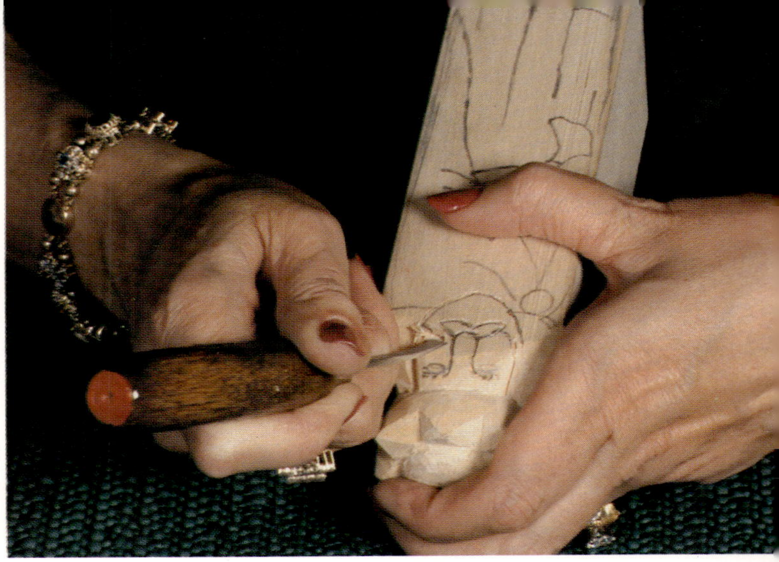

With a small chisel, start creating his little cheeks, by angling down to mustache.

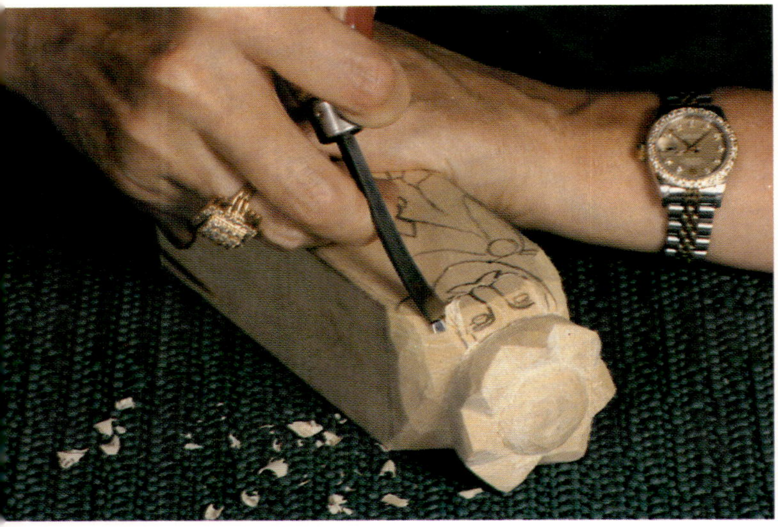

With your chisel, start removing wood from around the sides of the face.

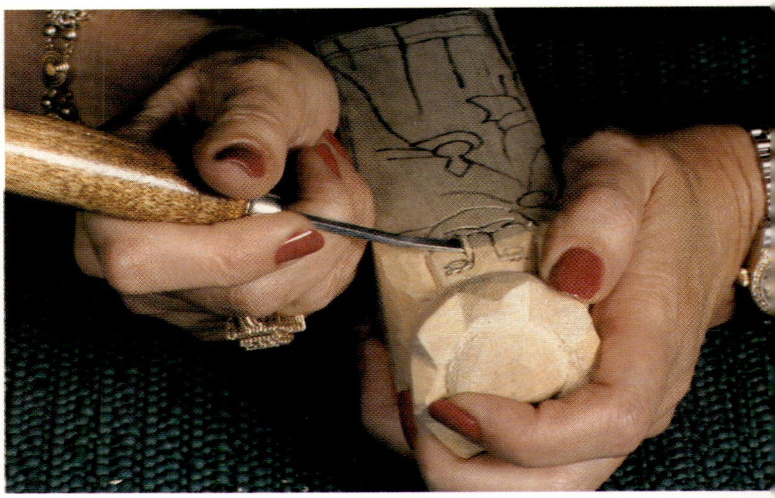

Come up the side of the nose.

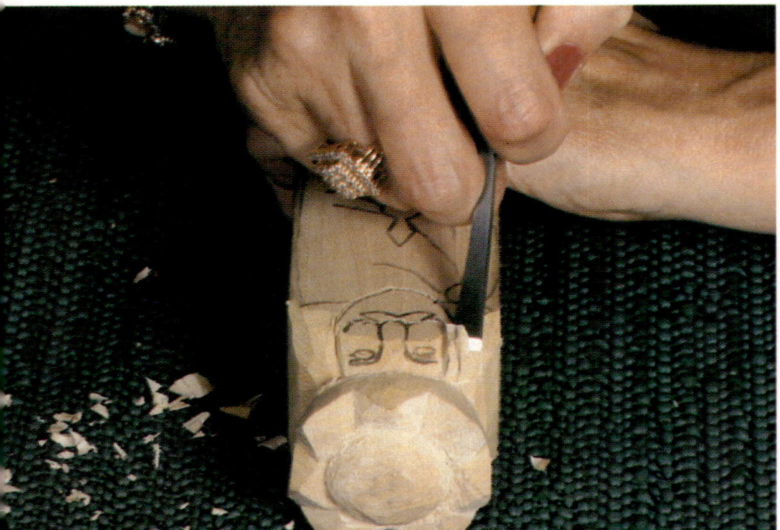

You will be taking the hairline back, revealing the face.

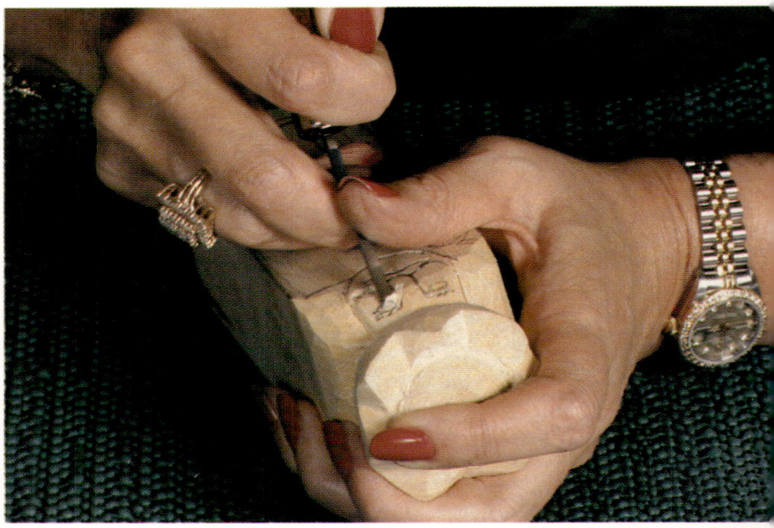

Go into the eye socket. Once again you will remove the eye you drew. Even though you remove and redraw certain lines again and again, it is sometimes necessary in order to know where you are. Just redraw.

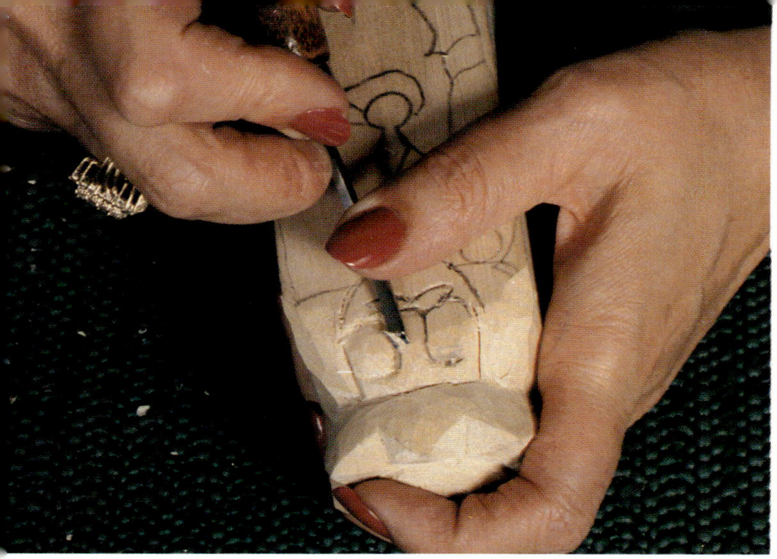

Round the sides of his nose by gently moving up the edge with your chisel.

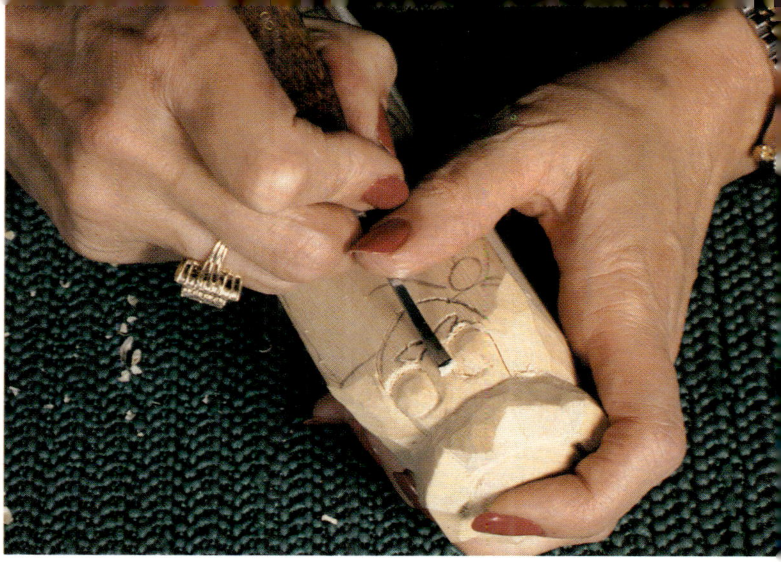

Round the nose.

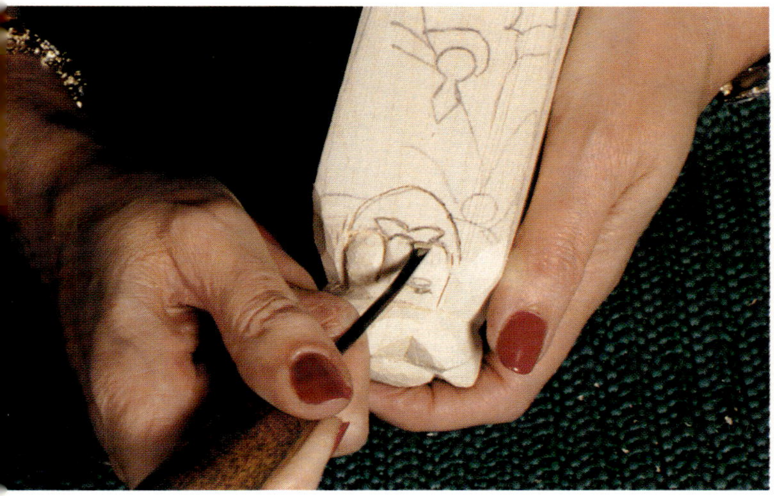

Start rounding the other cheek.

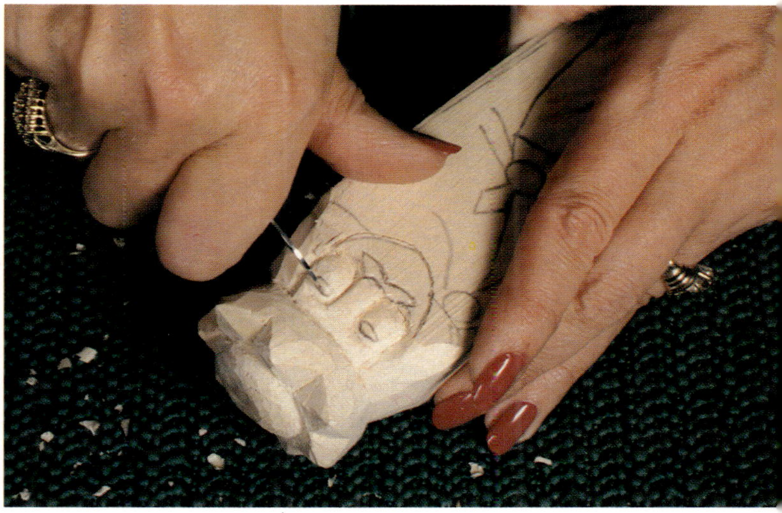

Redraw the eyes and carefully score the lines.

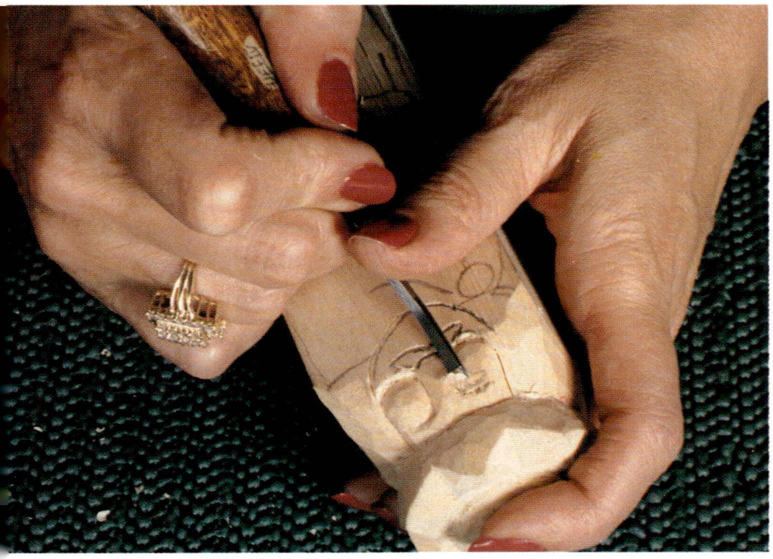

Move from the mustache up the side of the nose and into the eye socket.

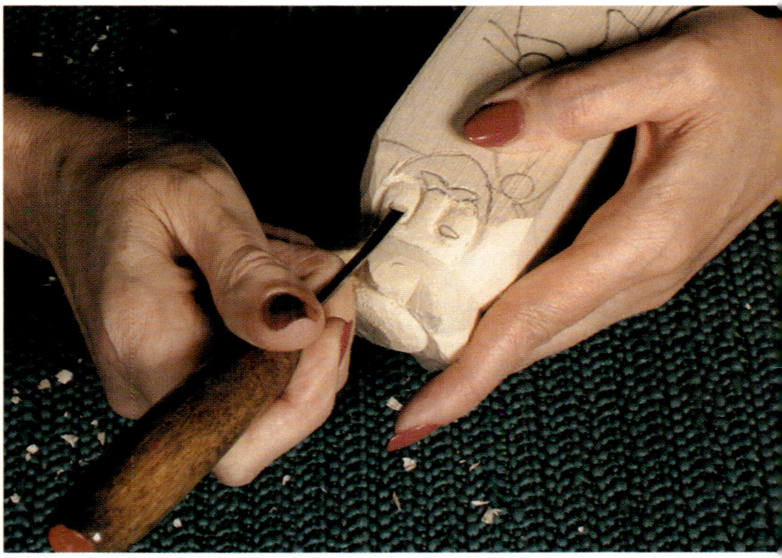

With your small chisel, remove wood inside the eye lines. Be careful to keep the area flat enough to paint an eye on it.

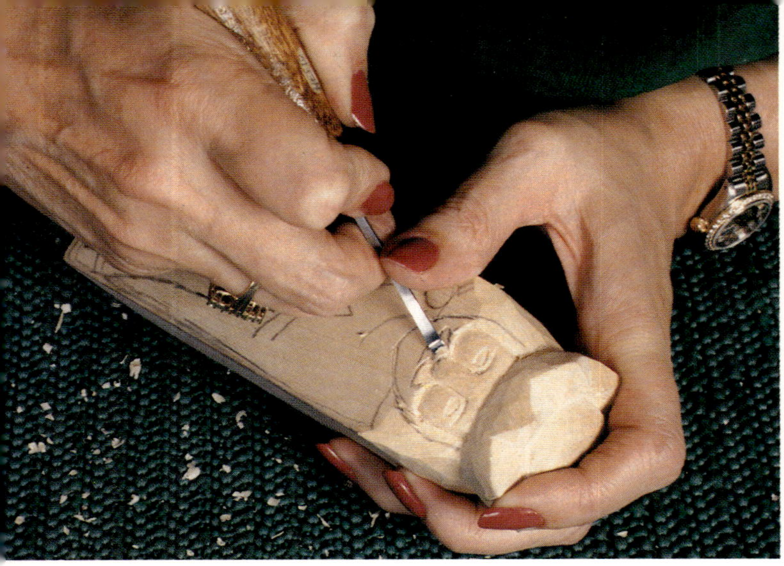

Remove wood from the mustache coming up under the nose, making sure to remove enough so his nose will be prominent. Don't go too deep.

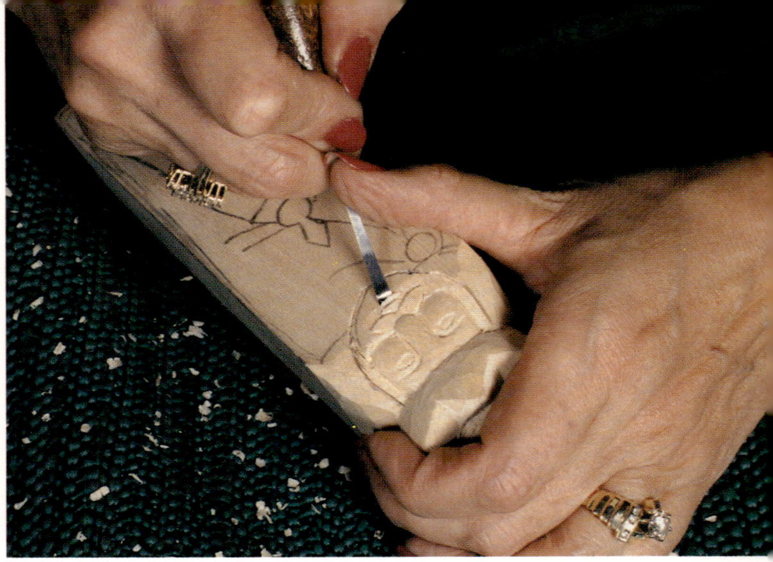

Again, with your small chisel, remove the wood under his lip.

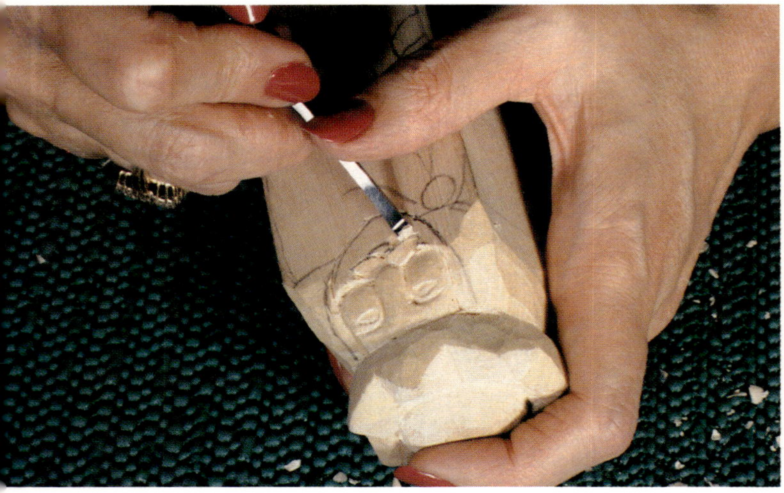

Check to see if the line is scored, then come up under mustache removing enough wood to reveal it.

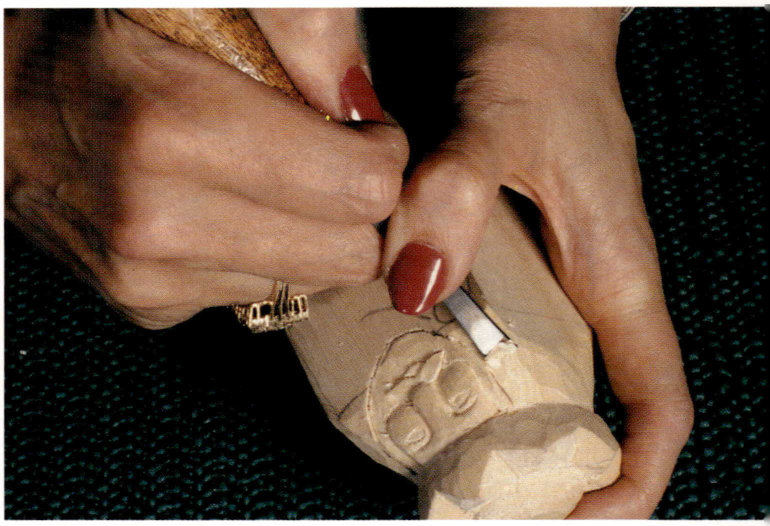

With your regular size chisel, start removing wood from his hair, revealing the beard.

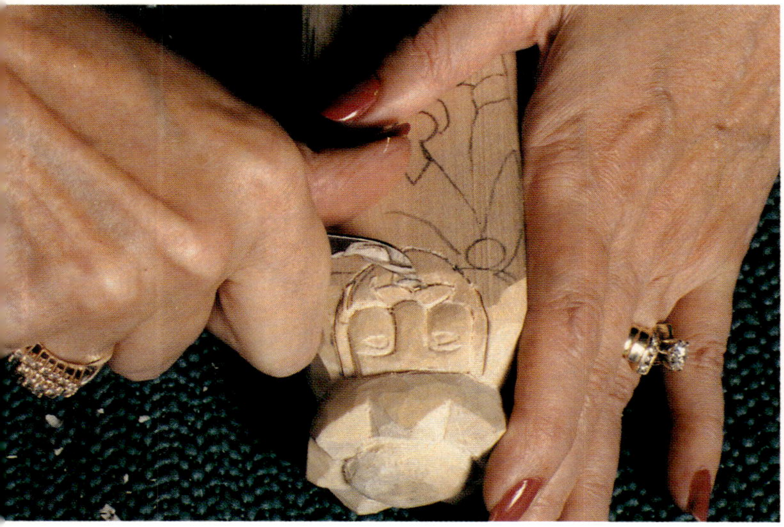

Next, score lip line.

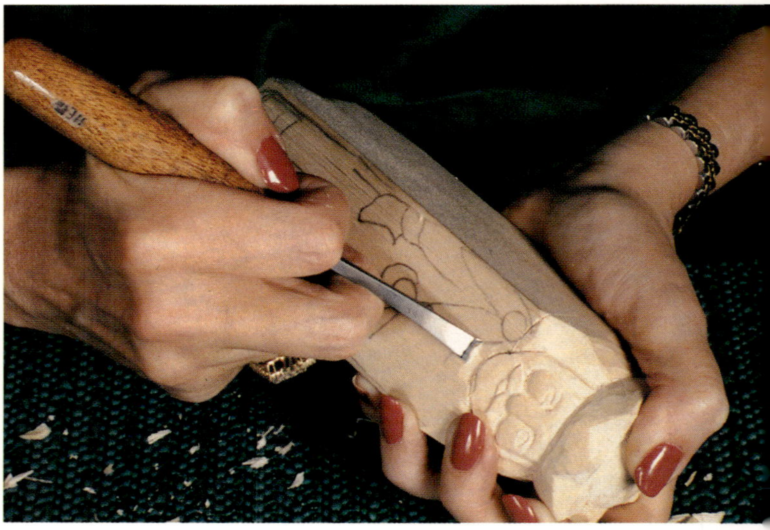

Come up under the beard cutting down about 1/4".

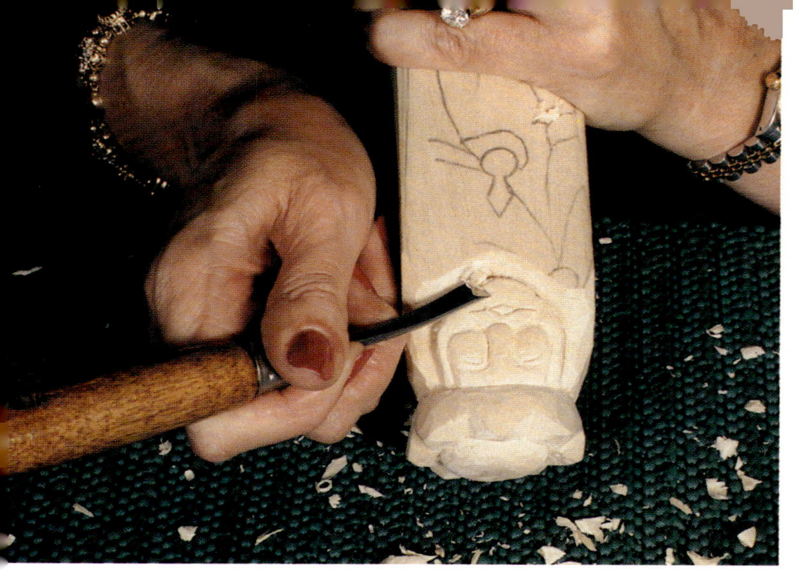

Round off the edges and surface of his beard.

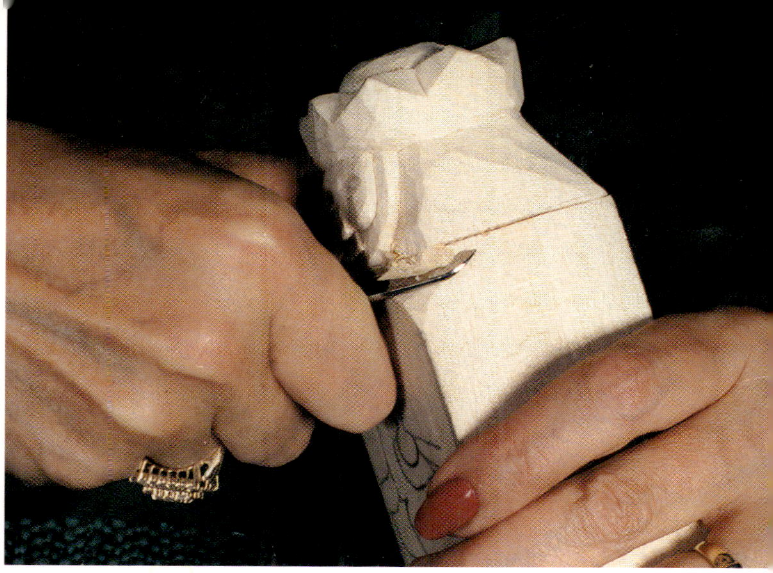

With your carving knife, come up under the hair line, from the shoulder to the stop cut. Re-score and repeat.

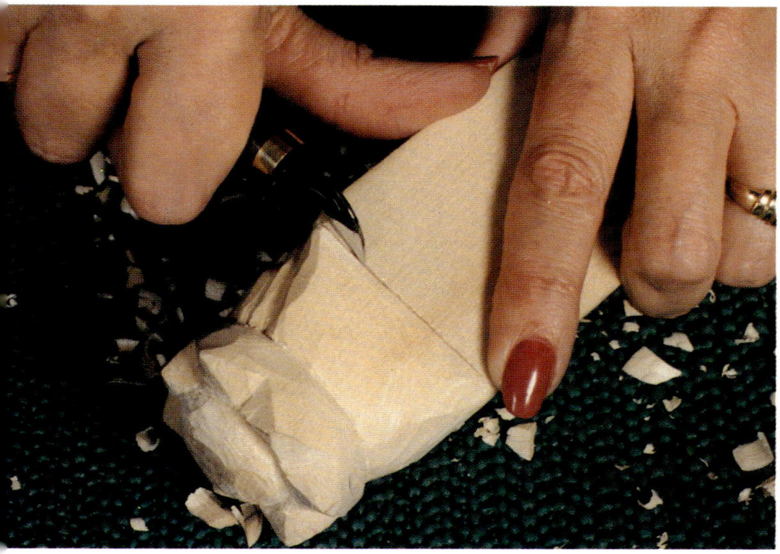

Next, score the hair line.

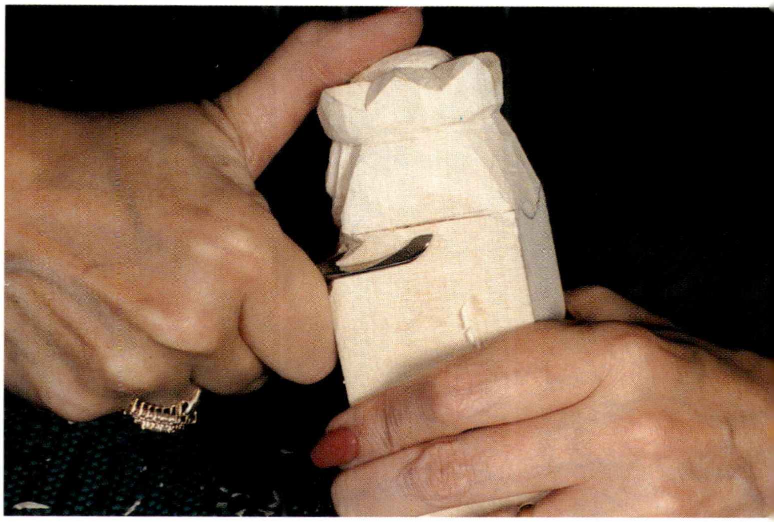

Work your way around the entire head.

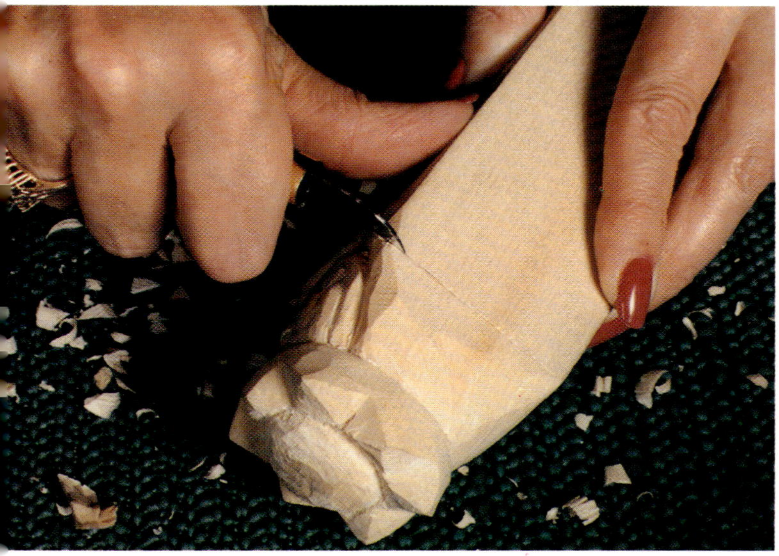

Go all the way around.

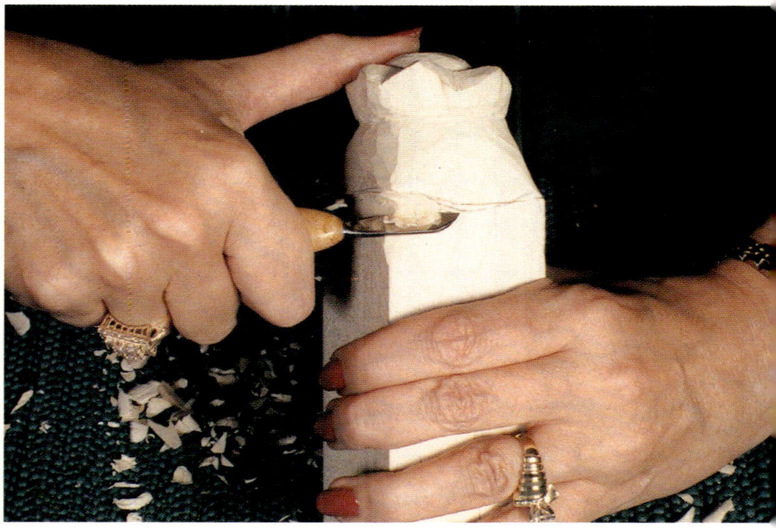

During this process, you are creating the shoulder line as well as the hair.

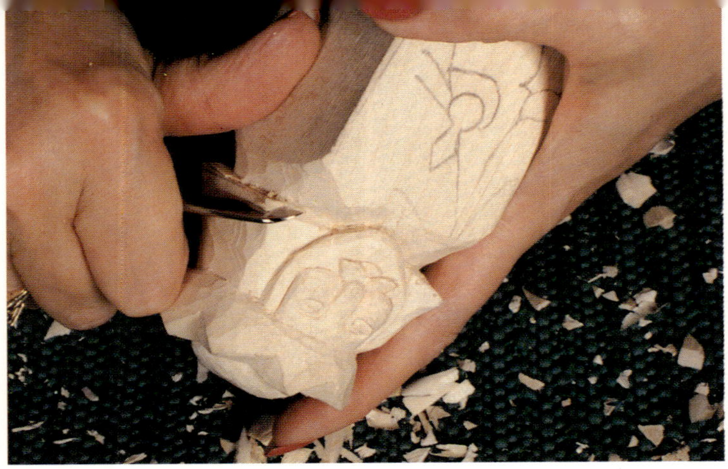

Now, start rounding off the bottom of the hair.

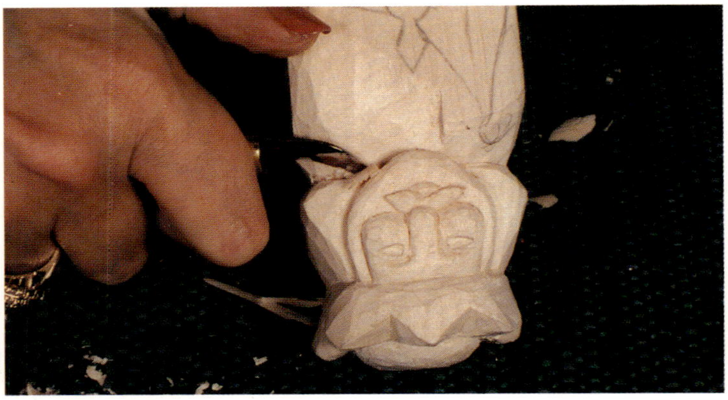

Using your scoring tool, clean up the lines under the beard and hair.

You should be at this point, ready to do the body.

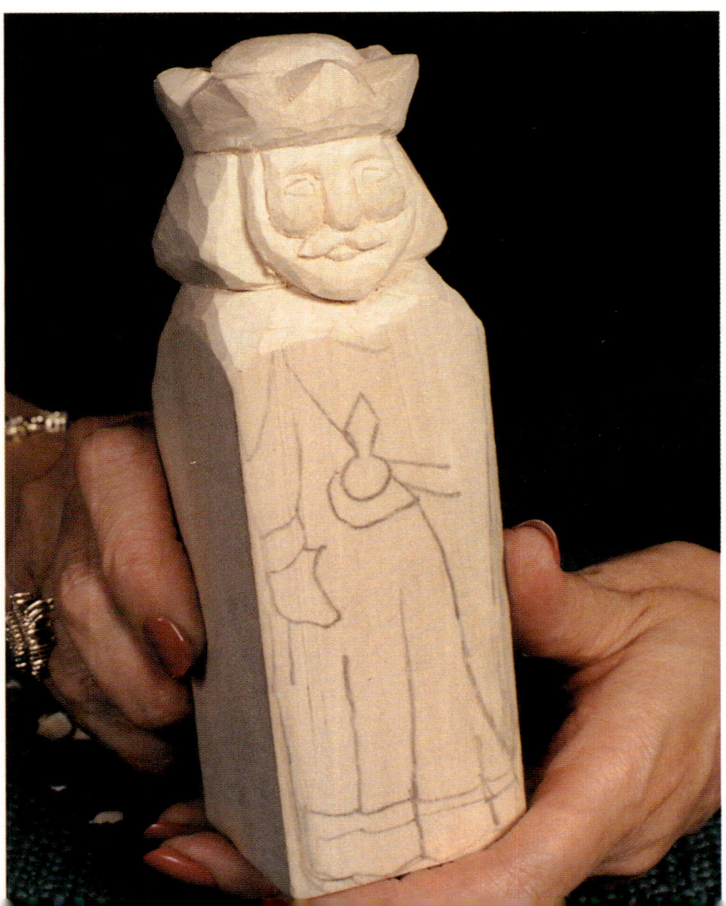

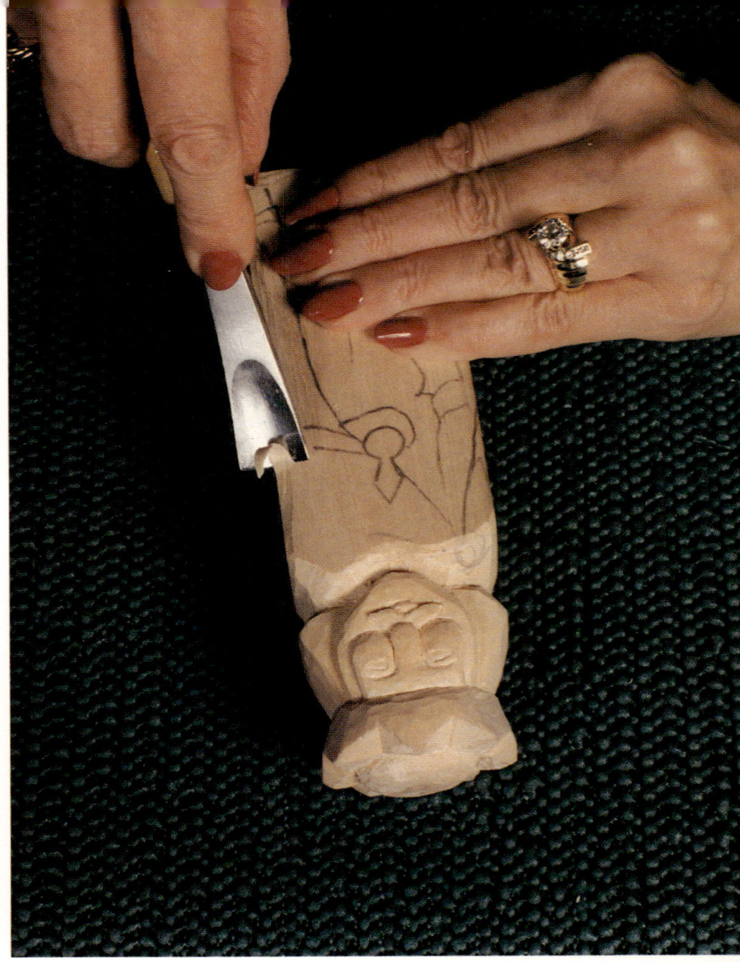

Using your large gouge, start at the front corner and round off the edges.

Continue around, creating nice big carve marks. Stop at opposite front corner, leaving the front for our next step. Carve marks are very desirable. This will give you the look of folk carving.

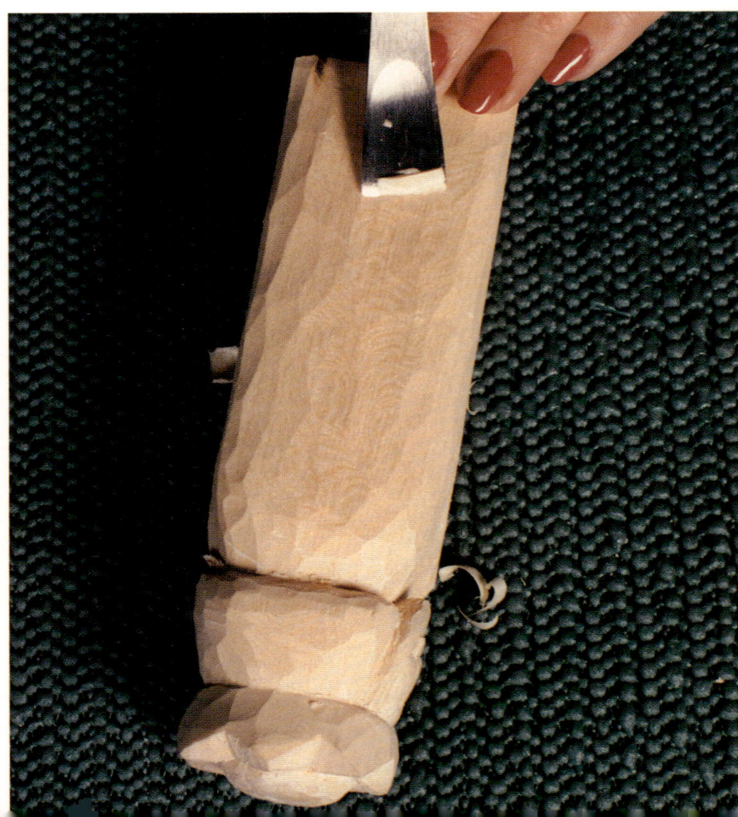

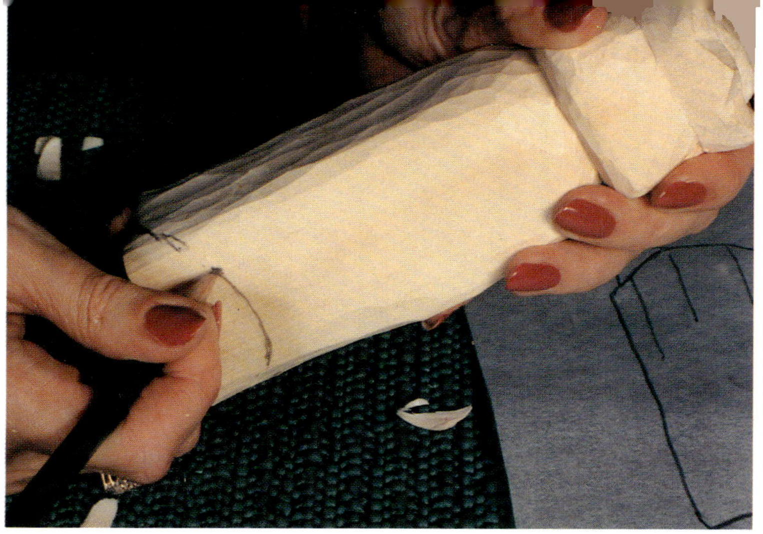

Refer to the pattern, then draw the gown and robe lines.

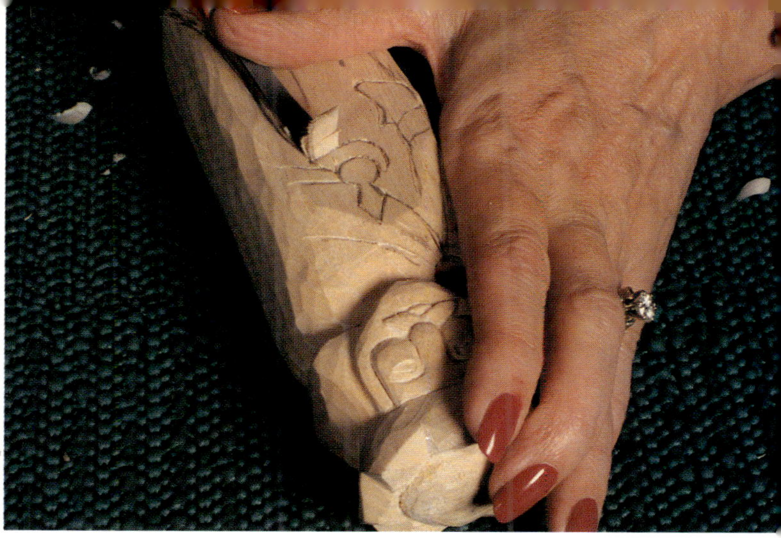

With your regular chisel, start removing wood from the opening of the robe up to the stop cut or score line.

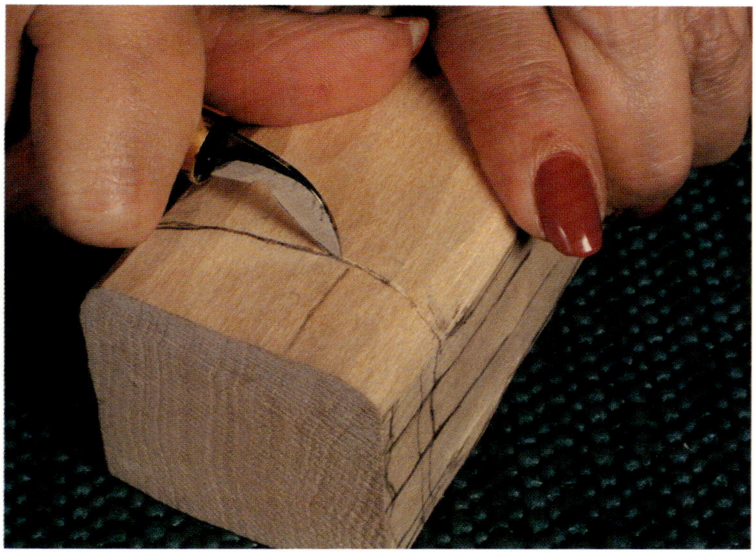

Score all remaining lines.

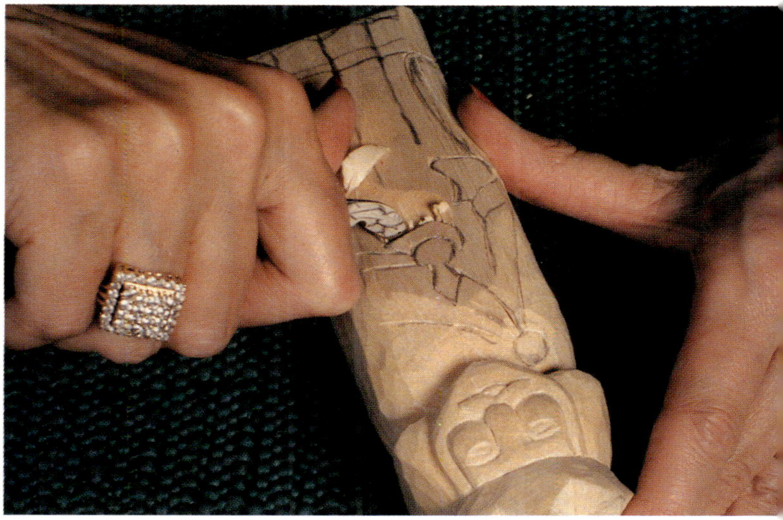

Be sure to re-score before going deeper.

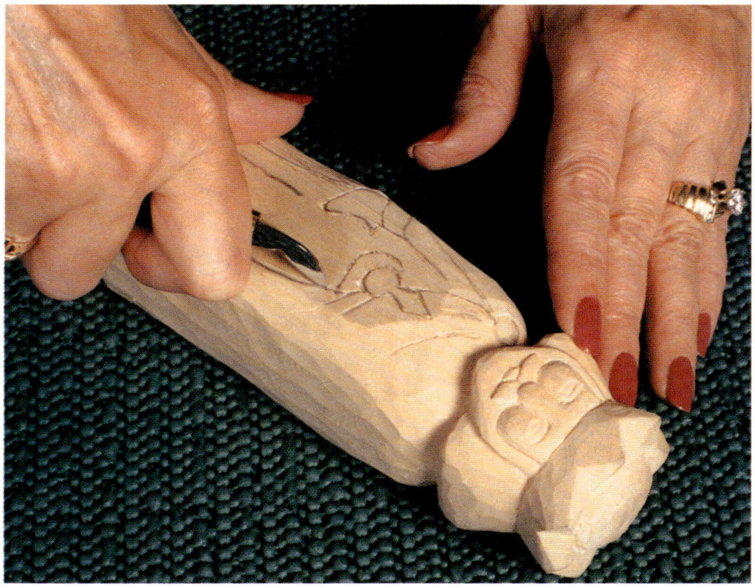

Be sure all details are included.

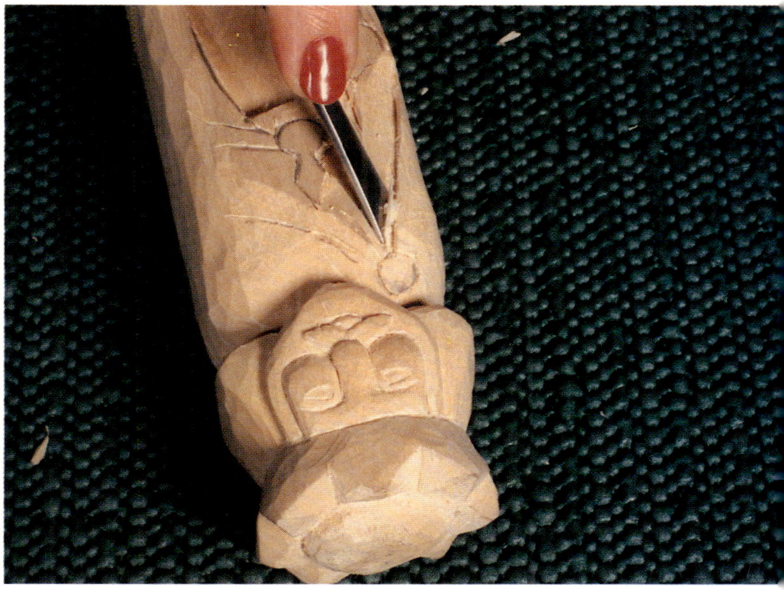

A skew chisel is used to reach this narrow corner with ease.

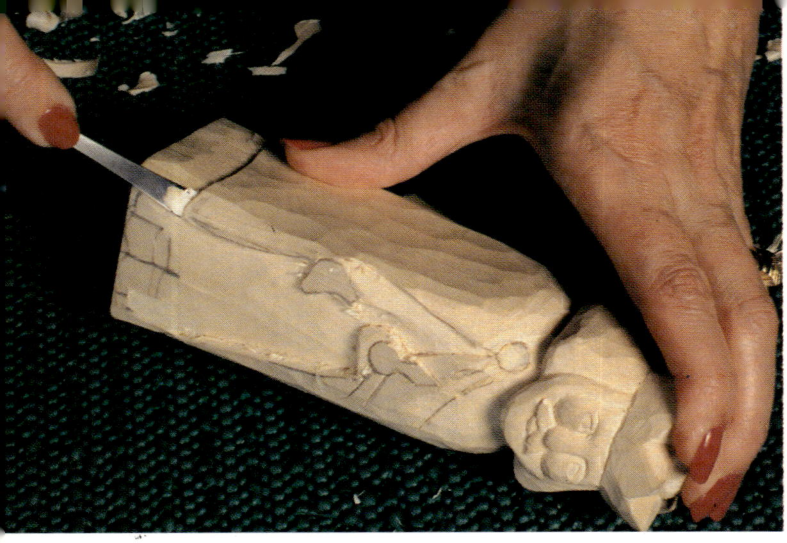

Use your regular chisel to approach the stop cuts. It gives you more control than your large gouge and you will be less likely to cut through the lines.

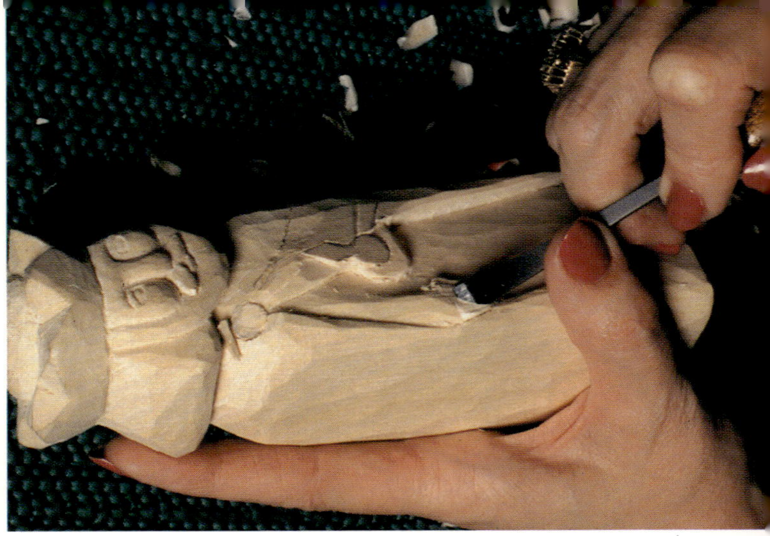

Continue scoring and removing wood.

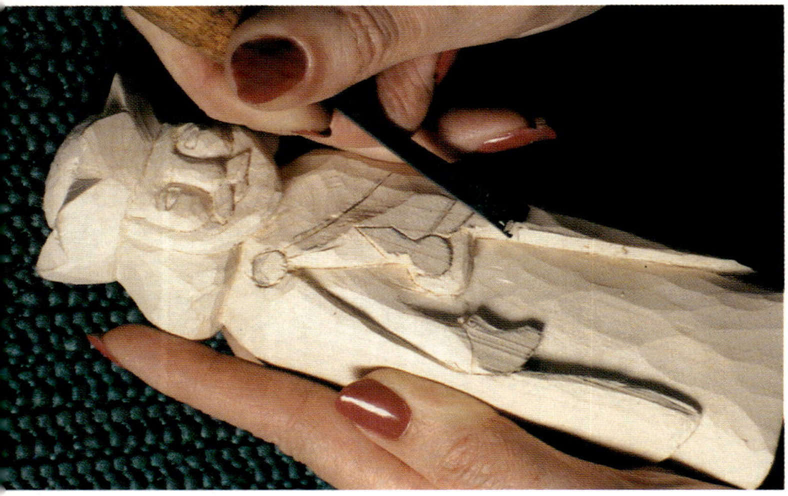

After removing wood from the gown, go ahead and round off the edges of his robe.

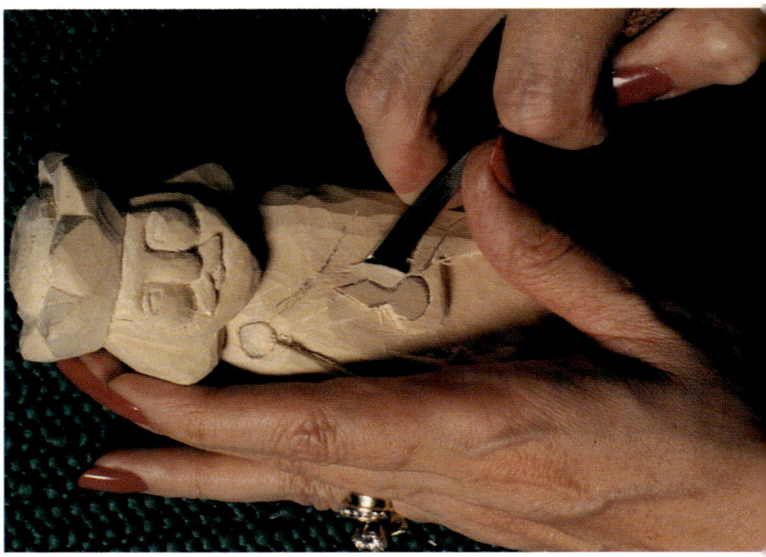

If the stop cuts are deep enough, you should have nice clean lines.

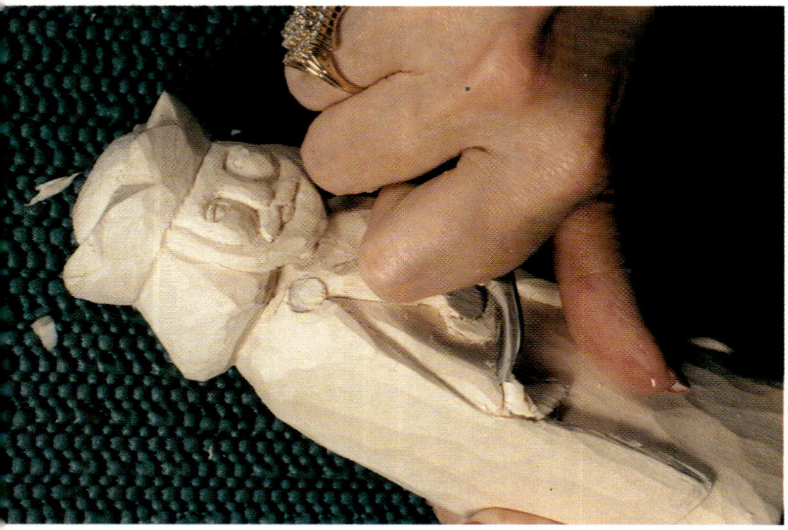

Finish the details carefully, making sure the stop cuts or score lines are cut in.

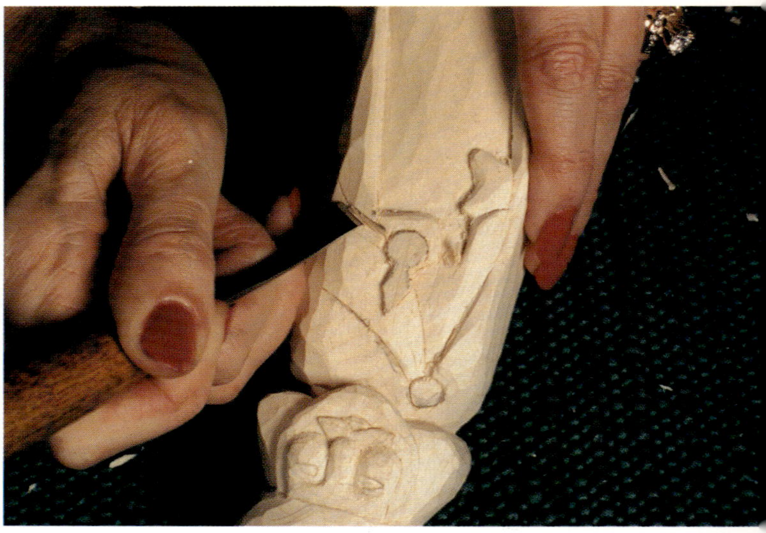

Because the folds are not deep, they can be rounded in with your regular chisel.

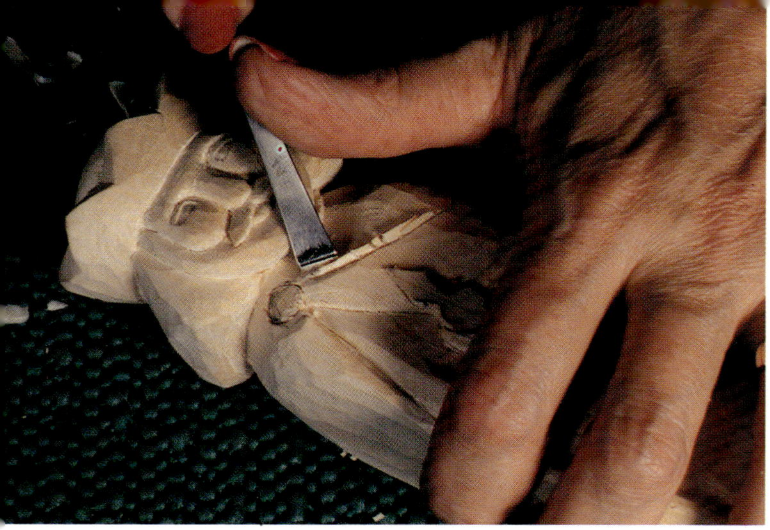

Finish the folds.

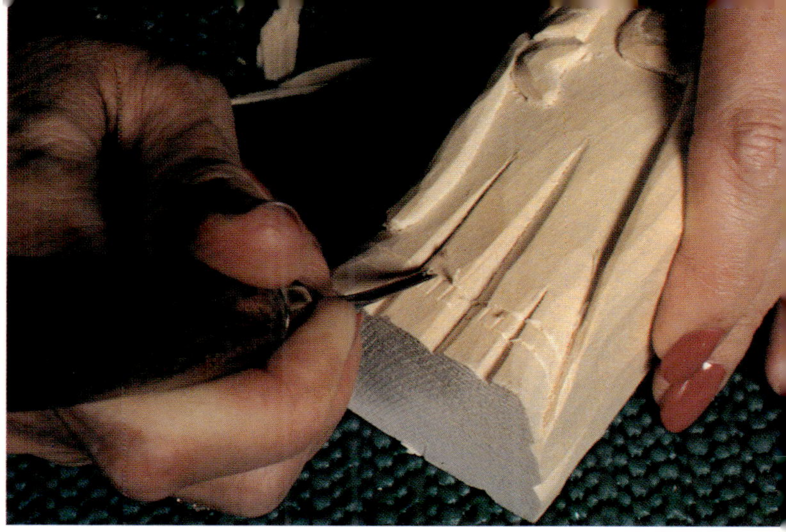

With your small V-parting tool, start cutting in detail.

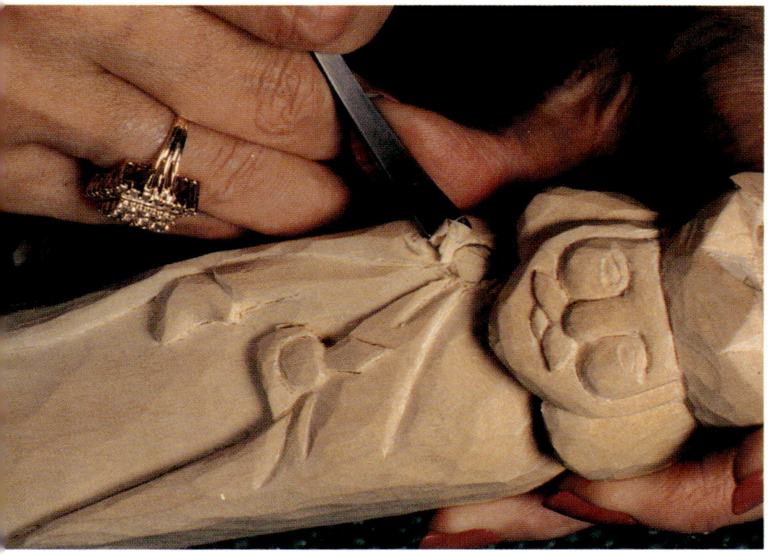

Round off all the small details.

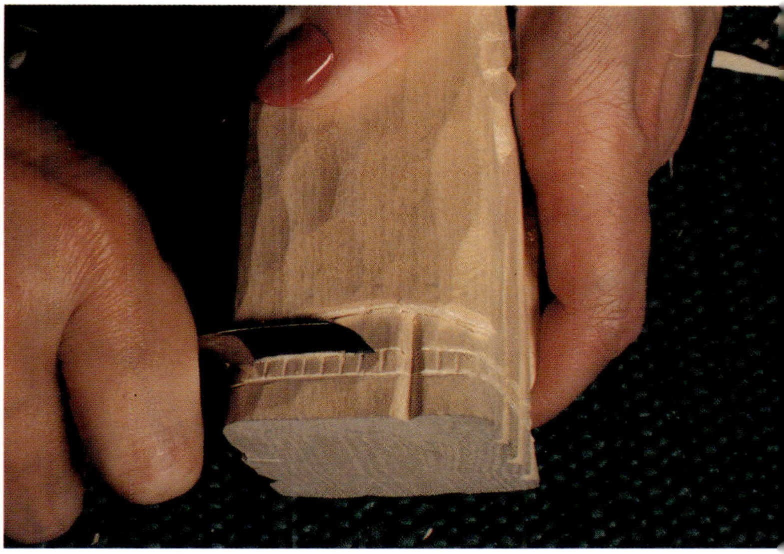

Your carving knife will make clean, well-defined lines to complete this detail.

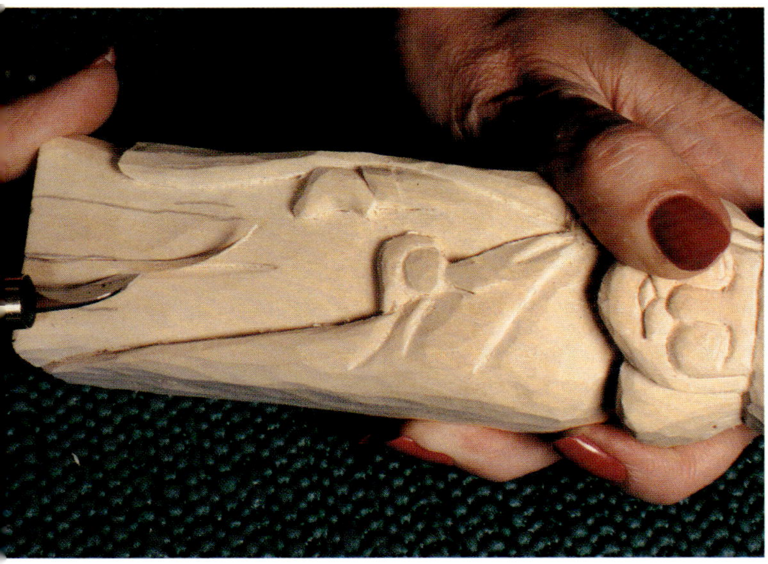

Using your scoring tool, cut in pleats with an angle cut along each side of the scored line as shown.

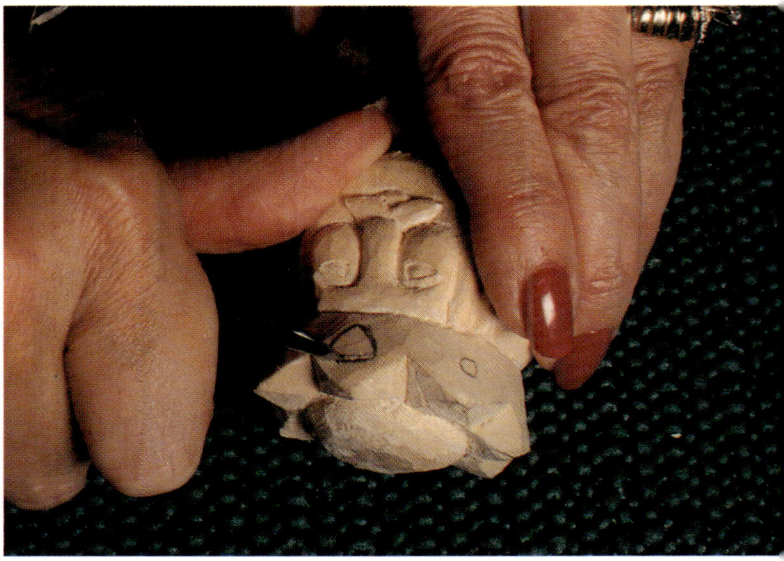

Score the hat details.

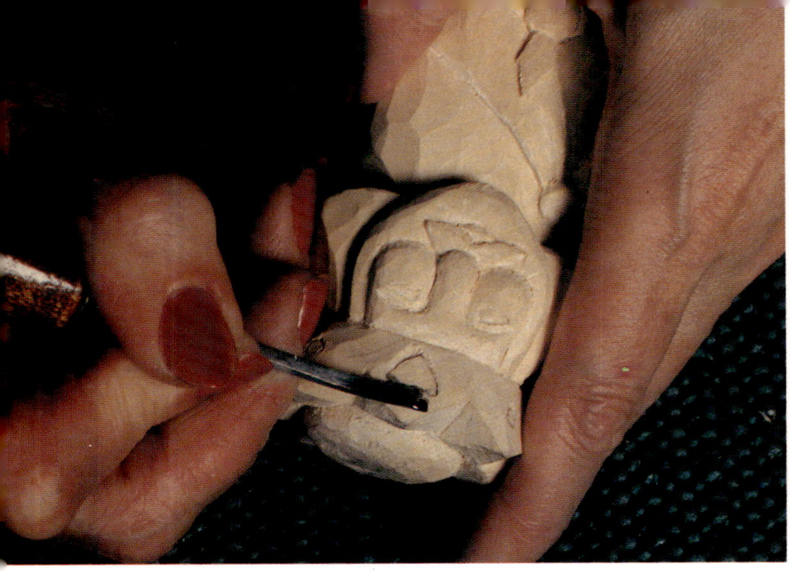

Remove wood from around, making the ornaments stand out.

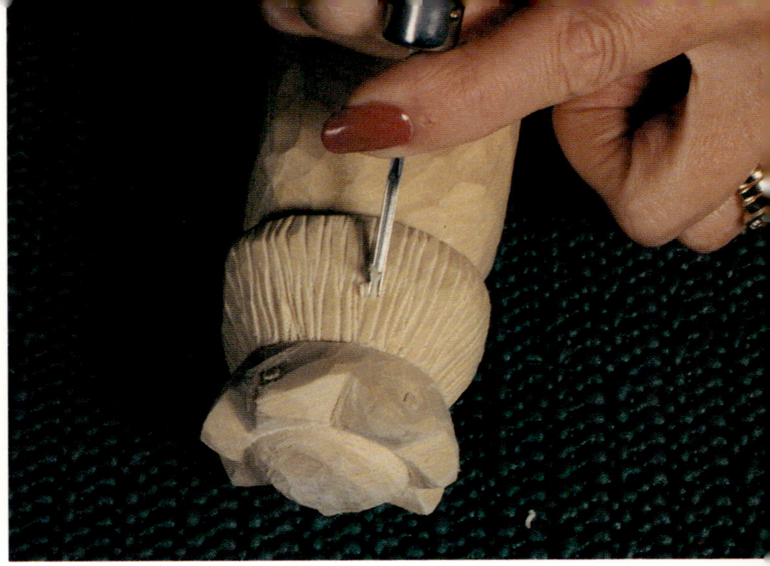

Go on around entire head and finish his hair.

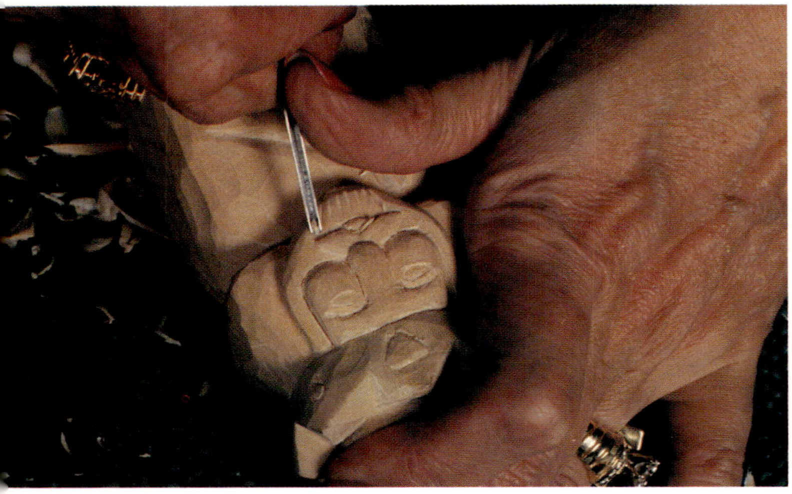

Finish hairlines with your V-parting tool, starting with the beard.

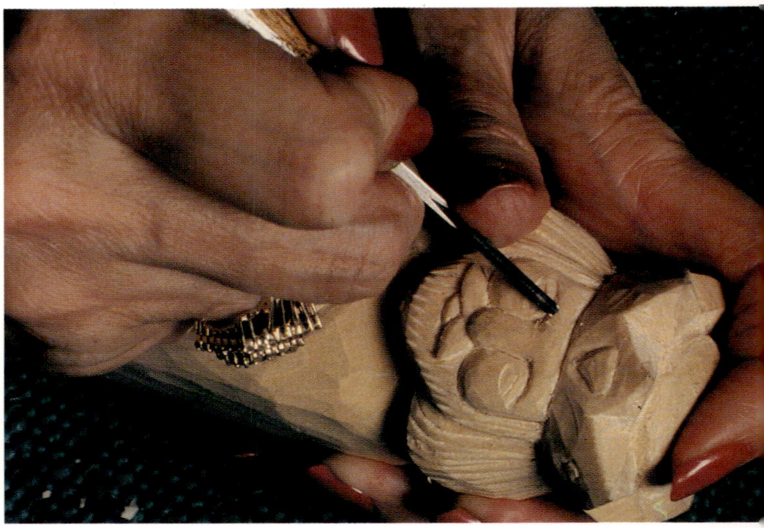

With the V-parting tool, carefully make fine little lines for his eyebrows.

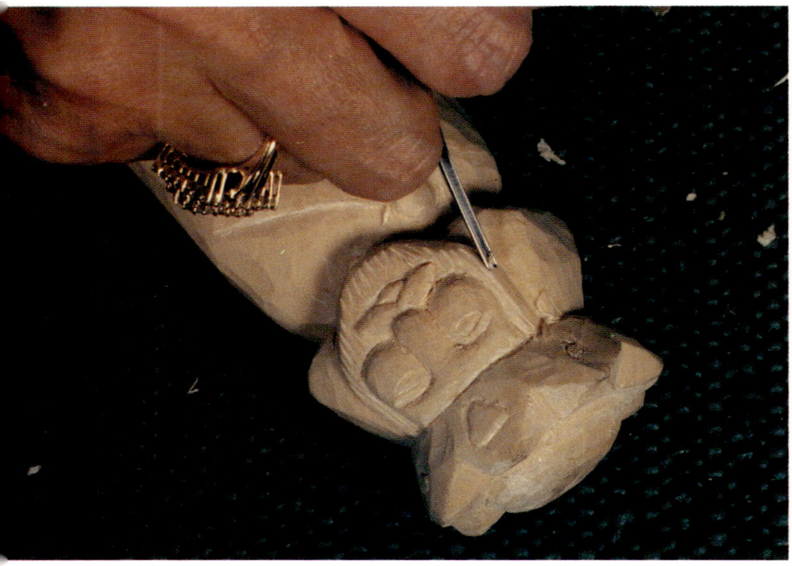

Continue up the side of beard with random strokes.

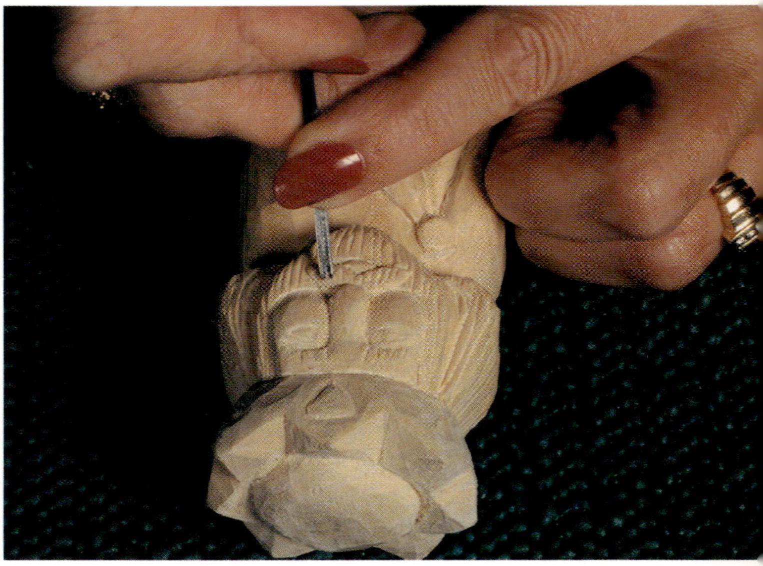

End by completing his mustache lines.

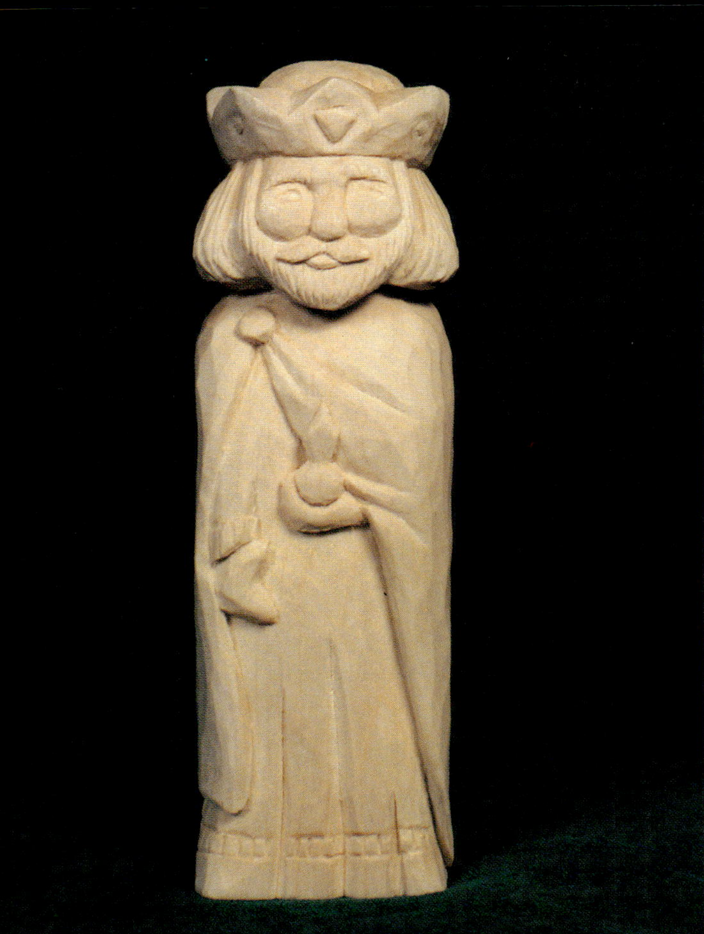

Front.

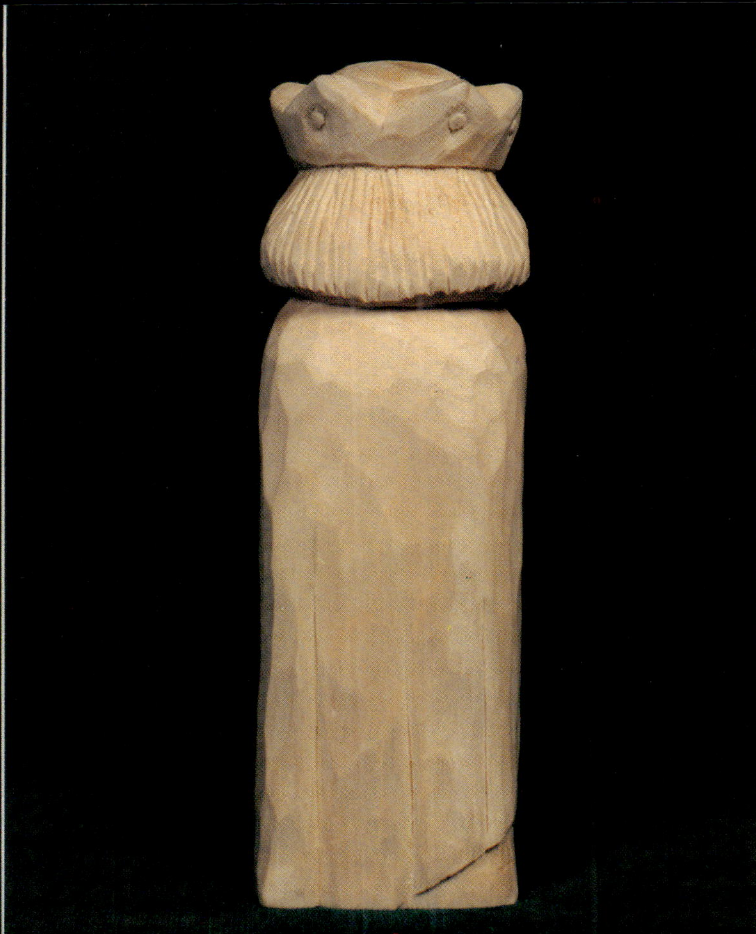

Back.

Side.

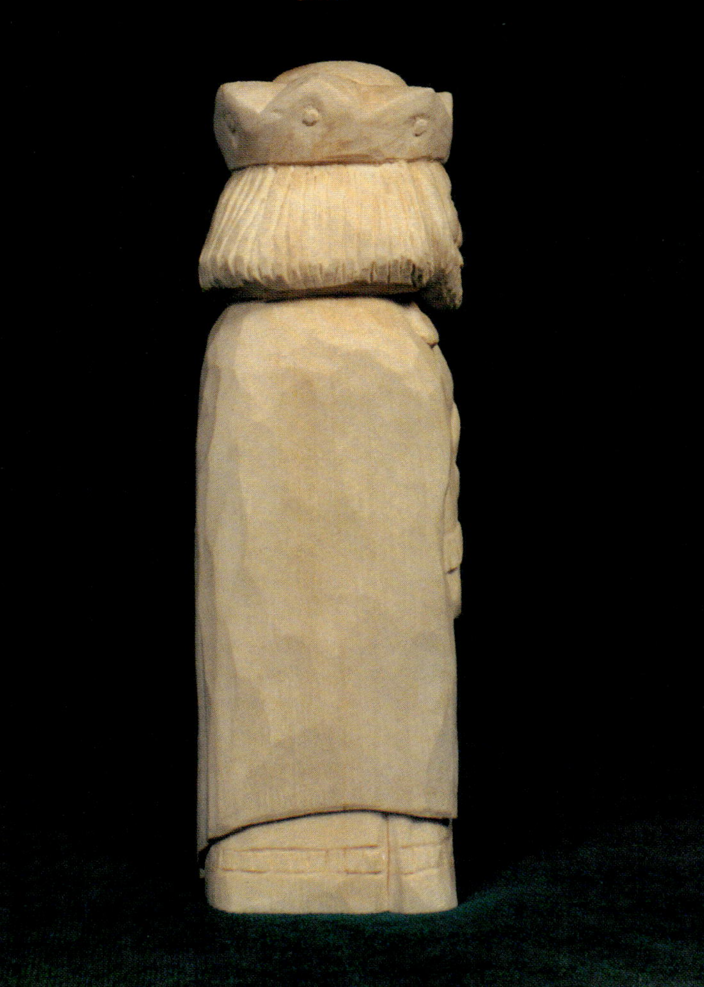

Side.

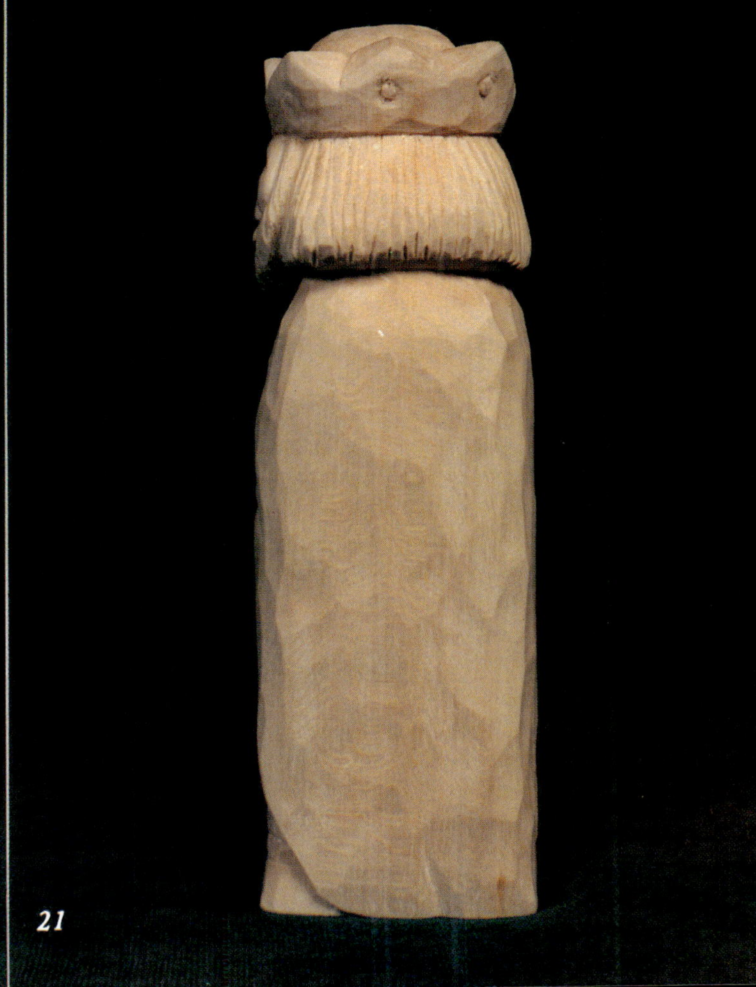

CARVING DONKEY

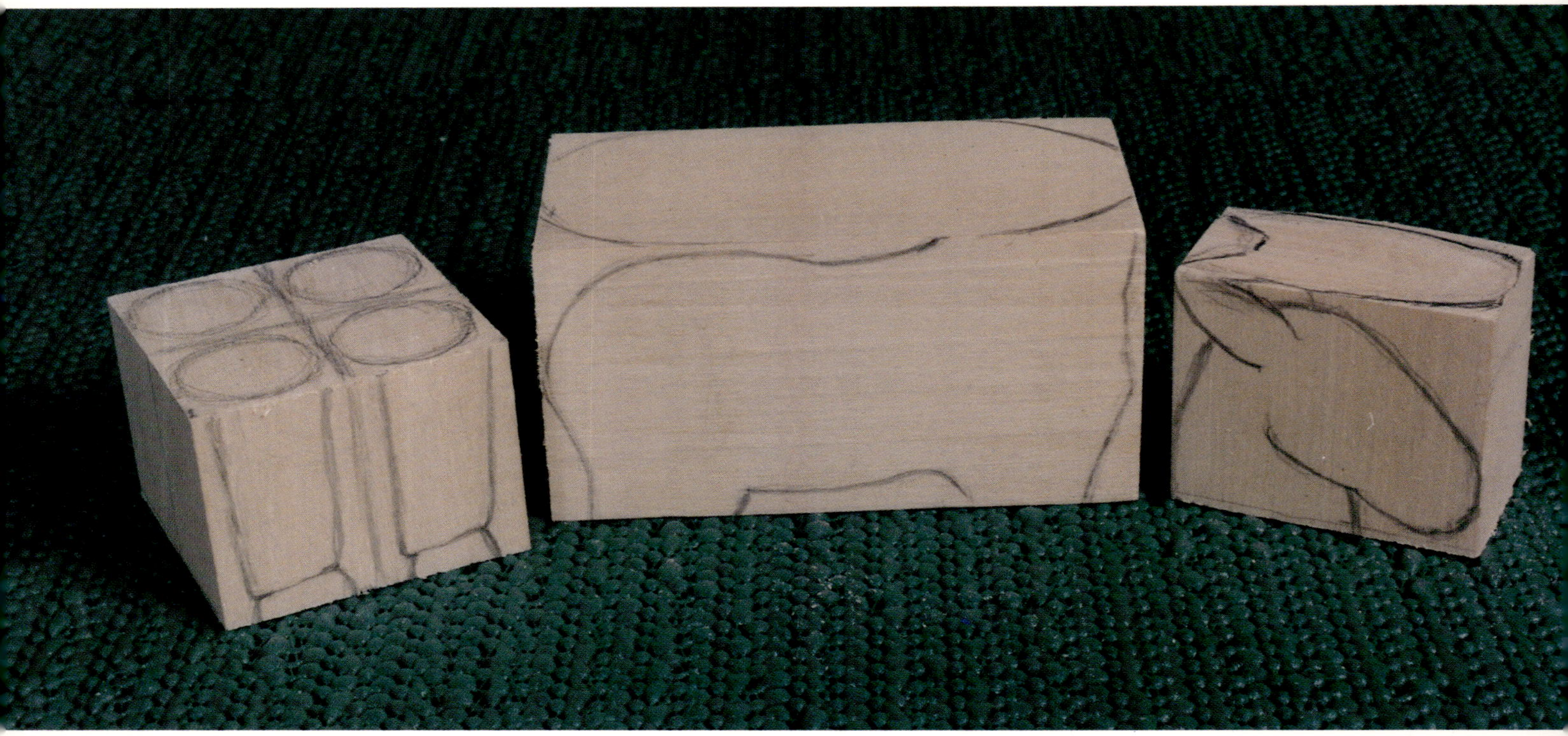

We are ready to start our donkey. I've cut the wood and transferred the pattern to a piece of 2″ x 2″ x 12″ bass wood, which is then cut into three pieces, the legs, the body, and the head.

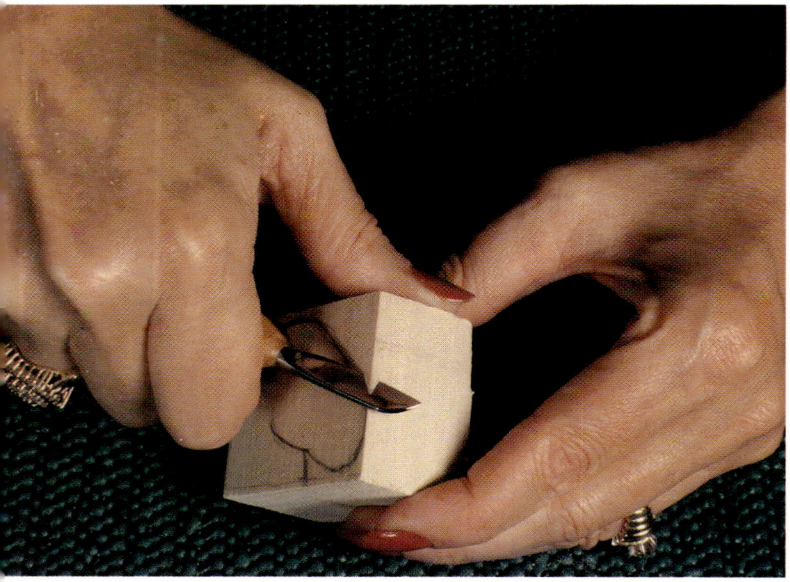

Start with the head. At top of the nose, cut in and start removing corners. We will not be scoring much on this piece. It is mostly rounding.

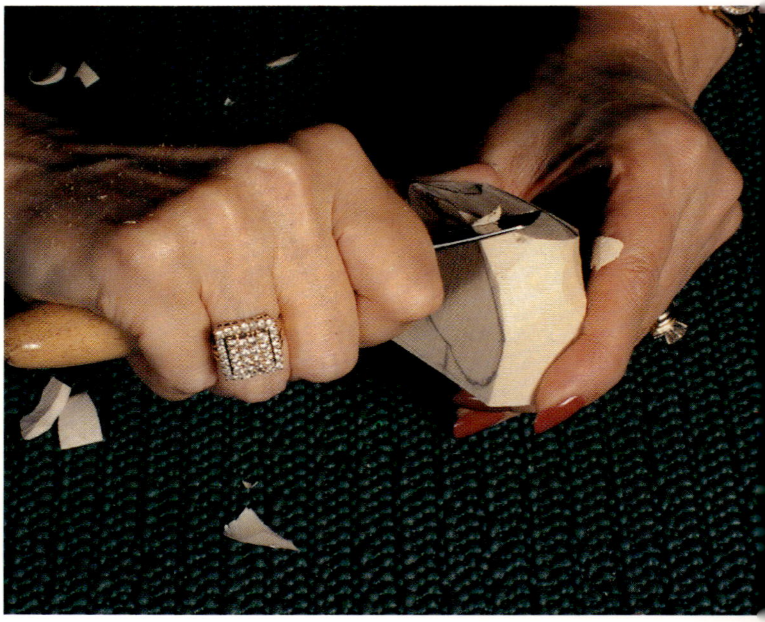

Draw your knife up over the entire nose to the base of the ears.

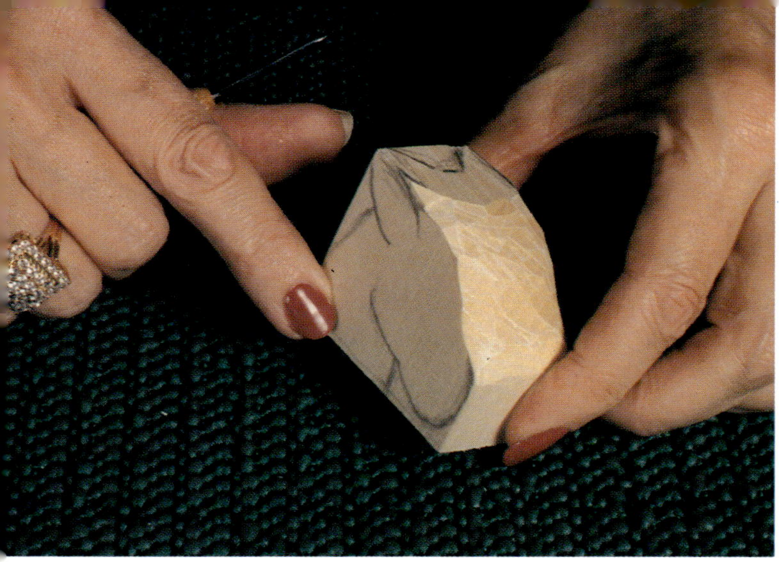

The piece should look like this.

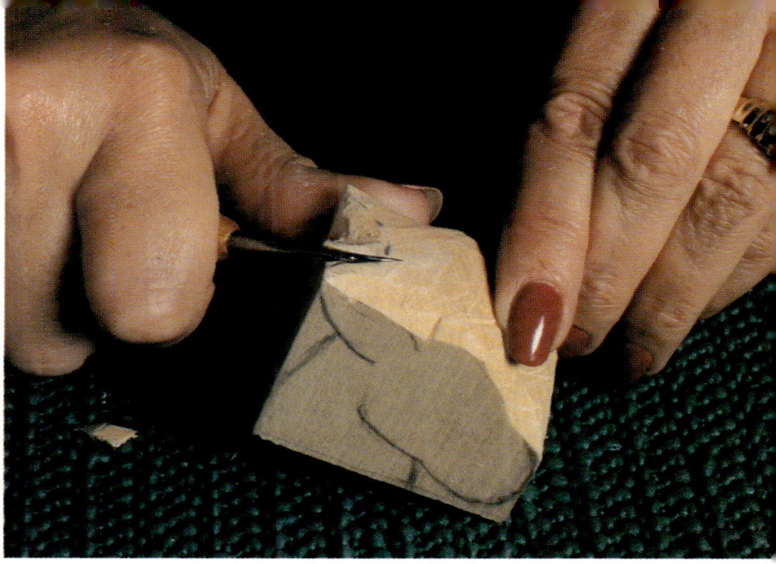

then the other.

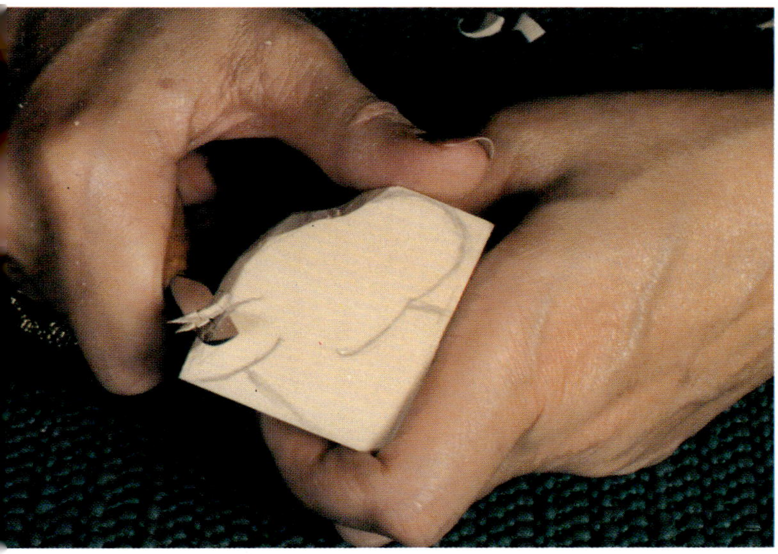

Starting at the top of his ears, carve down to the head.

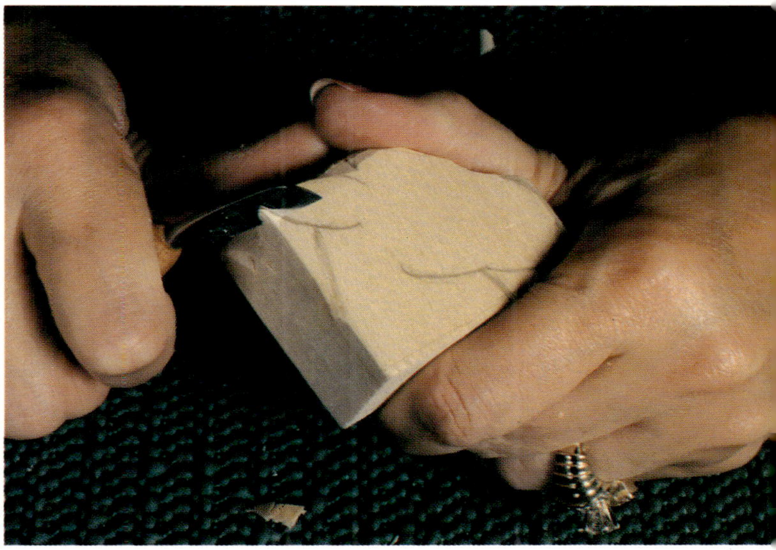

Make a stop cut on the back of his ear.

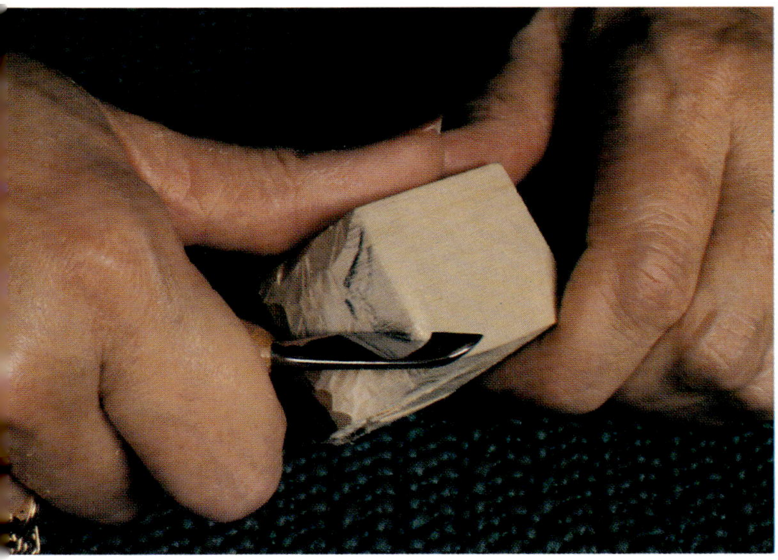

Make an angle cut to start separating the ears. Do one ear...

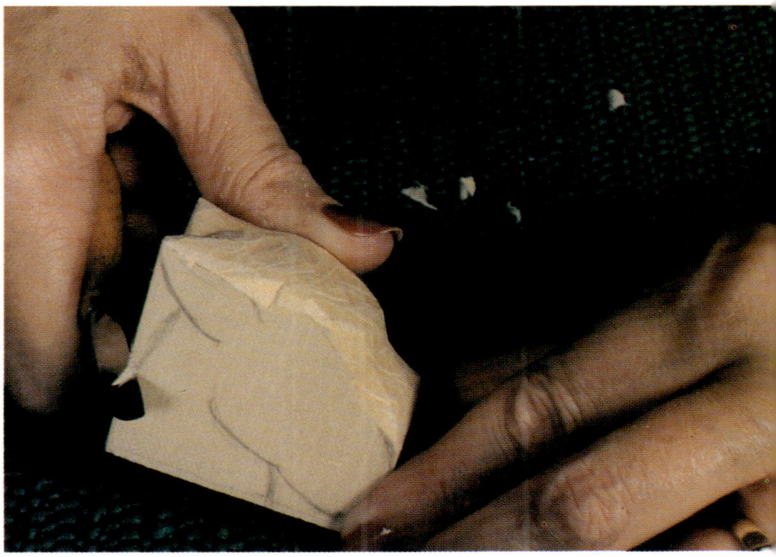

Draw your knife up to that cut from the neck.

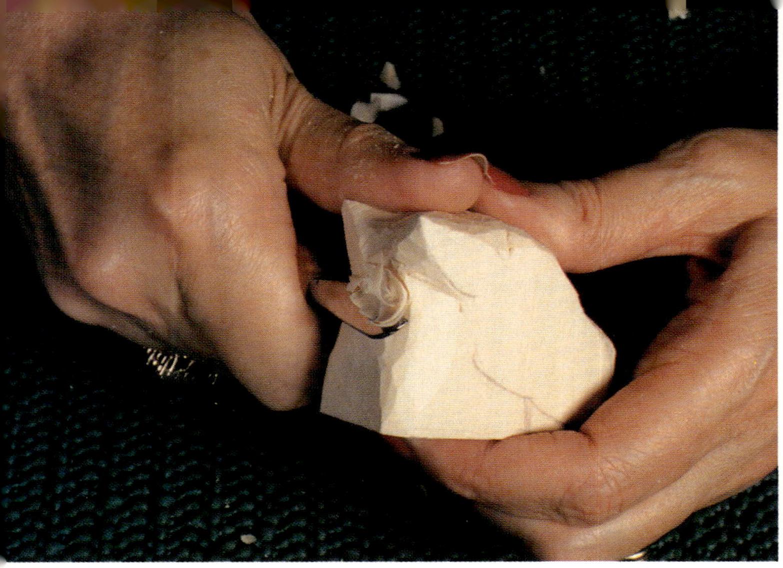

Start rounding off the back of the neck and head. REMEMBER to keep the base flat and carve-free. You must have this flat in order to glue the head to his body.

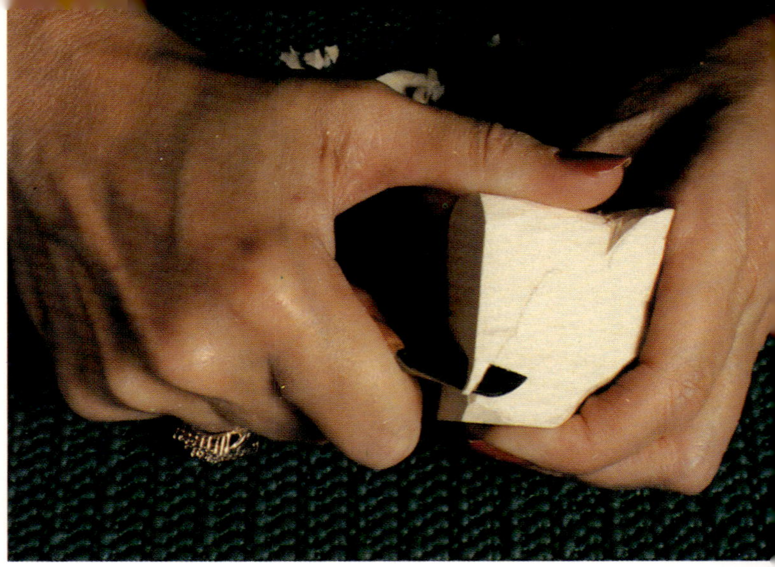

Still following the line, start rounding under the chin.

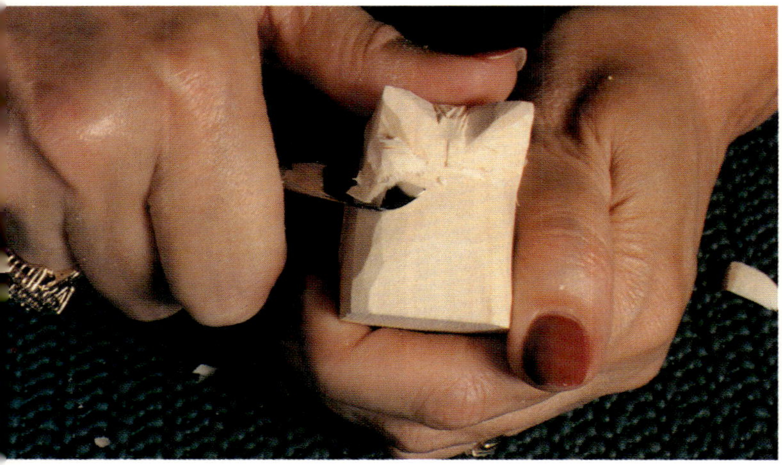

Do the same on the other side.

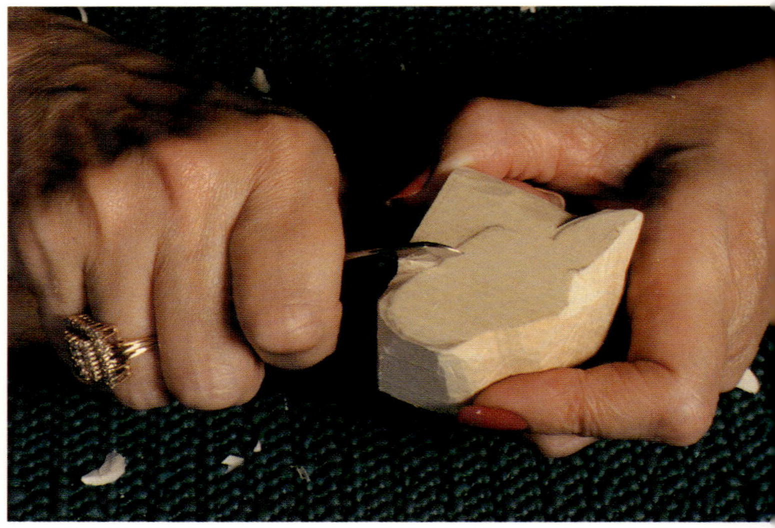

Cut a stop in the neck line.

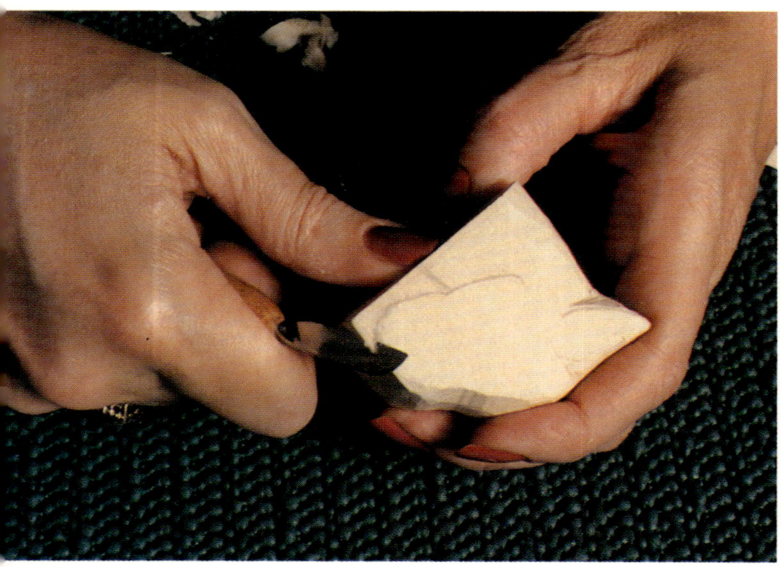

Come down the front of the nose, following the line and round it off.

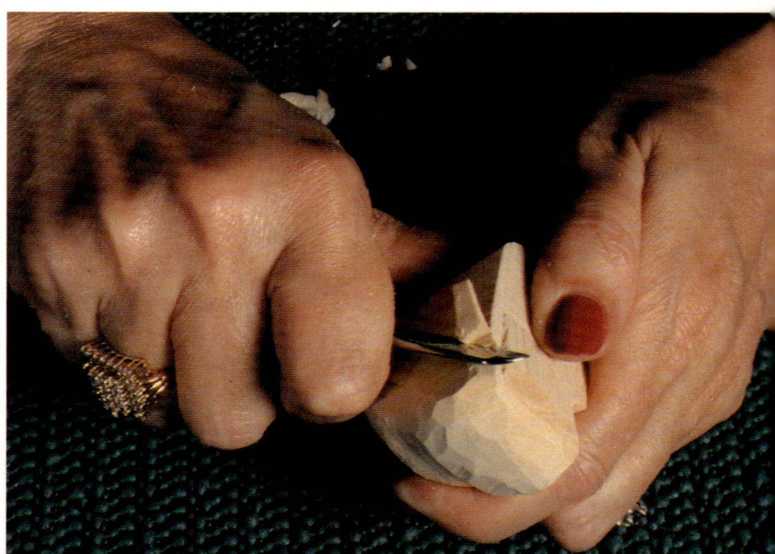

Draw your knife down under the chin to that cut.

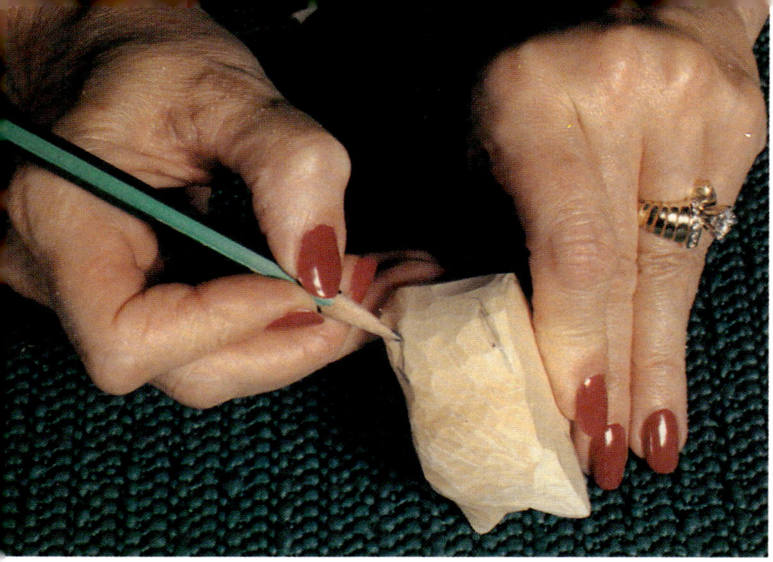

Draw in the nose line as seen from above, so you can see where you are going.

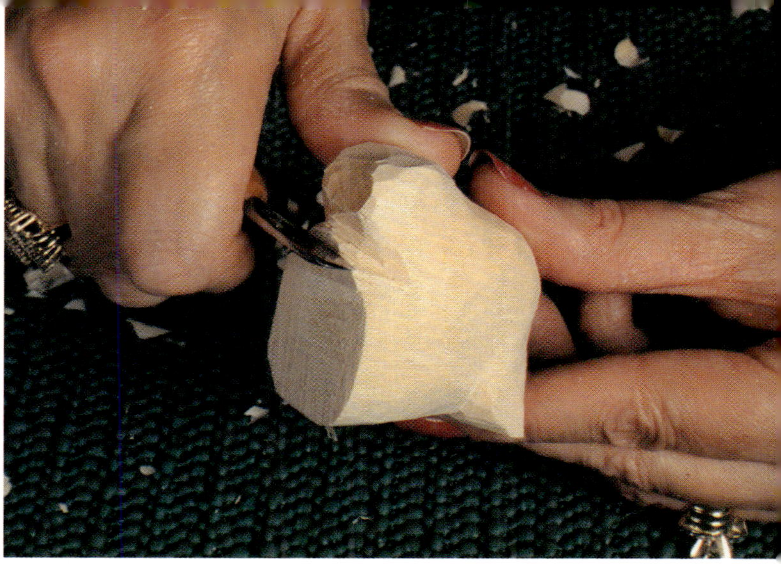

Finish the neck area under the chin.

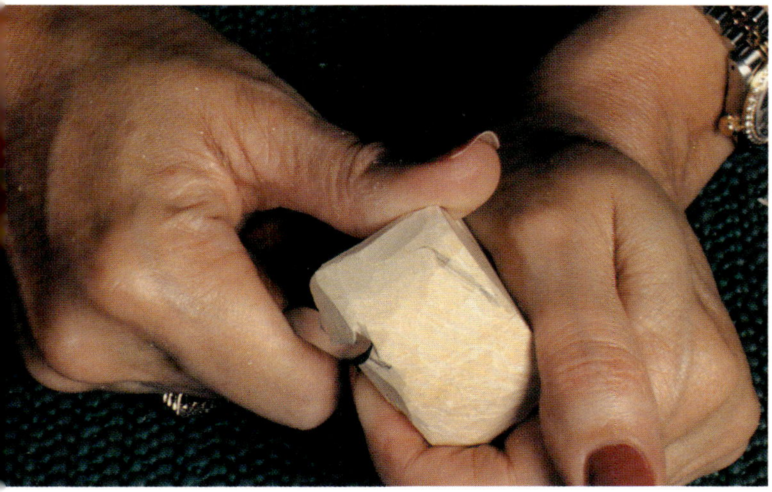

Now remove the wood to that line.

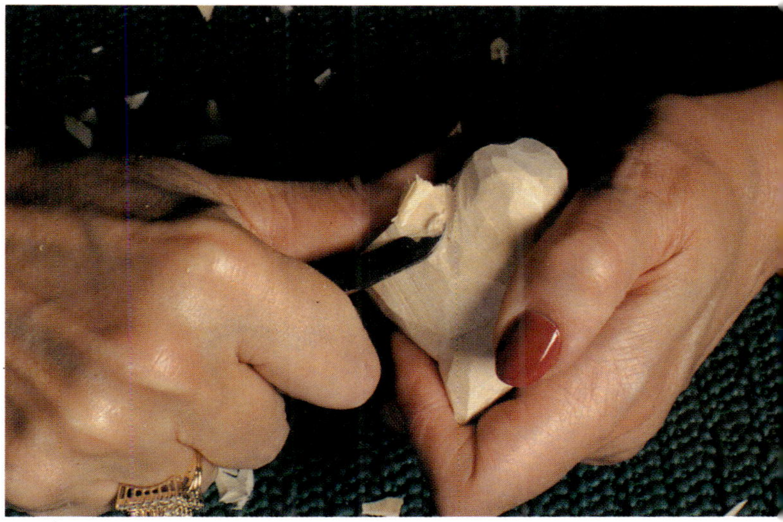

Continue to round all the way around the side.

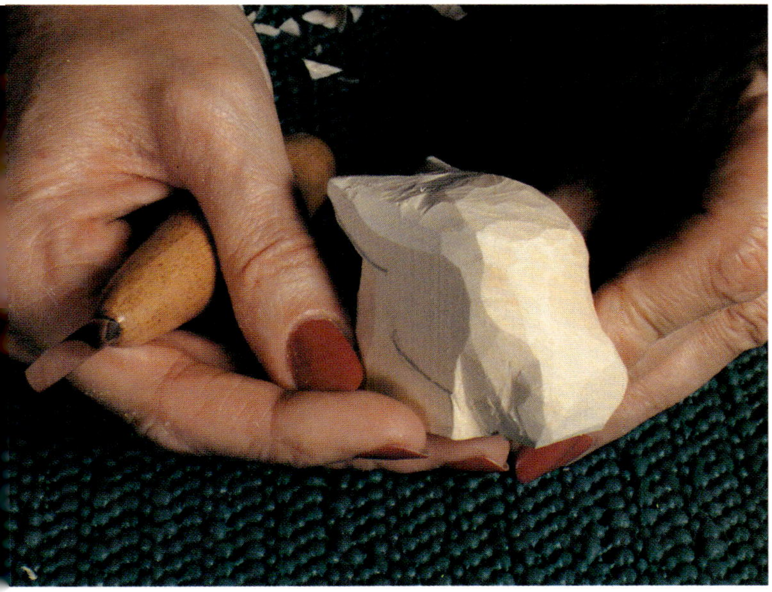

This is where you should be.

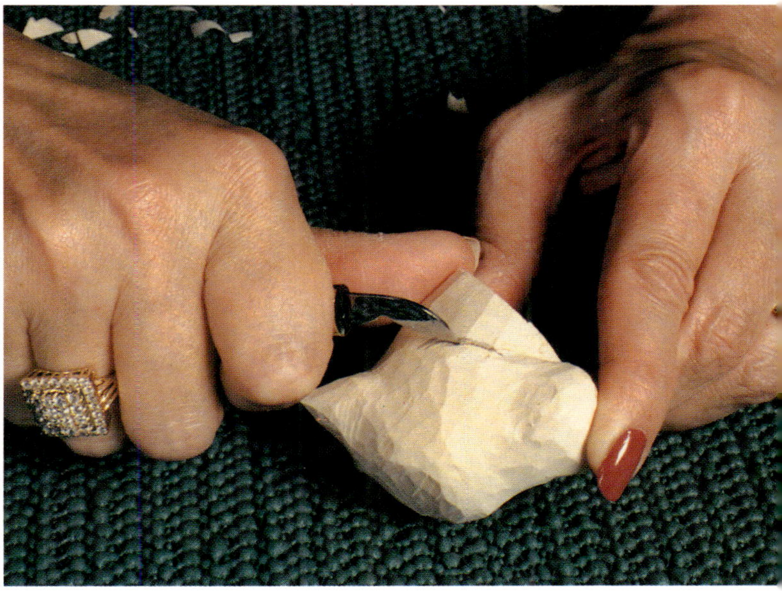

Score the jaw lines.

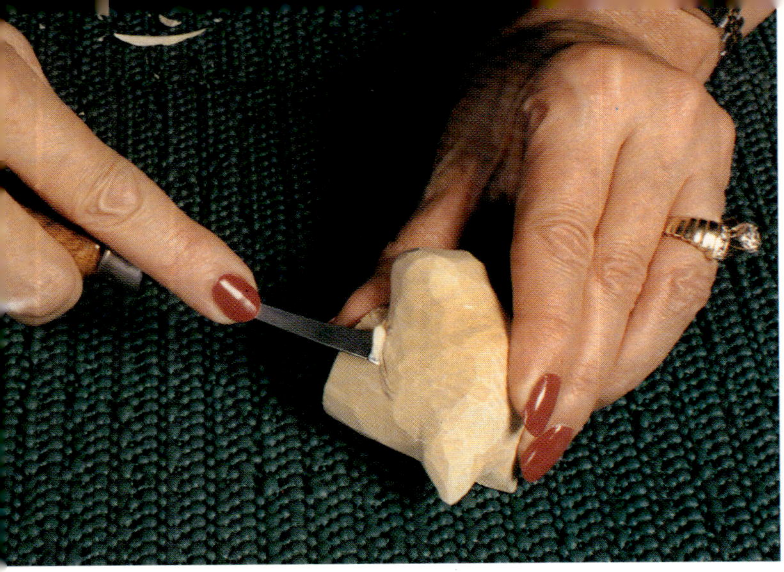

Carve up under the score line, then round to finish the head.

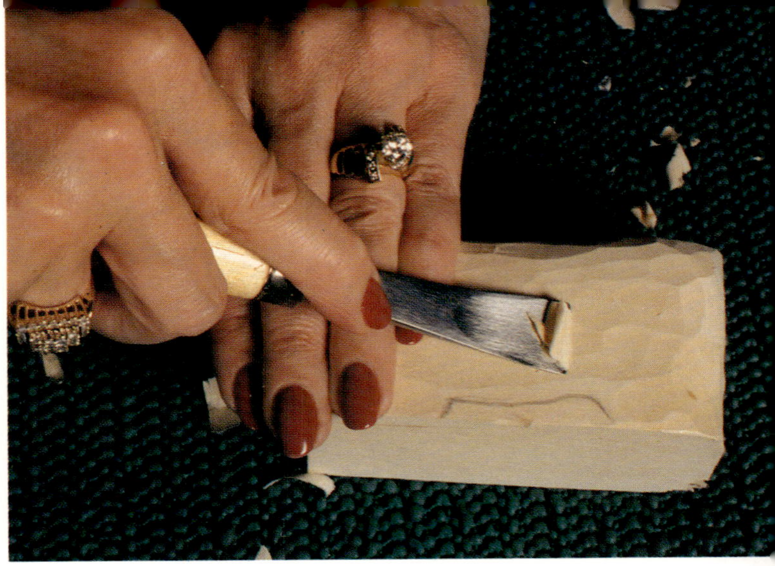

Again, use your large gouge and round off the body leaving the carve marks.

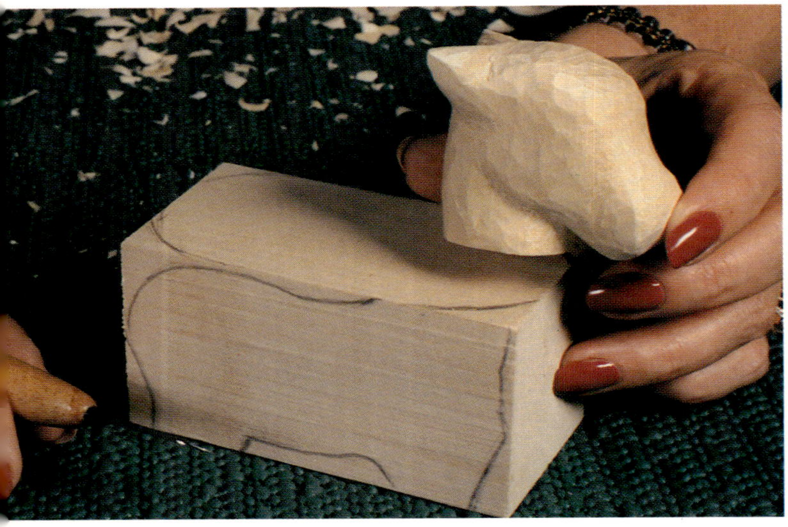

This is what it should look like at his point.

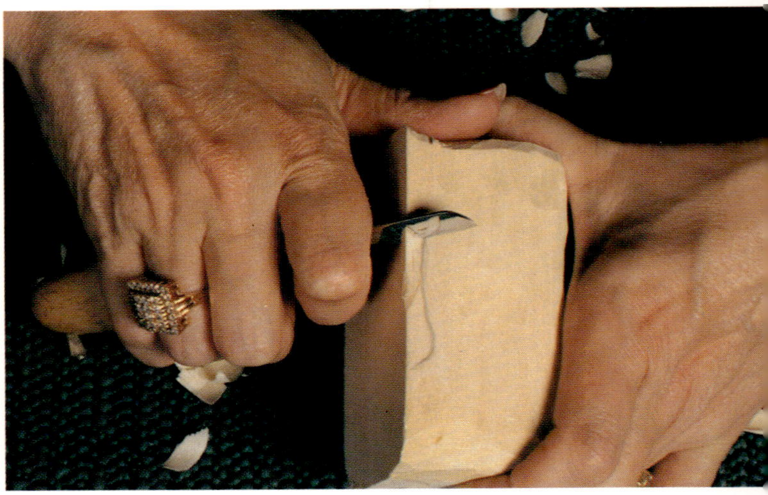

On the bottom edge make in a stop cut behind the front leg.

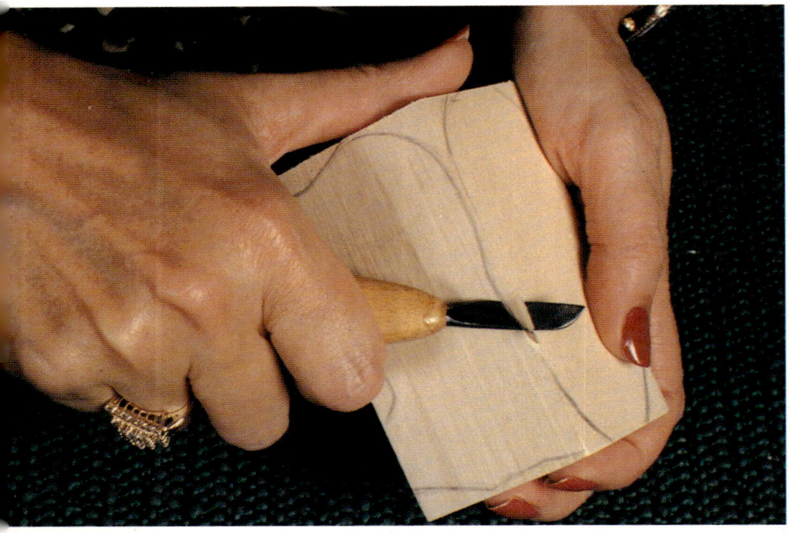

With your carving knife and start rounding the edges of the body. Be sure to draw a circle where the body and head will be glued. Keep this area smooth and carve free.

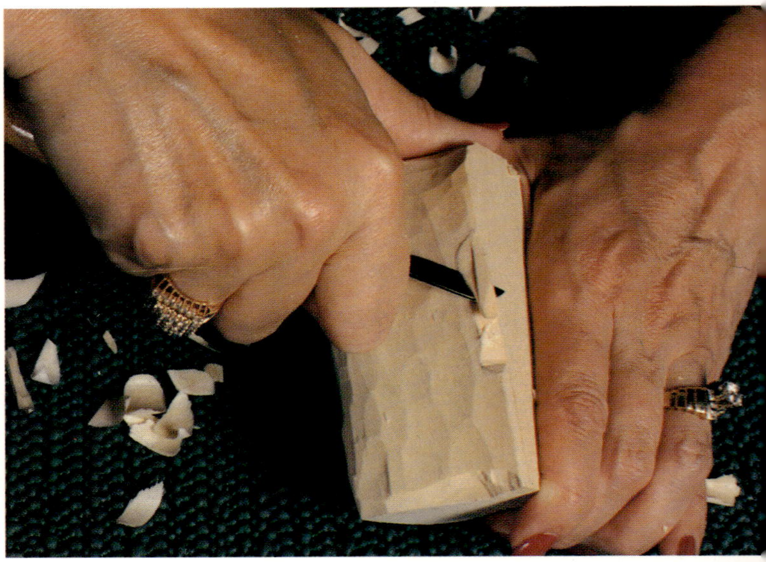

Cut back to the stop along the edge to remove the wood, starting his stomach area.

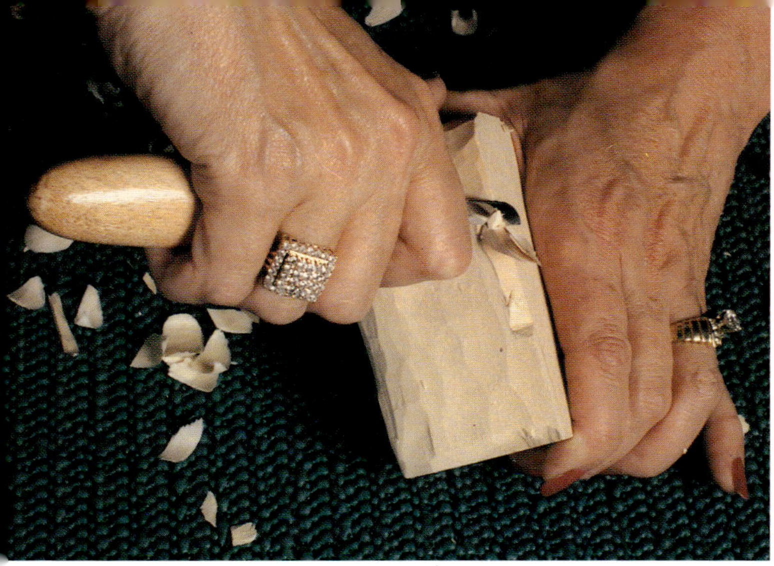

Make another angle cut for definition.

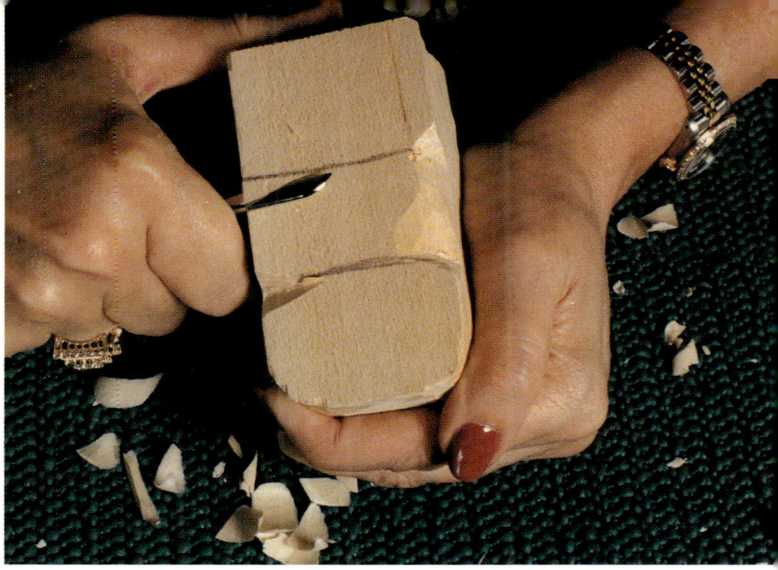

Do the same at the back legs. Angle into the line at the corner...

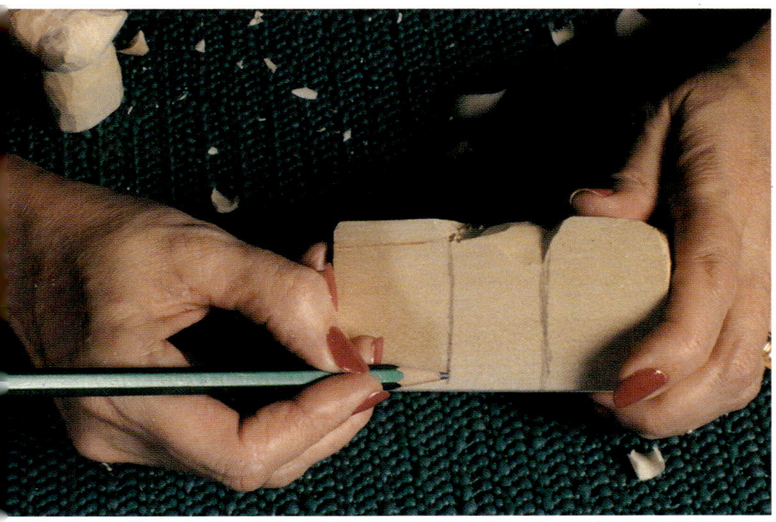

Turn the piece upside down and draw the the area of the legs. This defines the stomach and shows you what needs to be left carve free and flat for gluing.

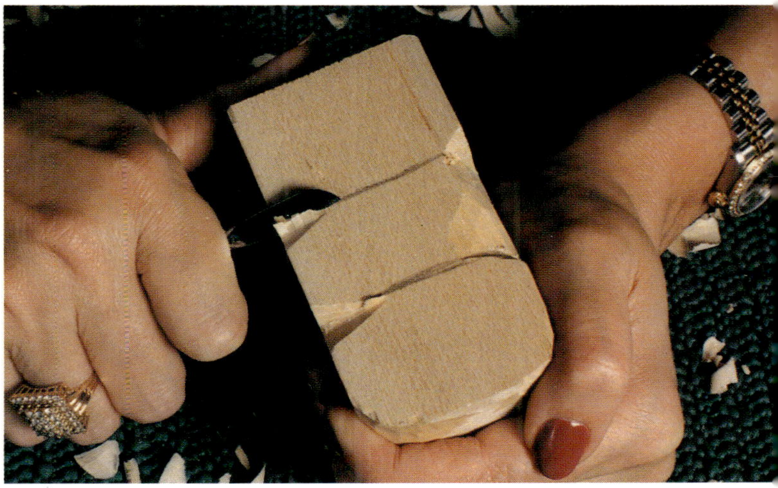

Then cut down on the line to finish the cut.

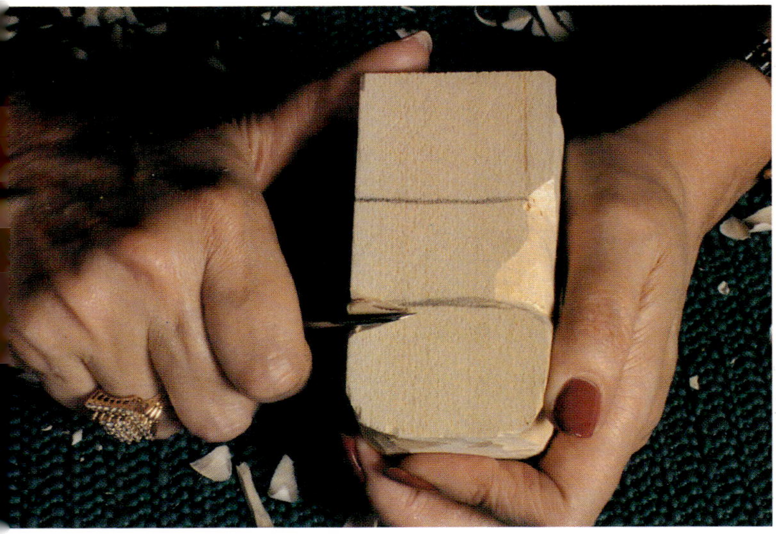

Using the line as a guide, cut a wedge behind the front legs.

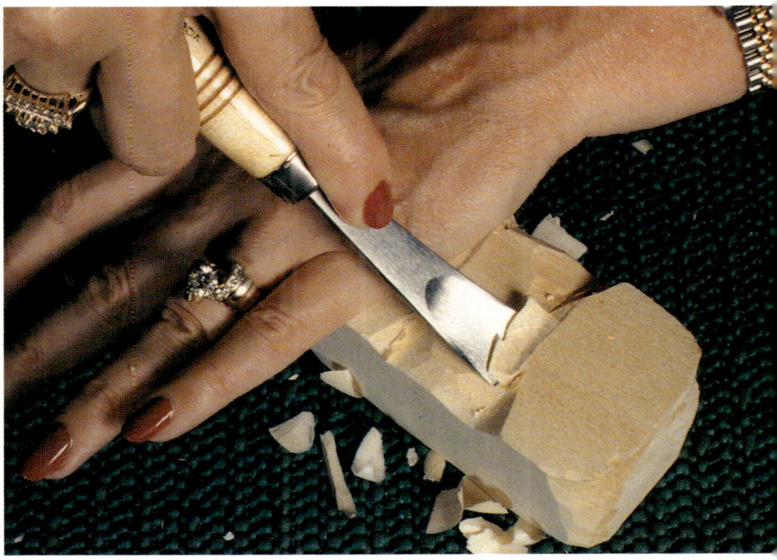

Start removing the wood on his stomach with your large gouge, leaving carve marks.

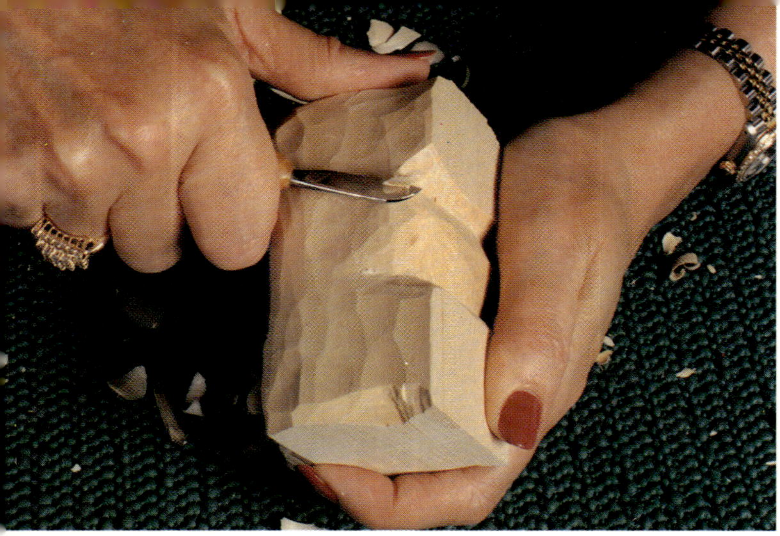

Finish rounding with your carving knife.

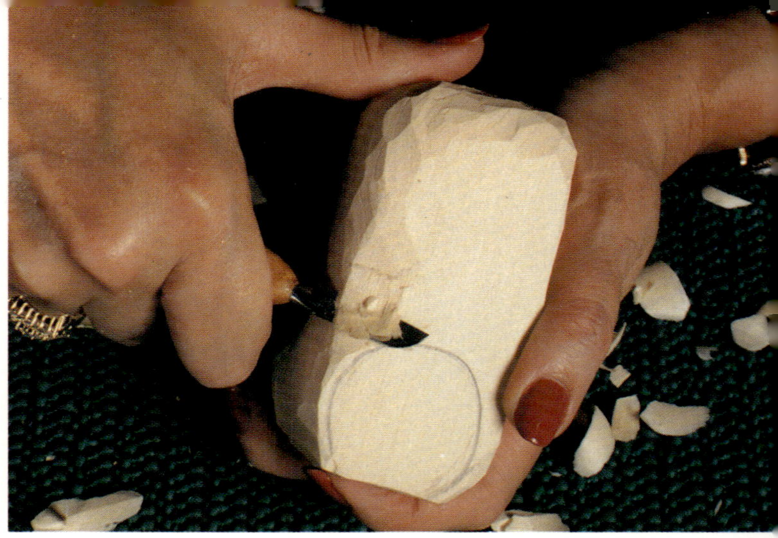

Finish rounding the body, leaving the neck base area flat and carve free.

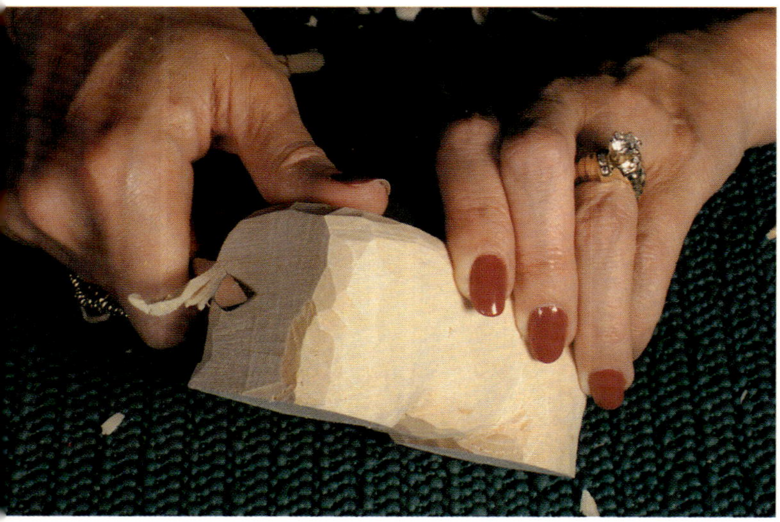

Now start rounding his backside.

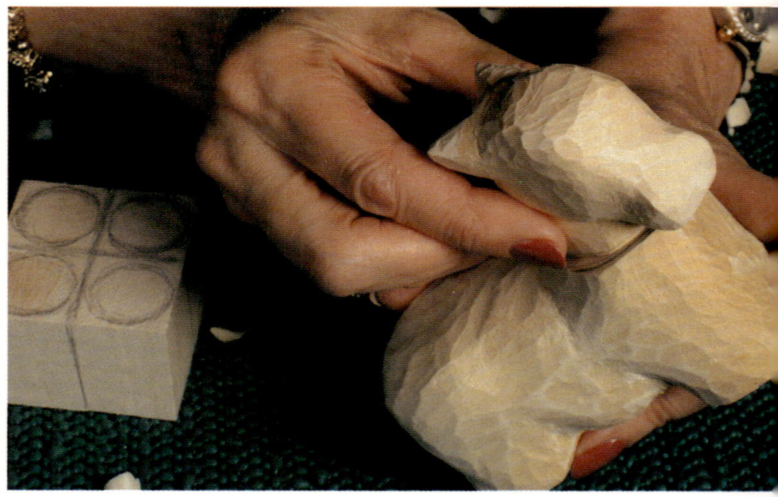

Now, position his head the way you would like. I have turned it slightly, so he is looking off to the side.

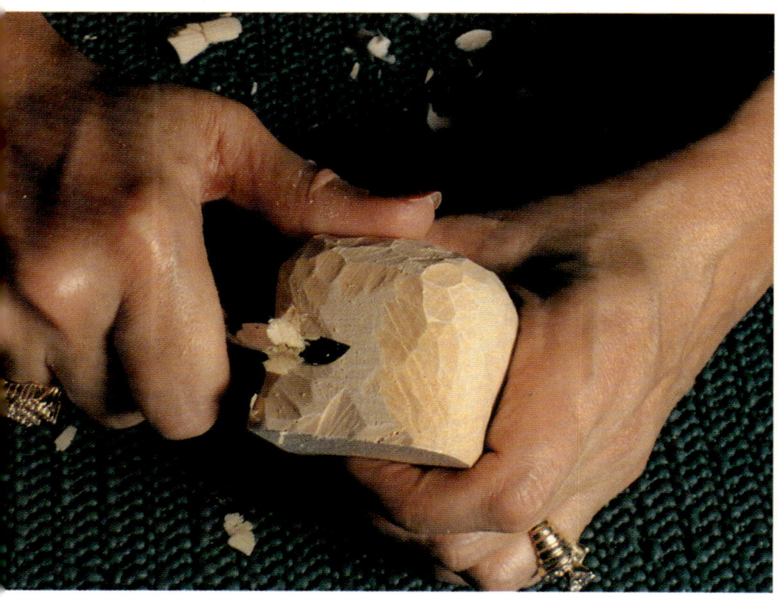

Make sure to curve in a bit to suggest the top of his leg.

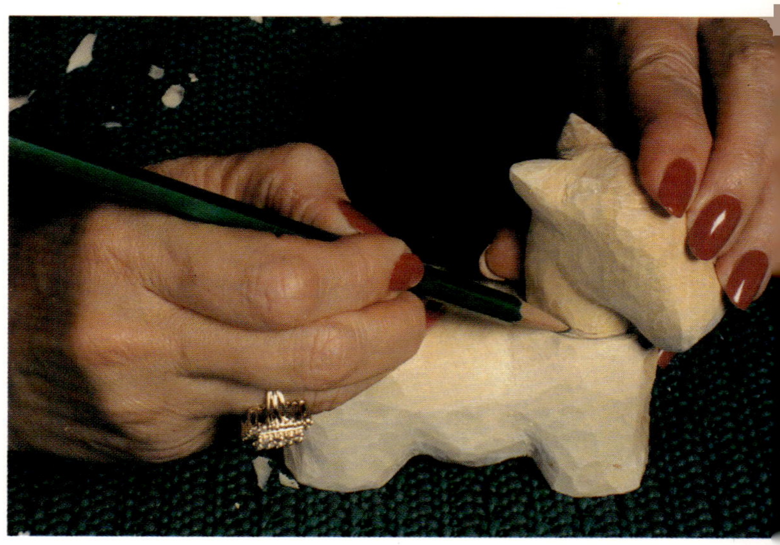

Draw the outline of the neck on the base, so you can make the cuts closer.

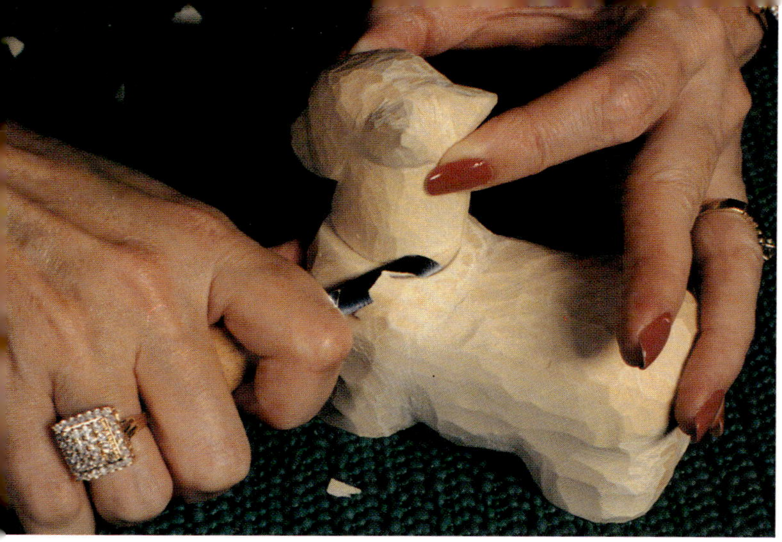

Do the final fitting. Hold his head on and cut as close as possible.

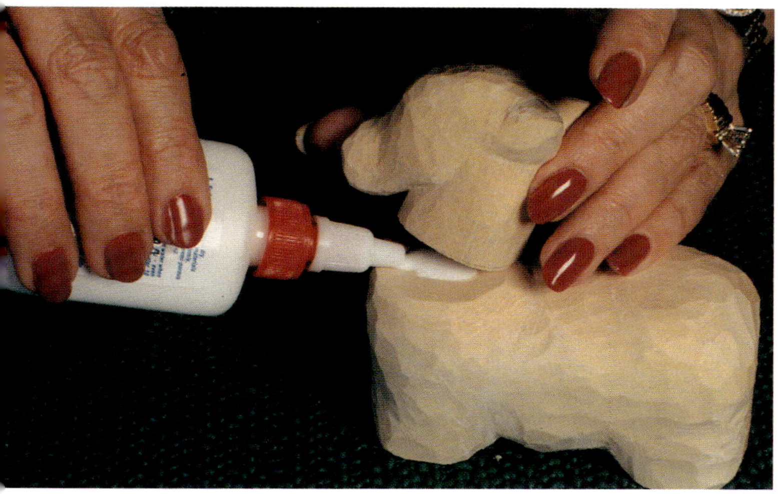

Using the wood glue, glue the head in place.

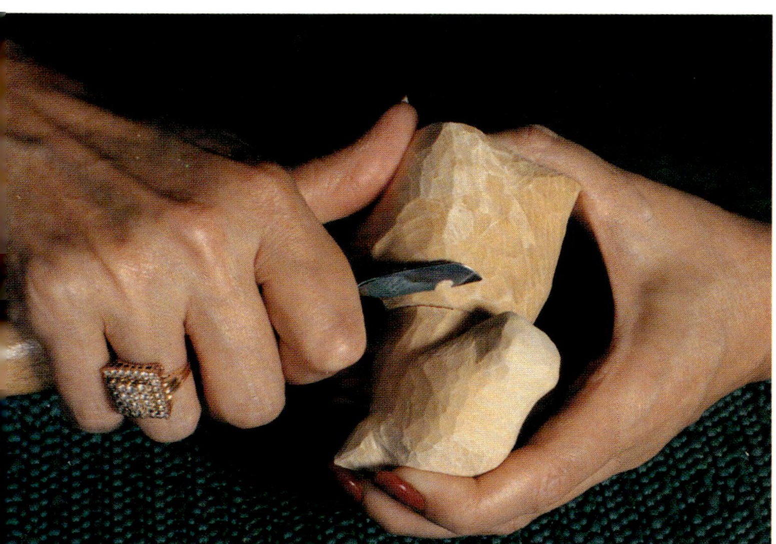

Once the glue is dry, you can fine tune the fit. Carefully carve to a perfect match. We will putty the seams later.

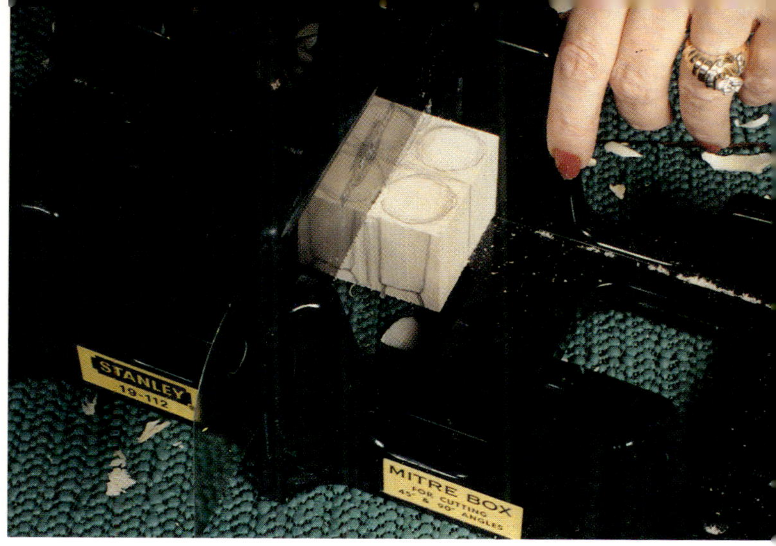

Separate the legs with a saw.

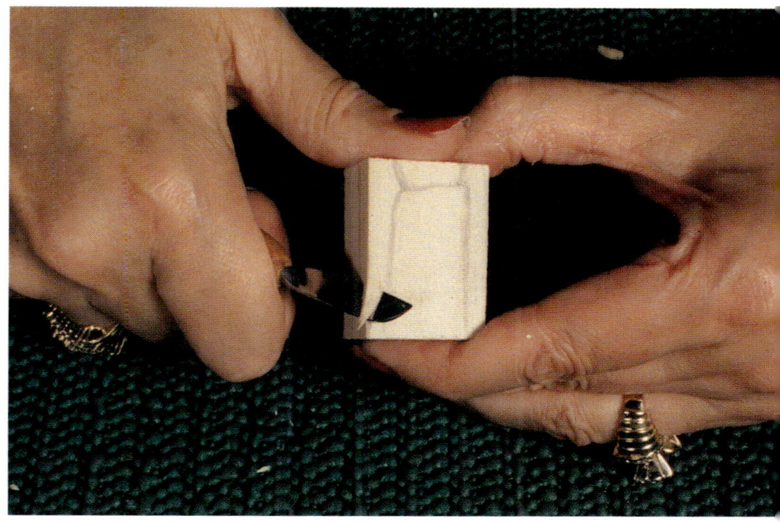

Round off each leg.

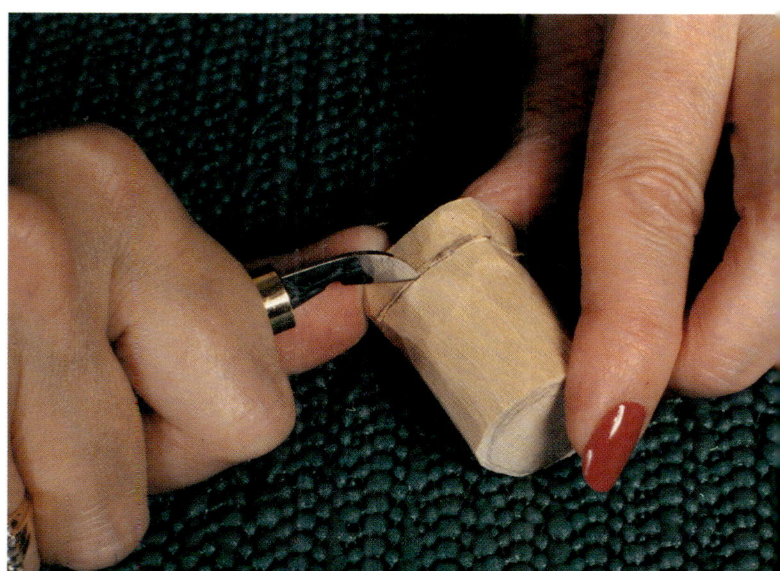

Score the top of the hoof.

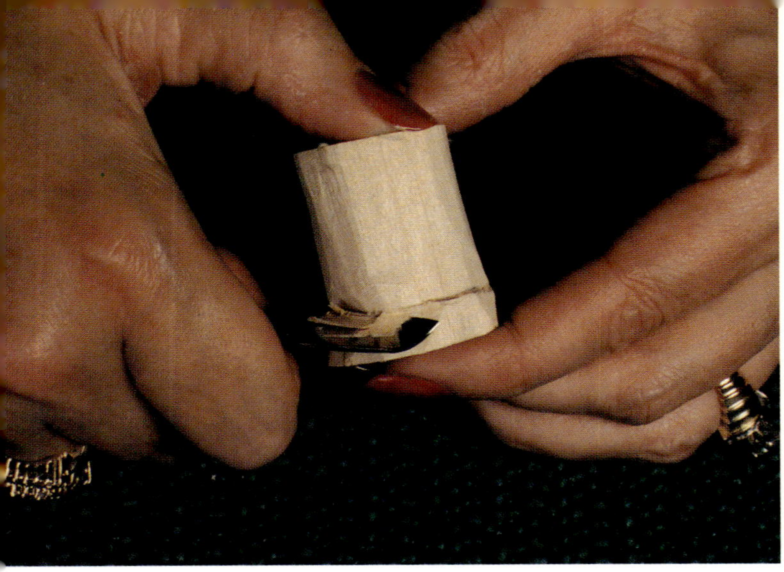

With your carving knife, cut up to the stop cut.

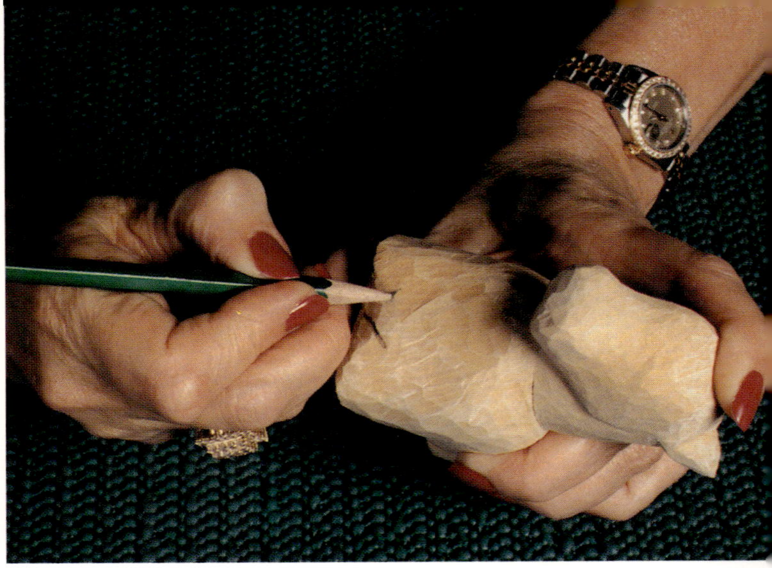

Draw a small V at the bottom of his chest area.

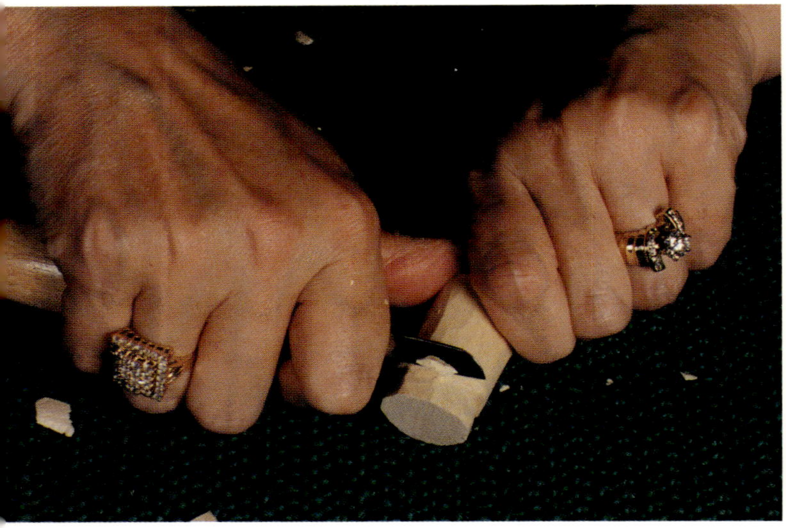

Come down and round off the edge of his leg into the hoof.

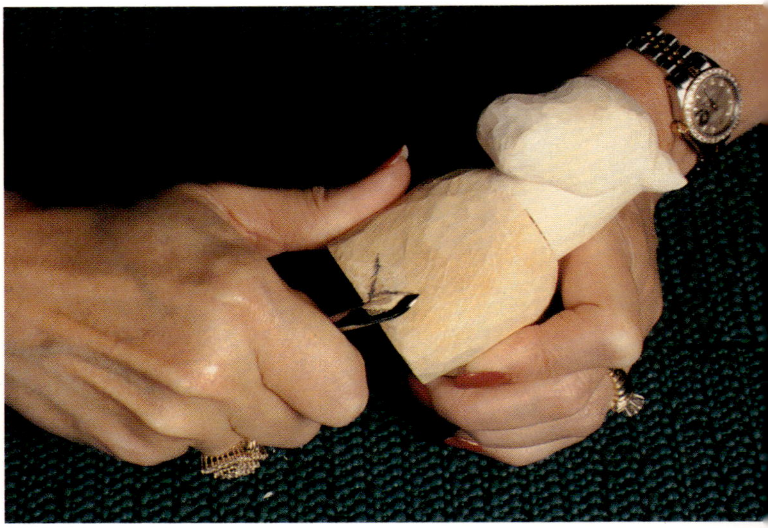

Cut in slightly to suggest the top of his legs.

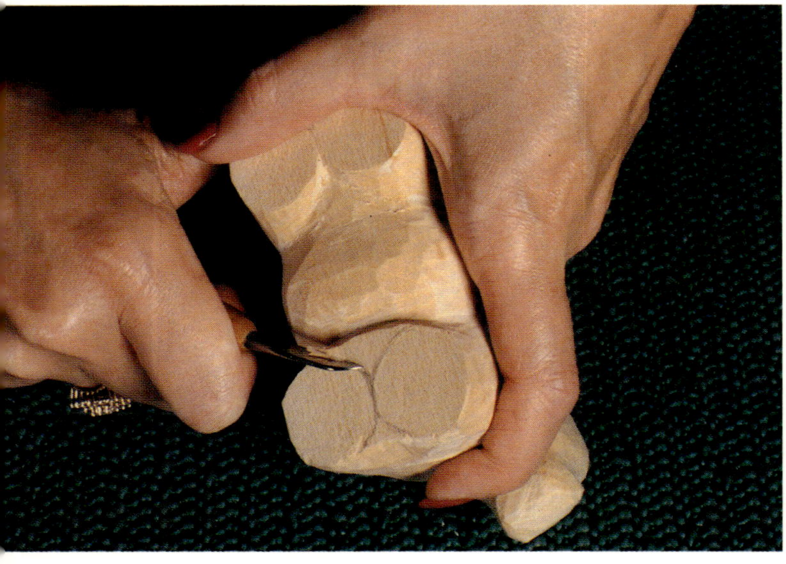

Draw the leg area on the body. Make sure to keep it flat and carve free. Do the fitting and make the cuts.

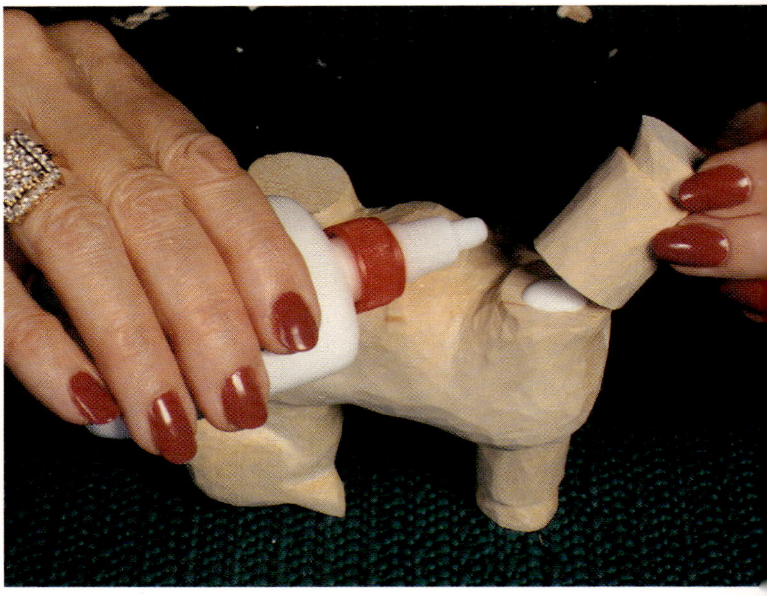

Glue the legs in place.

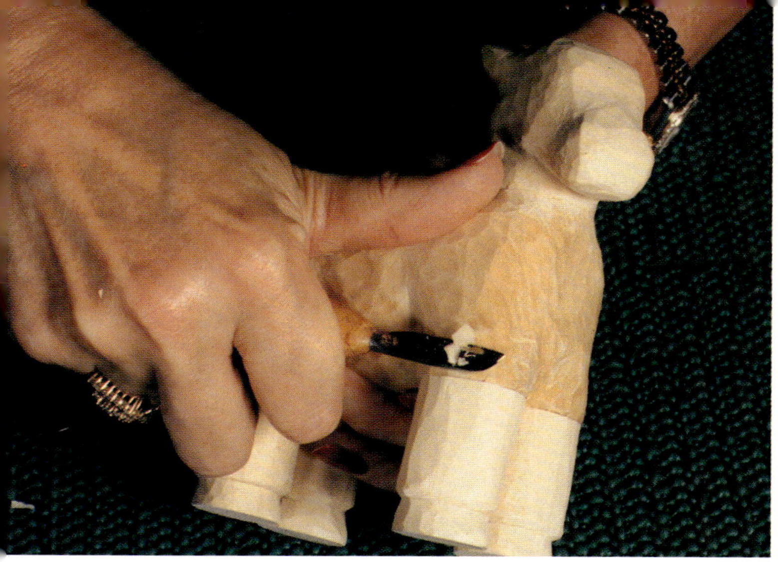
After they dry, fine tune the fit.

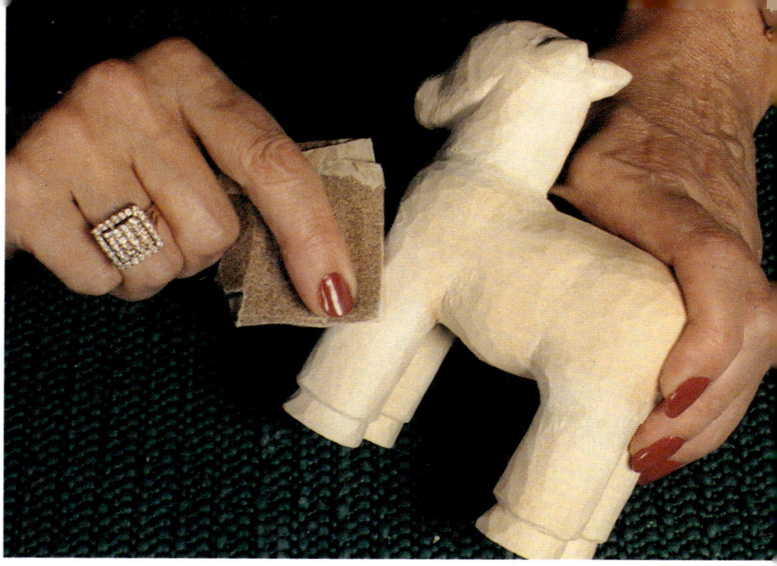
Sand the joints with fine sandpaper.

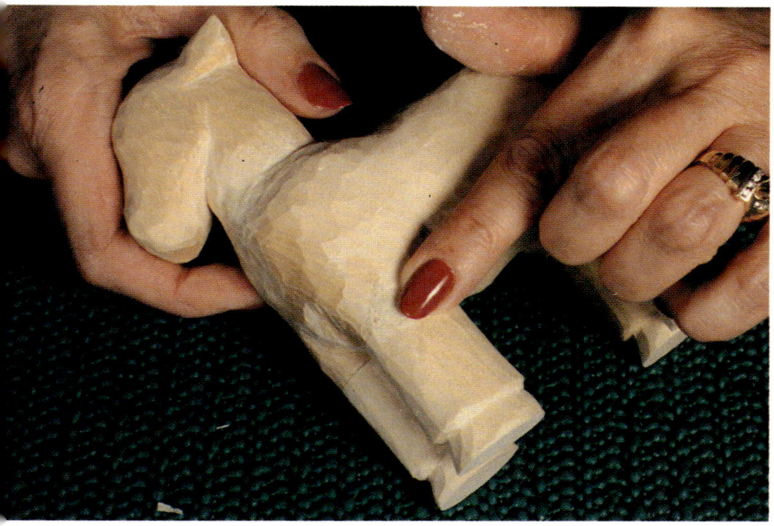
Apply putty to the joints of his legs.

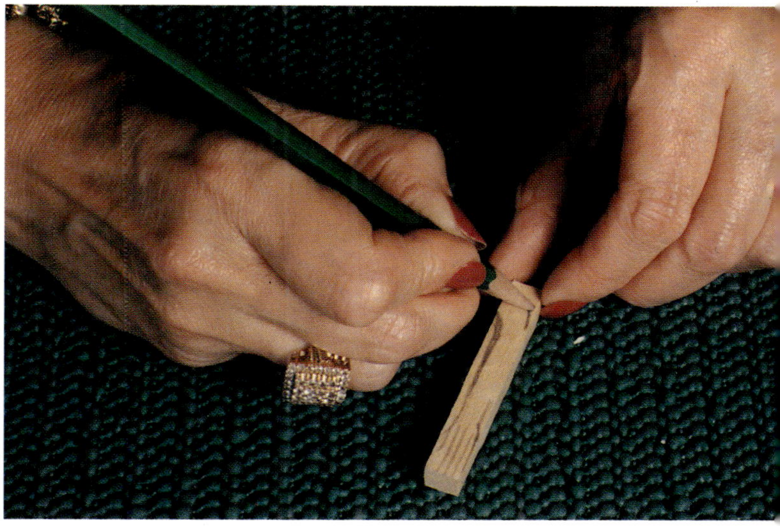
Draw the tail on a piece of scrap.

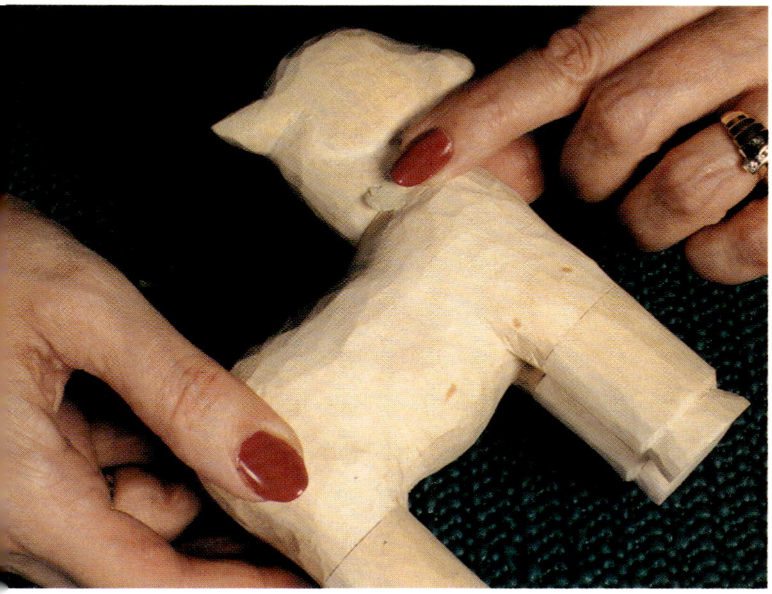
Putty his neck.

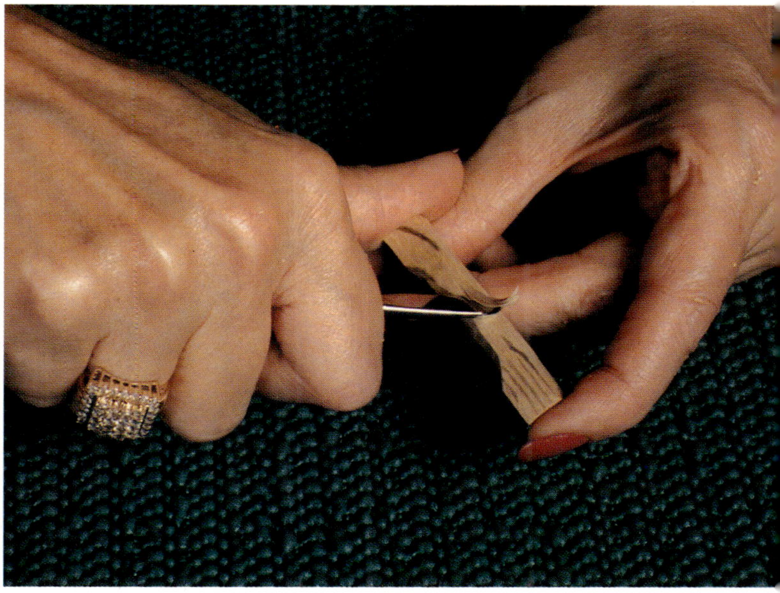
Round it off.

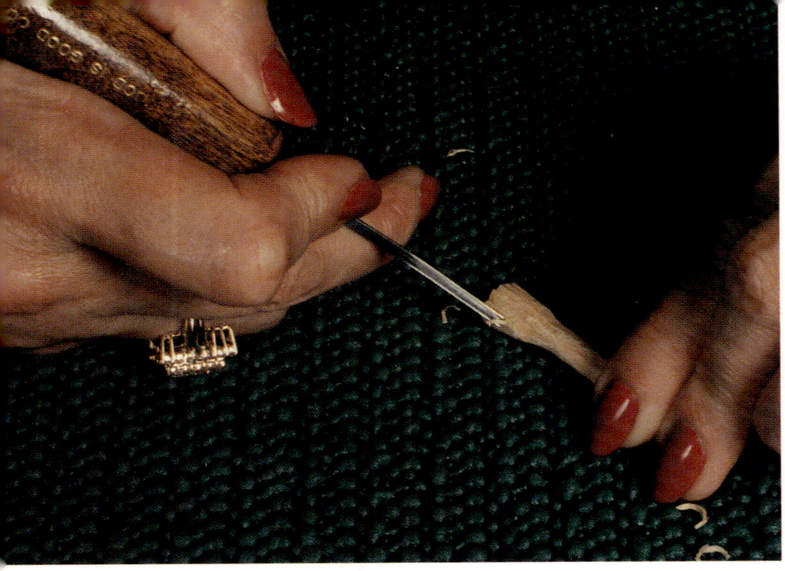

With your small V-parting tool, make hair lines at random.

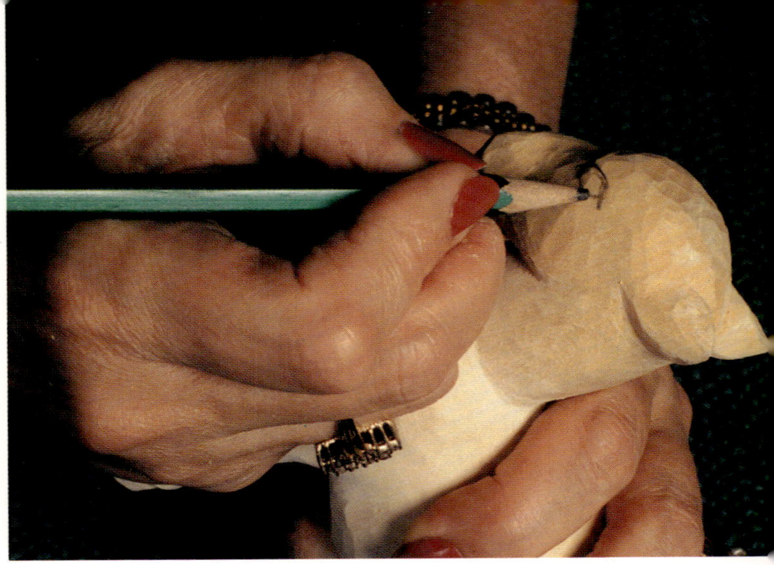

Draw on details: eyes, nose, ears, and hair.

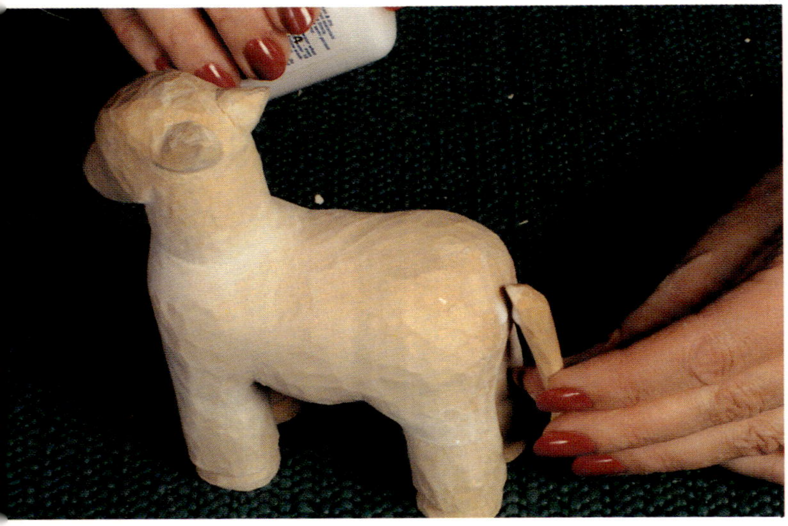

Fit and glue.

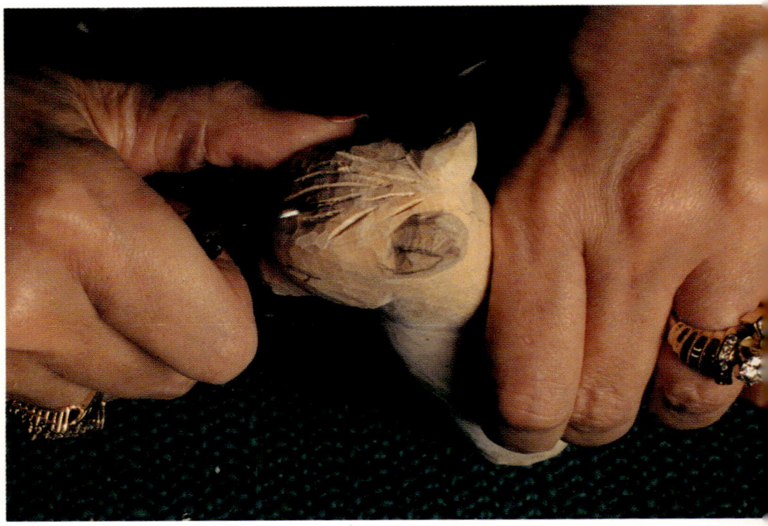

You need to cut in the hair marks on his head with a knife, because it is all cross-grain and too tough for your V-parting tool.

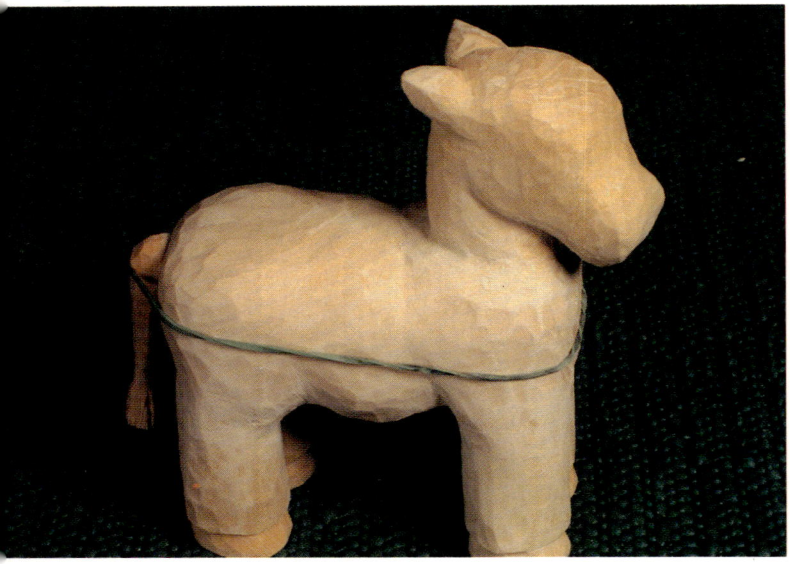

A rubber band works great for holding the tail in place while the glue dries.

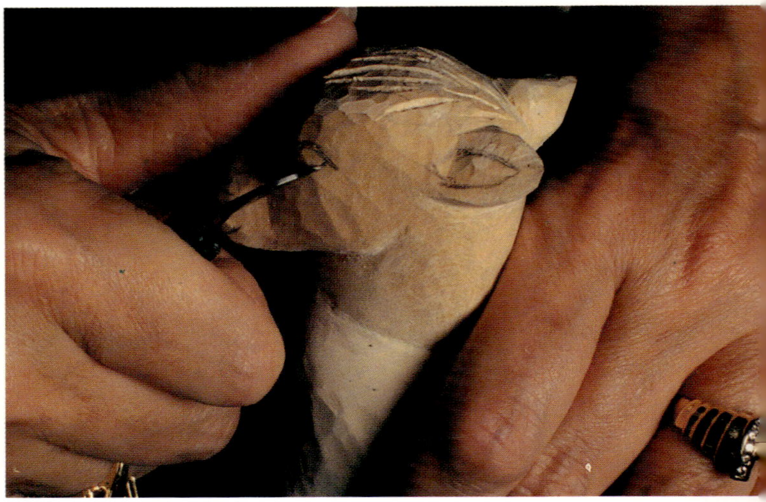

Score and carve the slightly rounded eyes. Keep them flat enough to paint.

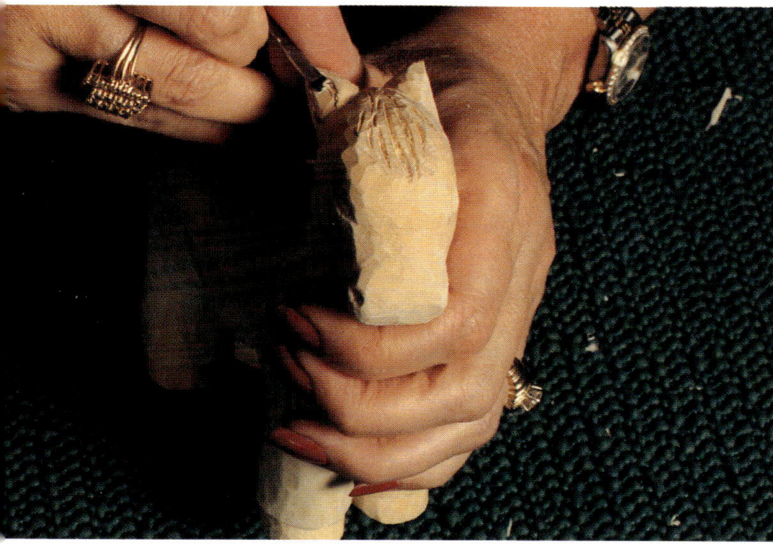

Finish with his ears.

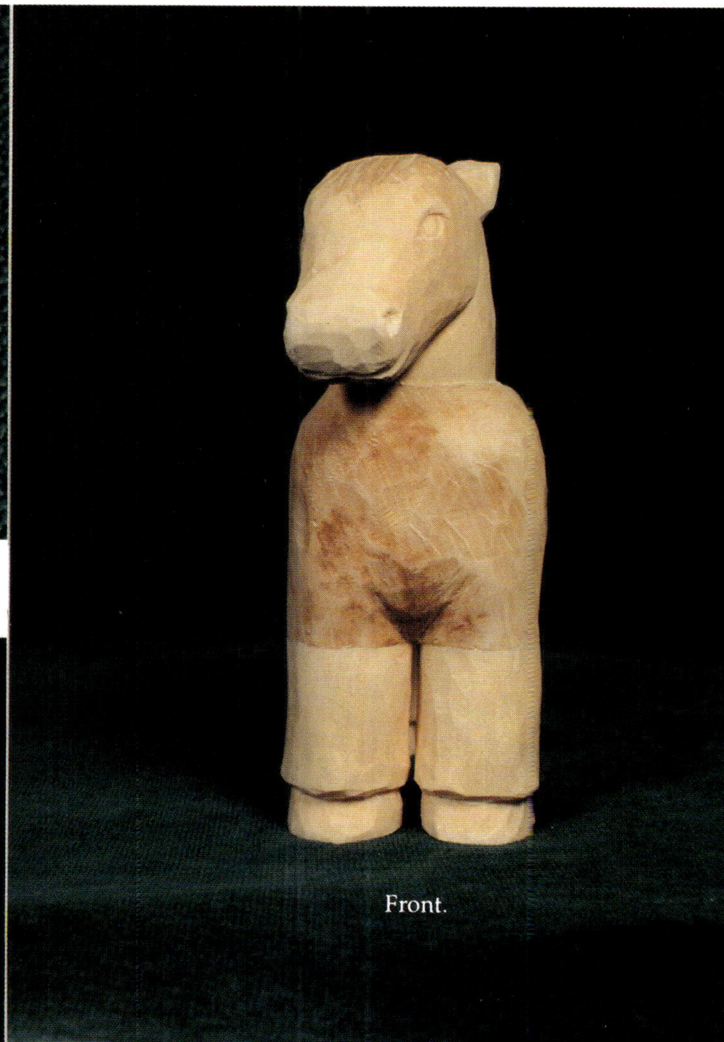

Front.

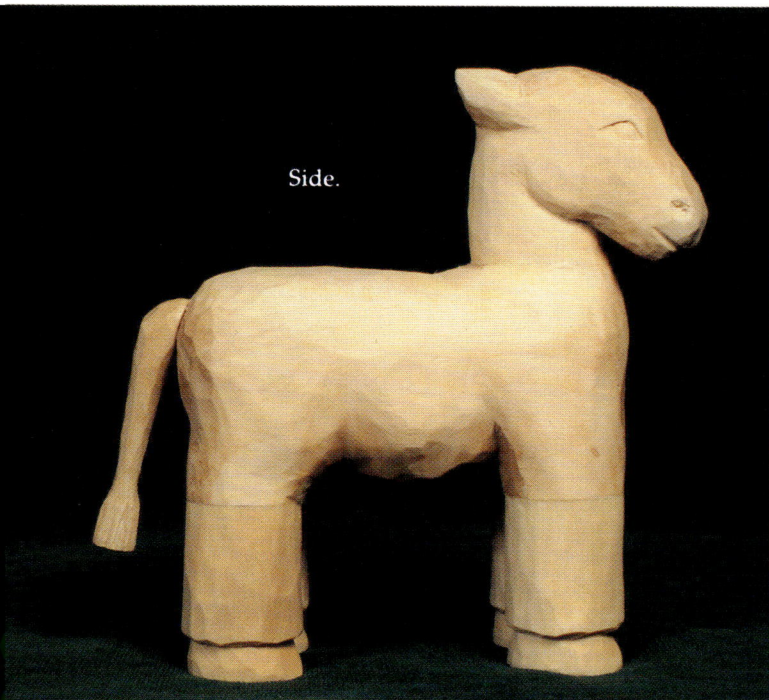

Side.

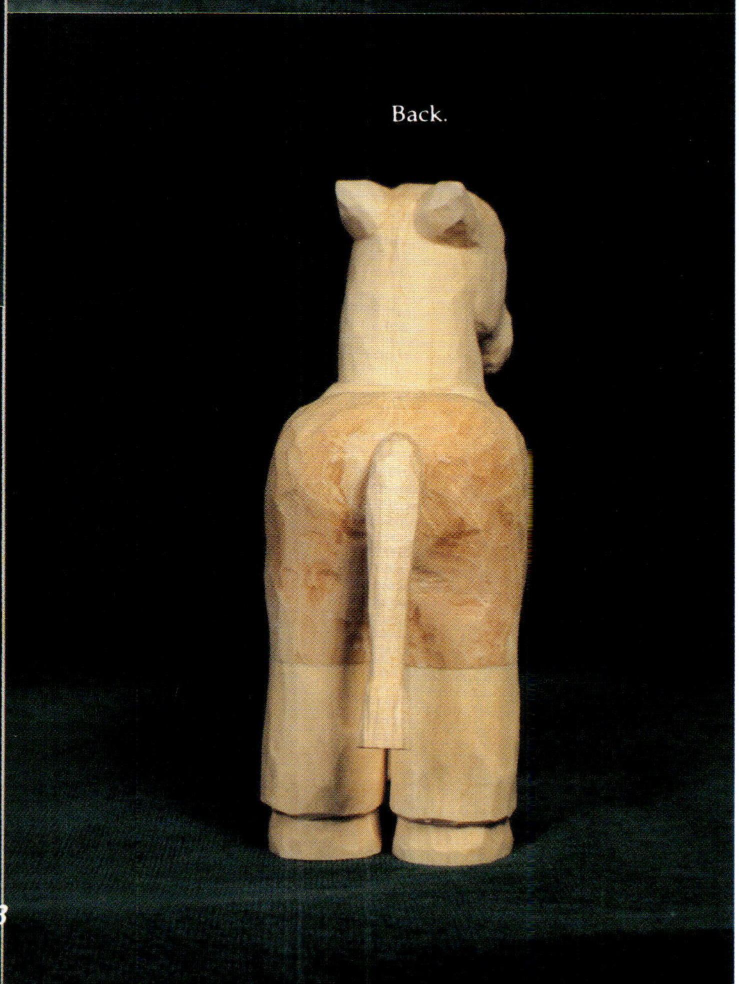

Back.

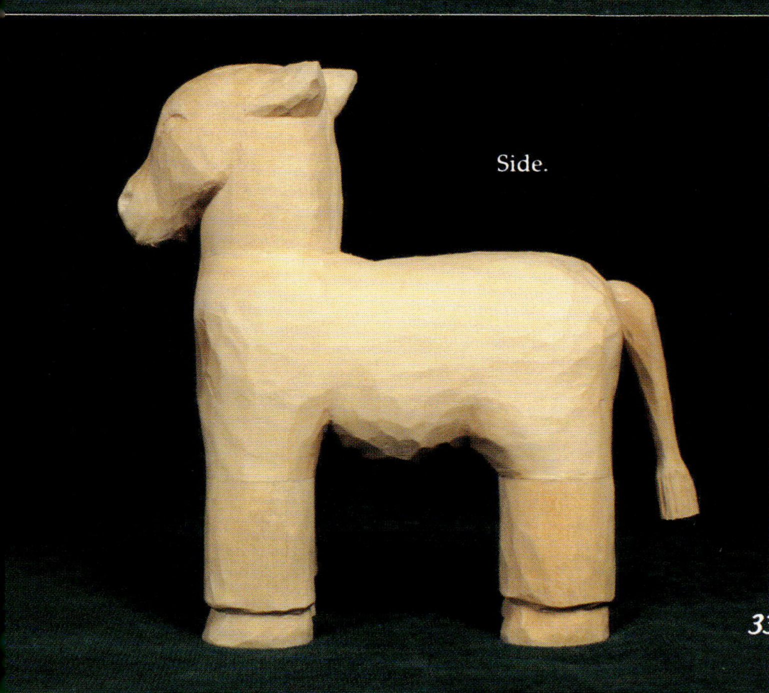

Side.

CARVING ANGEL

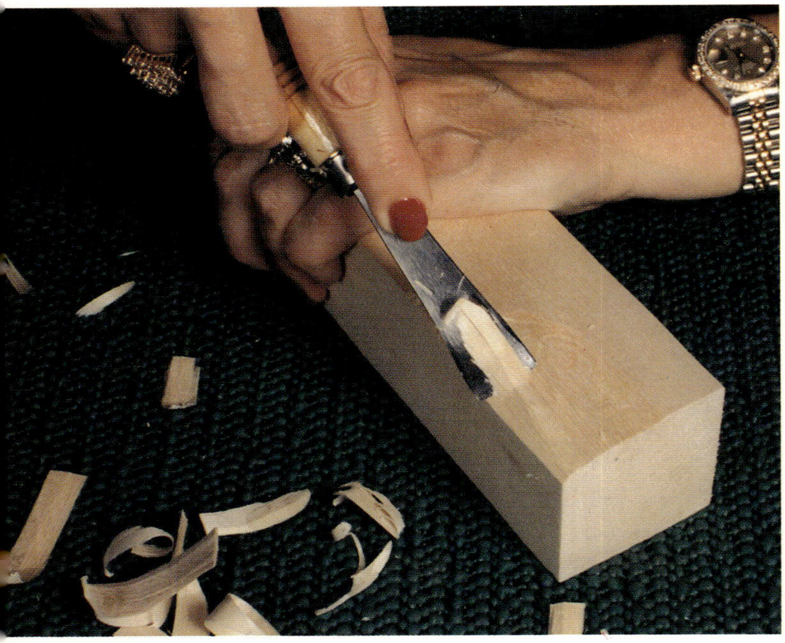

Begin carving the Angel by transfer only the front of the angel pattern. With your large gouge, round off the sides and back leaving carve marks.

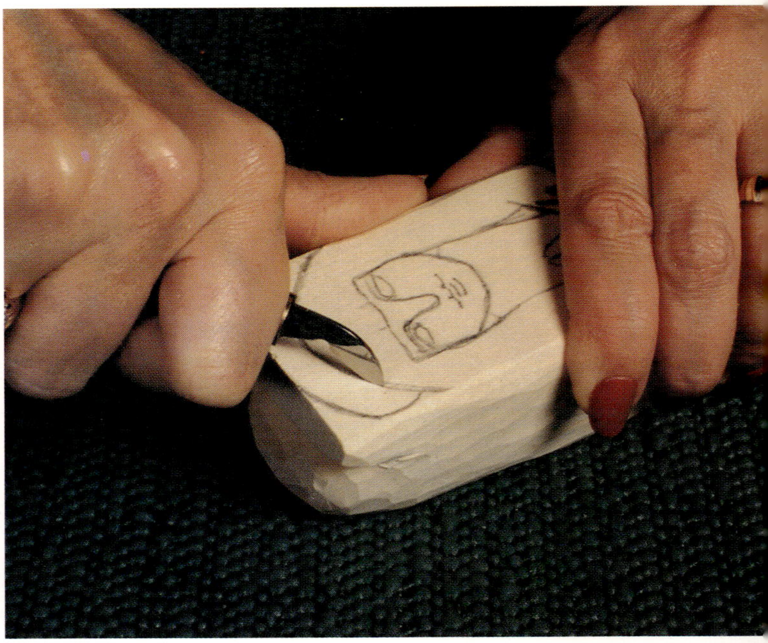

Score the base of her halo, creating a stop cut.

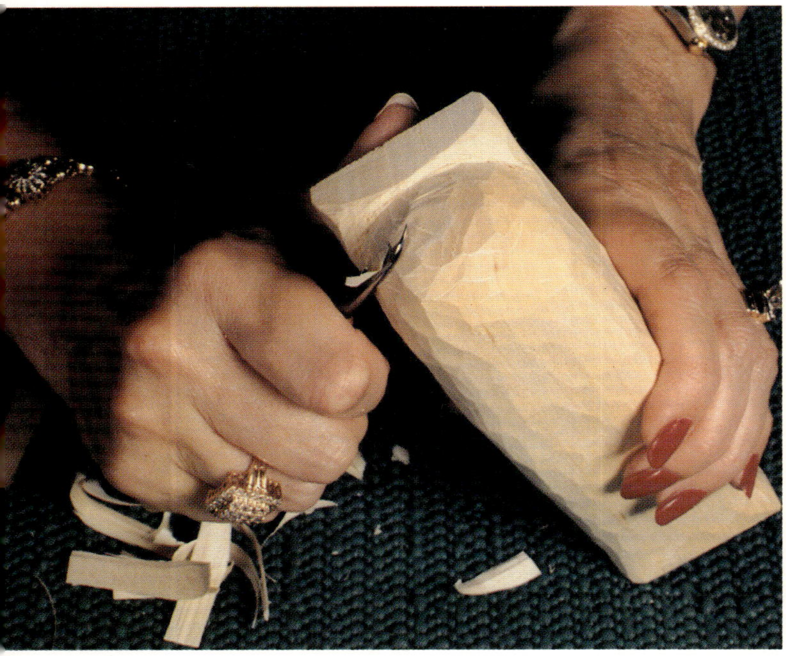

With your carving knife, continue rounding over the head leaving about 1/2" at the front for her halo and bangs as shown.

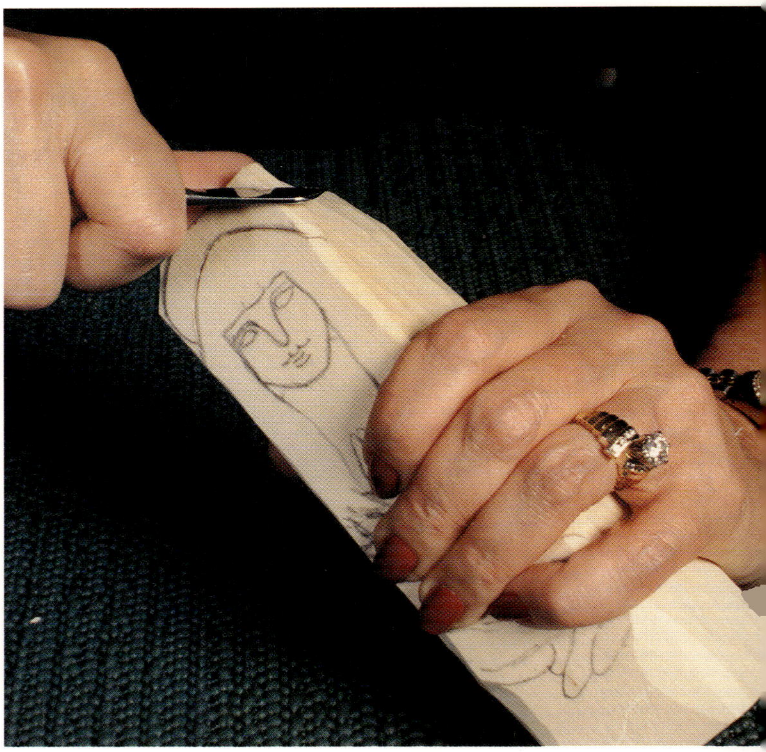

Round off top and corners of her halo.

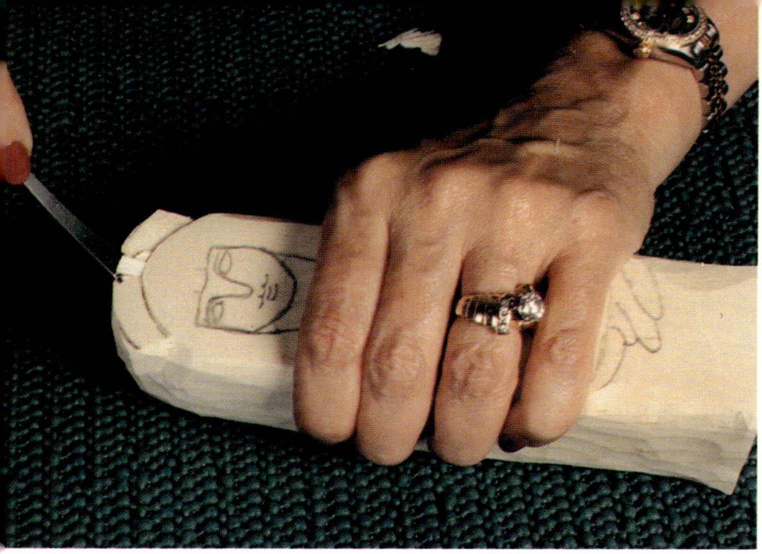

With your chisel, start removing the wood on her halo, taking it back about 1/4".

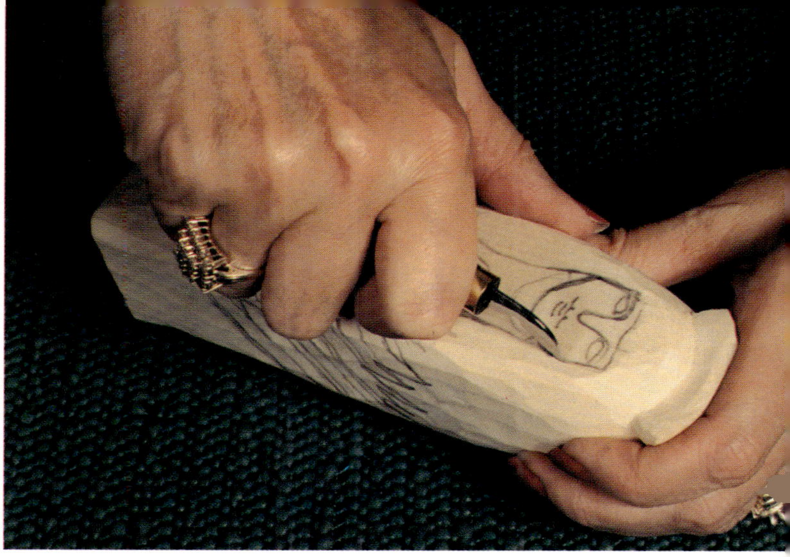

Score the outline of her face.

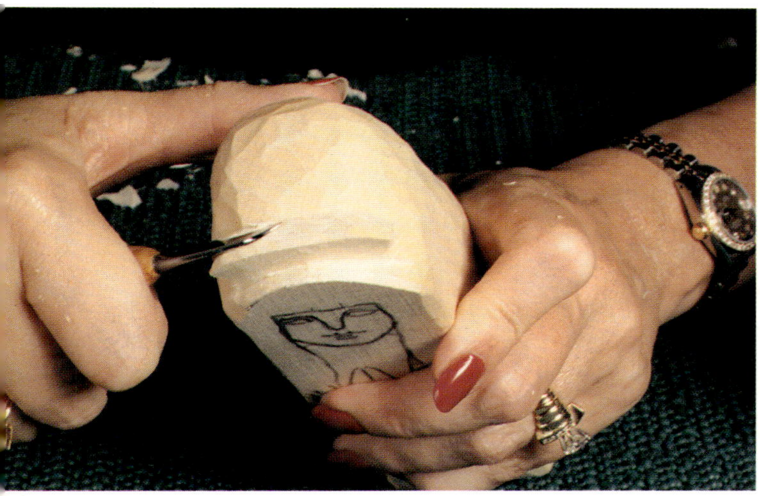

Round off the back of the halo with an angle cut.

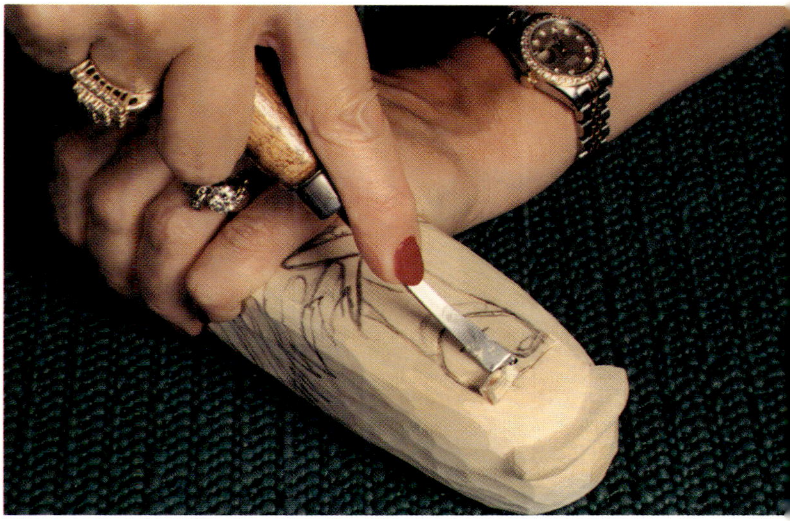

Again, with your chisel, come up under her bangs and start rounding her forehead.

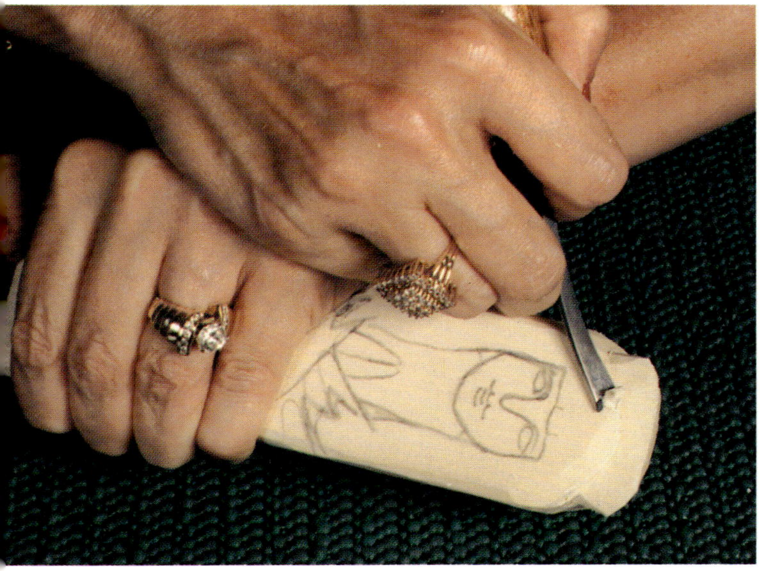

With your chisel, start rounding off the front of her bangs.

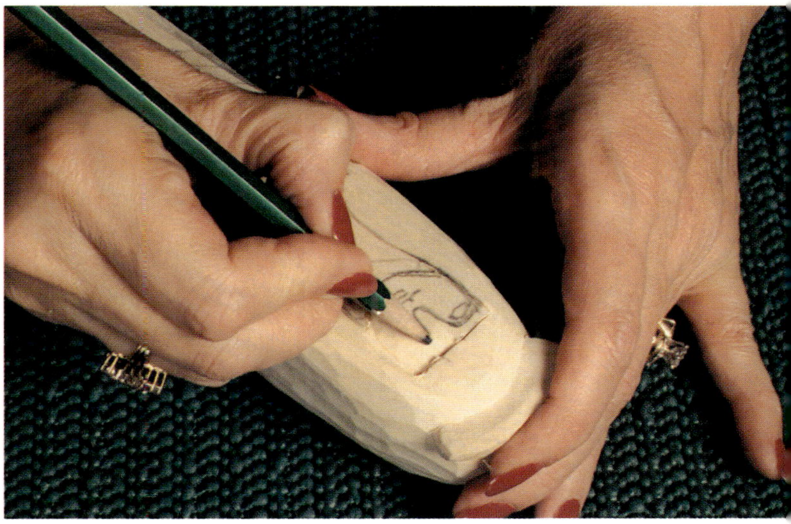

Remember your pencil! I like to do one side at a time, so I can redraw right away using the other side as a reference.

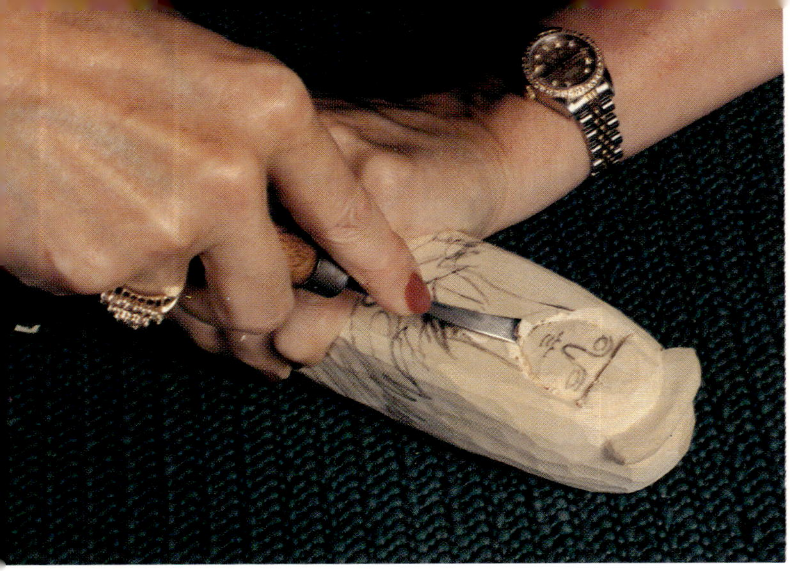

Remove the wood under her chin, revealing her face, hair and hands.

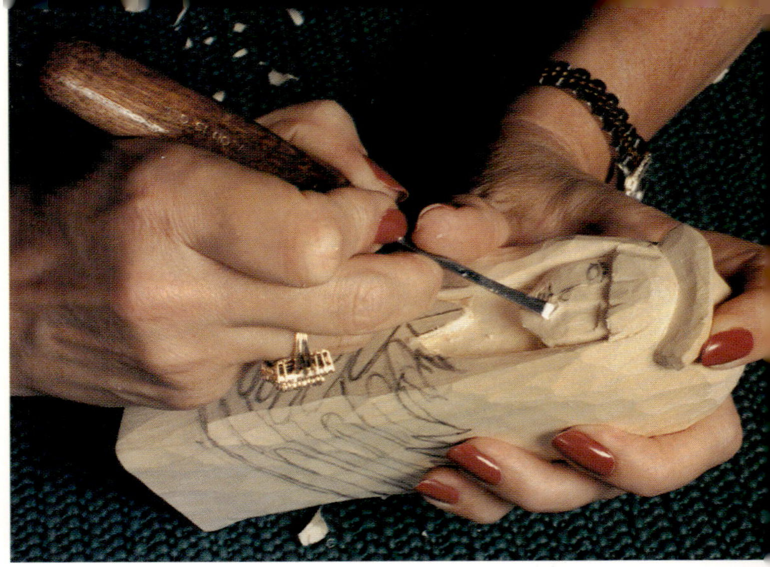

The mouth is tough. You need to start angling back from the top of her lip to the start of her cheek.

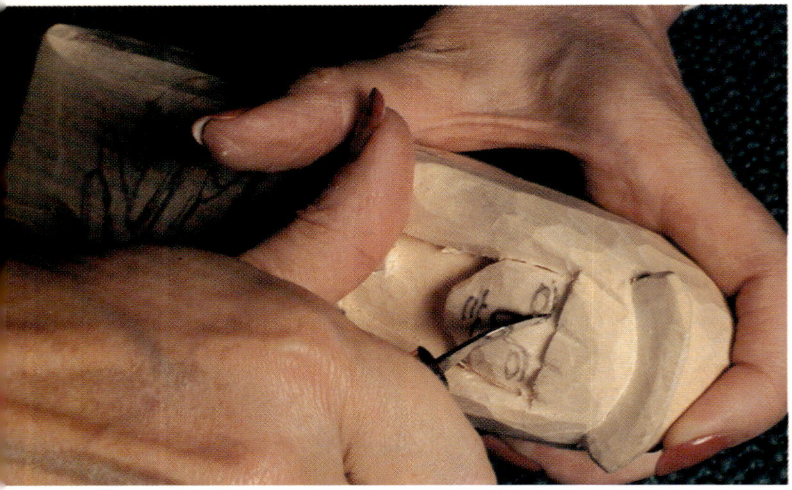

Once the basic shape of face is done, go back and detail her face by scoring the lines.

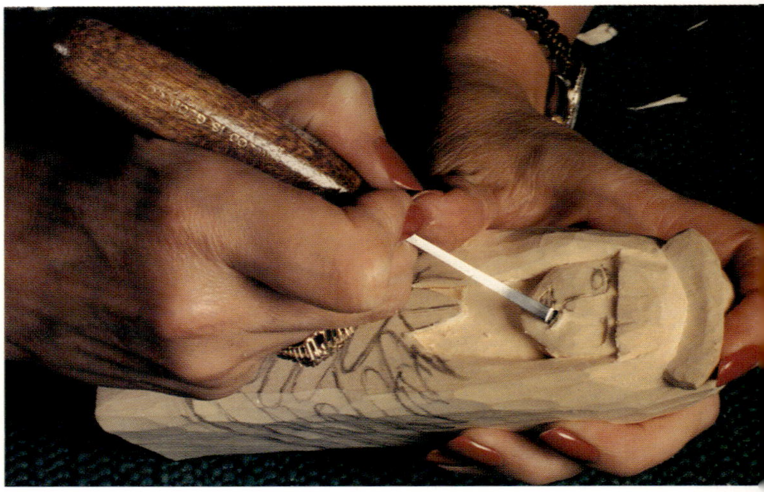

Repeat that cut and carefully create a slight dip between lips and cheek.

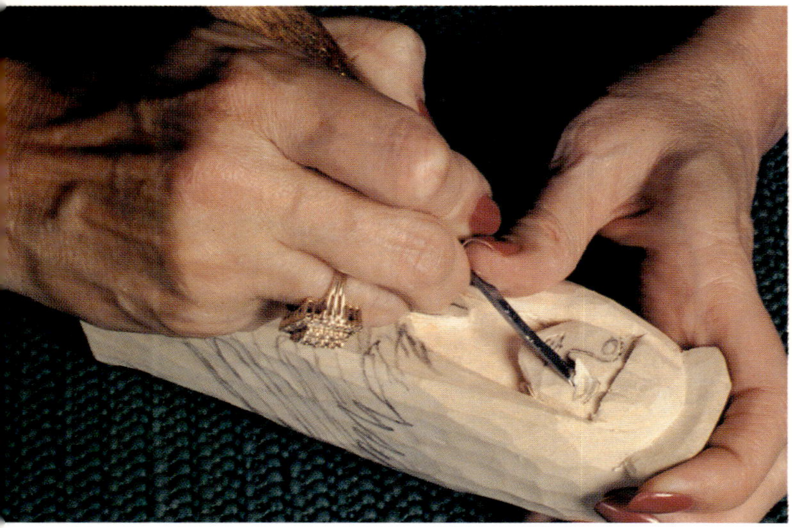

With your small chisel, start at the edge of her nose and trim up into the eye area.

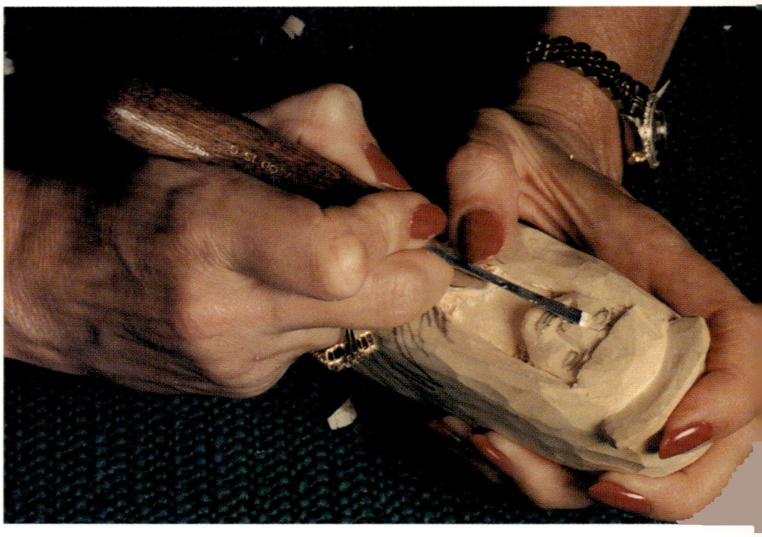

Continue under the nose and up the other side. Remember, this is folk carving. Don't worry about perfection.

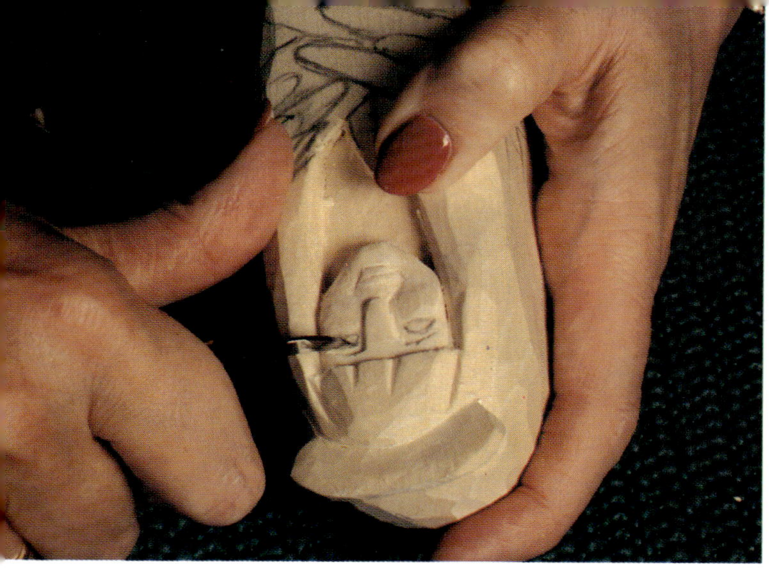

After removing the wood from around her mouth, you will score her eyes.

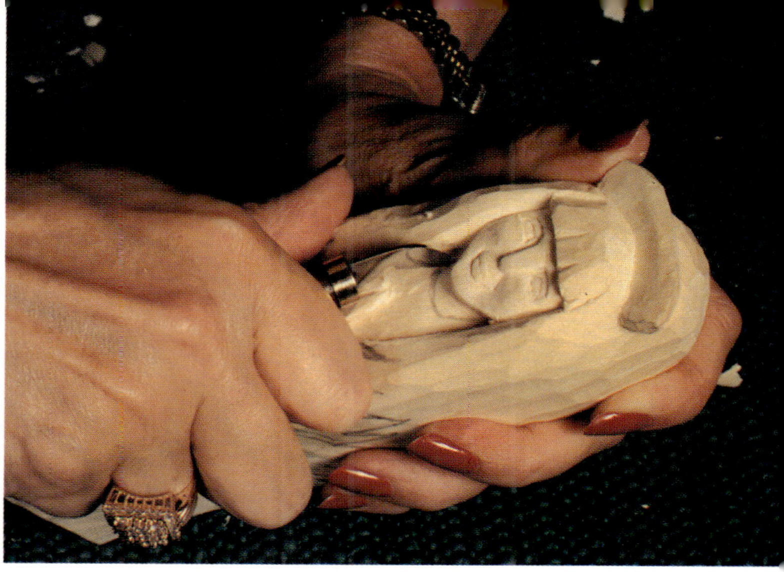

Score her dress line at the neck.

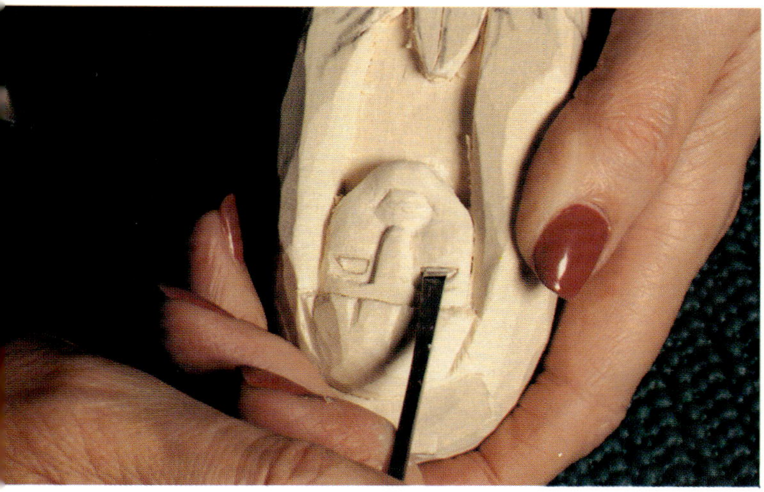

Keep this area flat enough to paint the eye (not too deep).

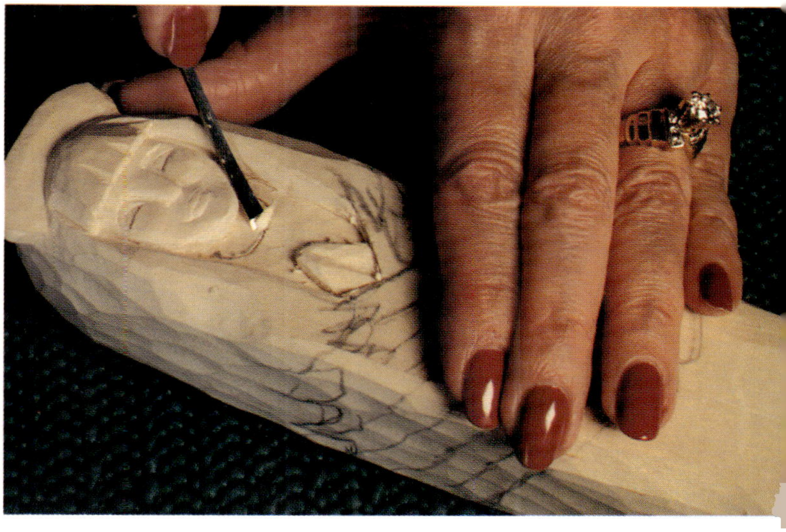

With your small chisel remove the wood from the neck.

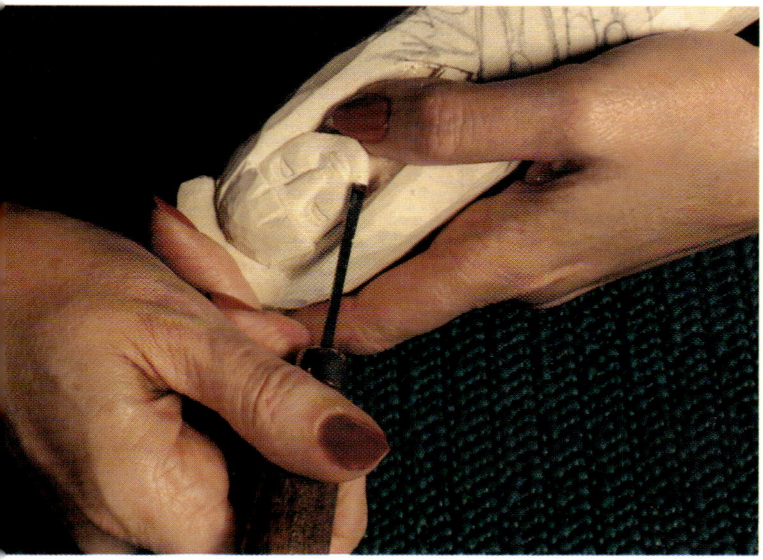

Finish her face with final rounding and shaping. A piece of fine sandpaper may help.

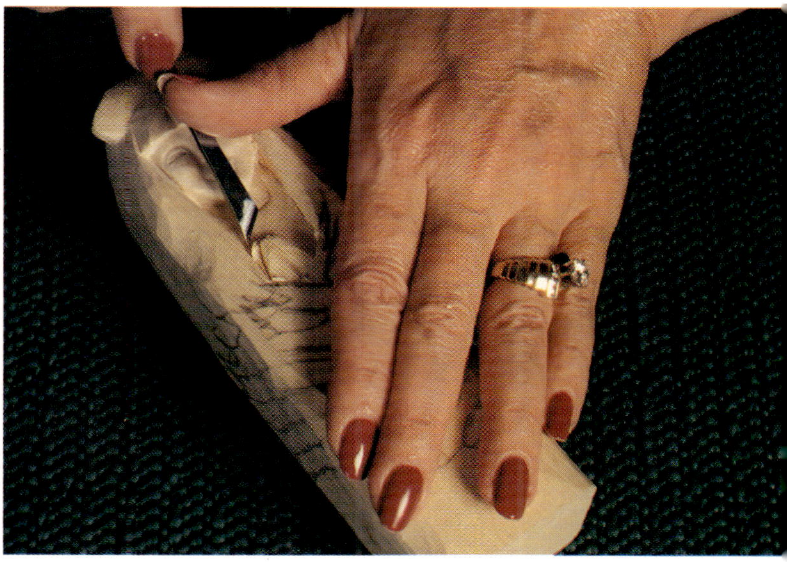

Re-score and continue to carve out the dress area. Your skew will come in handy for these hard to reach places.

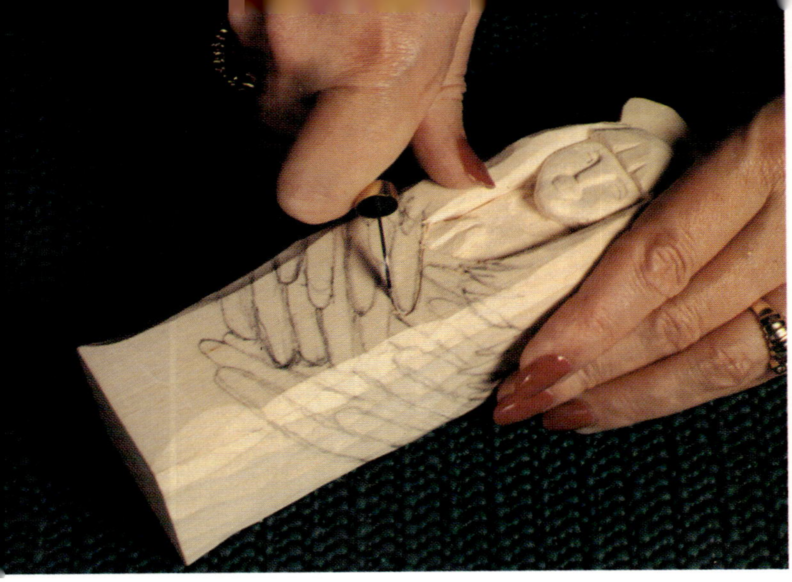

Score all of the feathers.

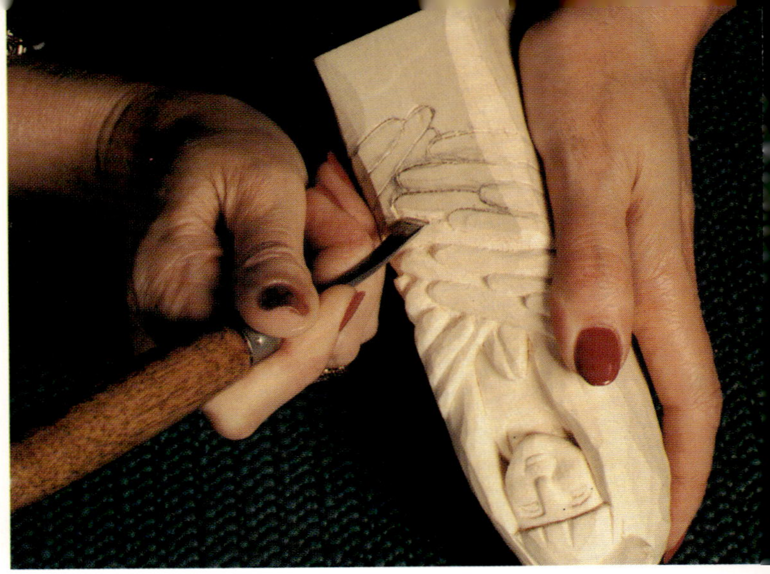

From the top of the feathers round down to that same cut.

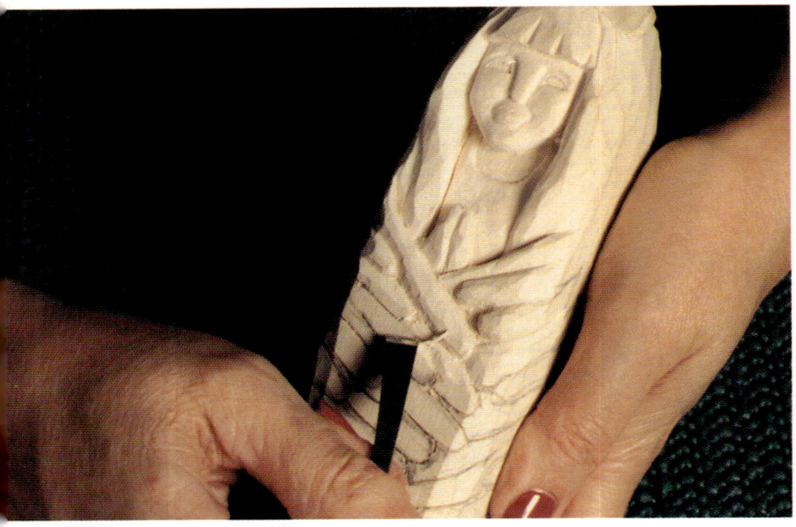

With your chisel, round the feathers.

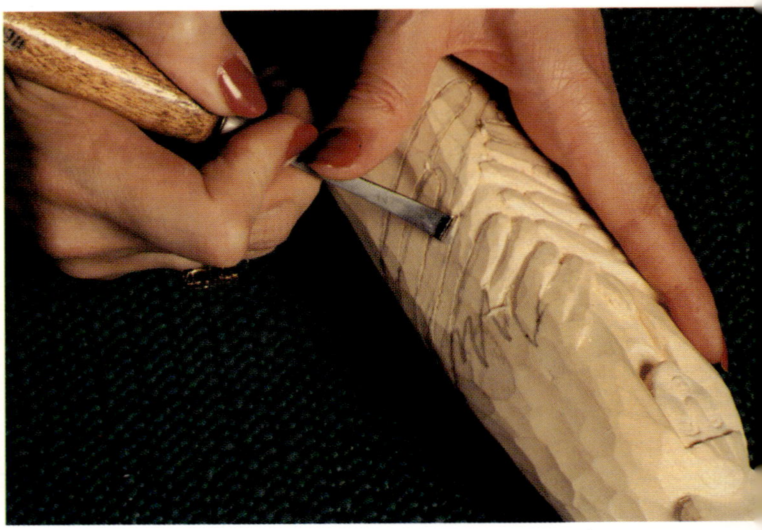

You will want to re-score and repeat. Complete all the feathers.

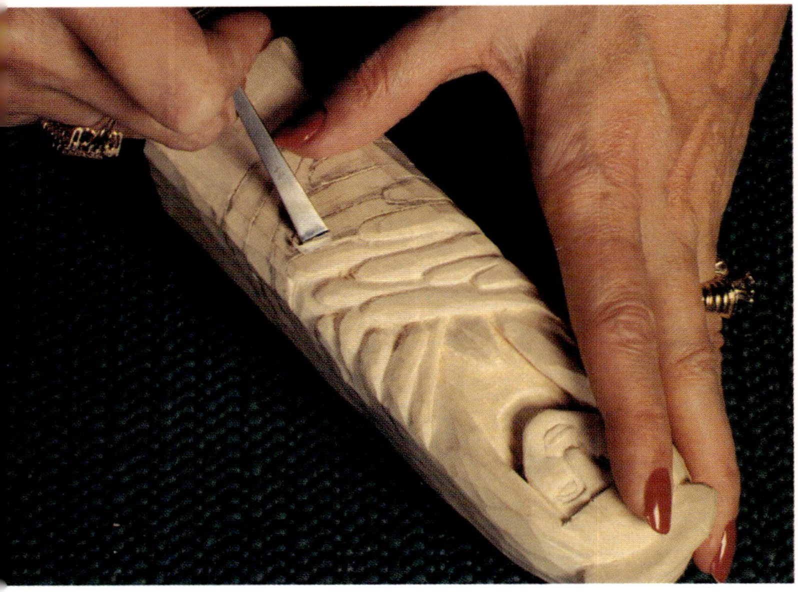

Cut up under the feathers to the stop cut.

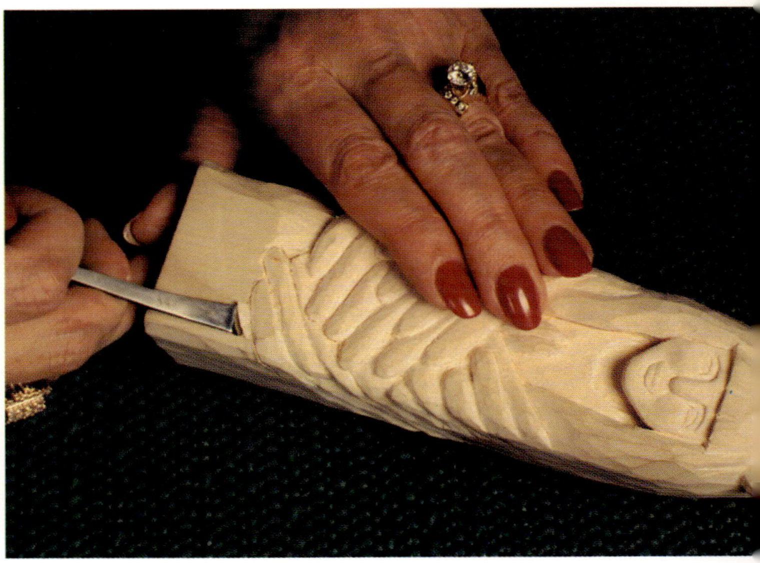

Cut up under the lowest line of feathers.

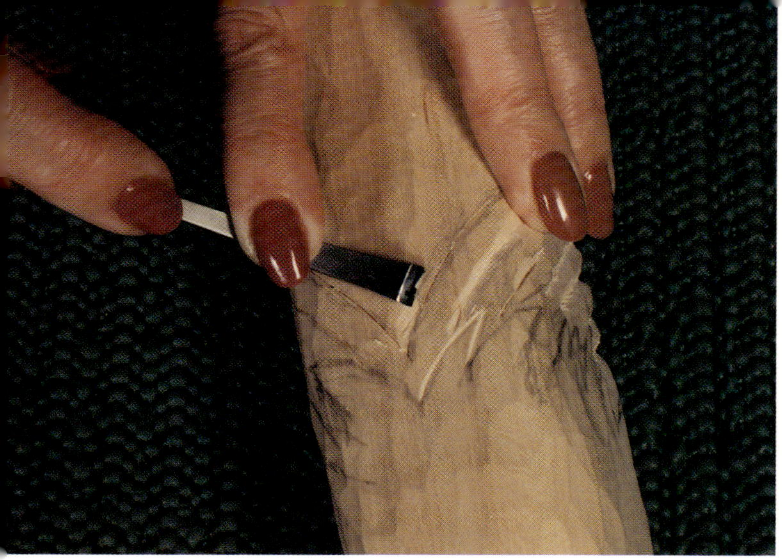

Move around to the back, removing wood and rounding.

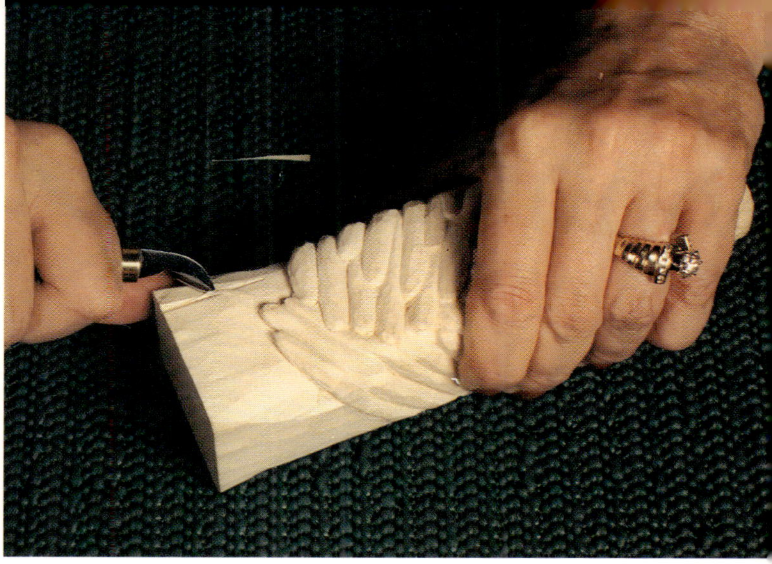

then the other side.

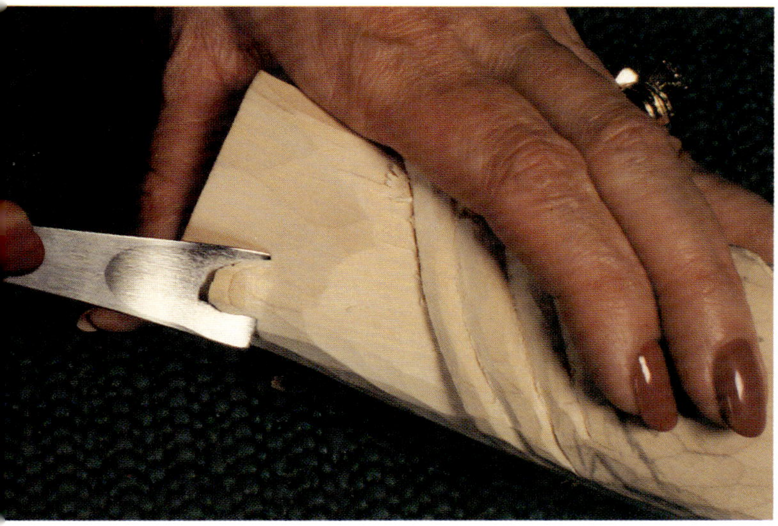

With your large gouge, angle her gown up under the wings creating those large carve marks.

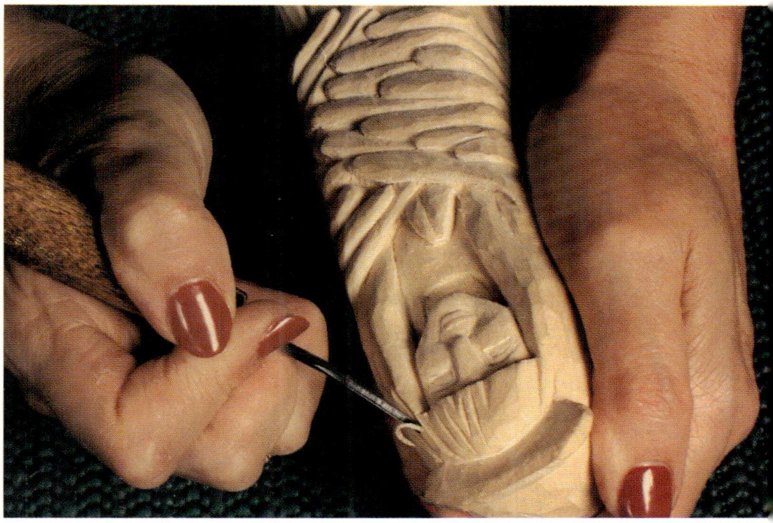

With your V-parting tool, start texturing her bangs.

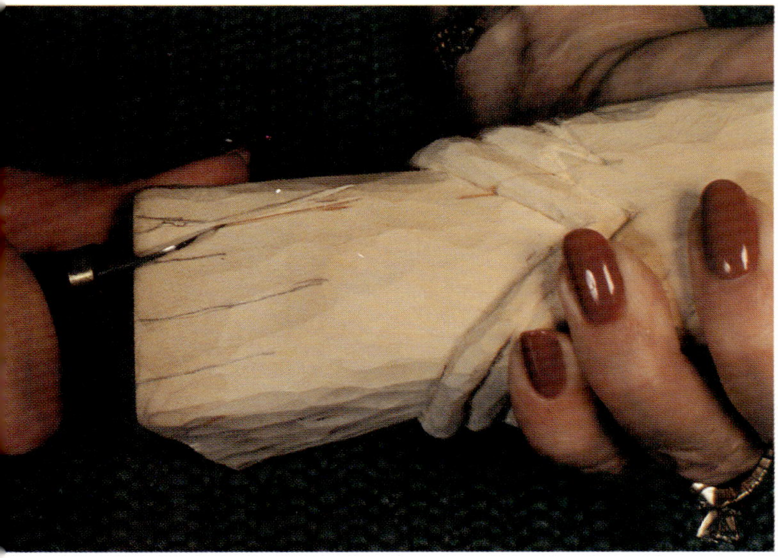

Start cutting in the pleats, angling down one side...

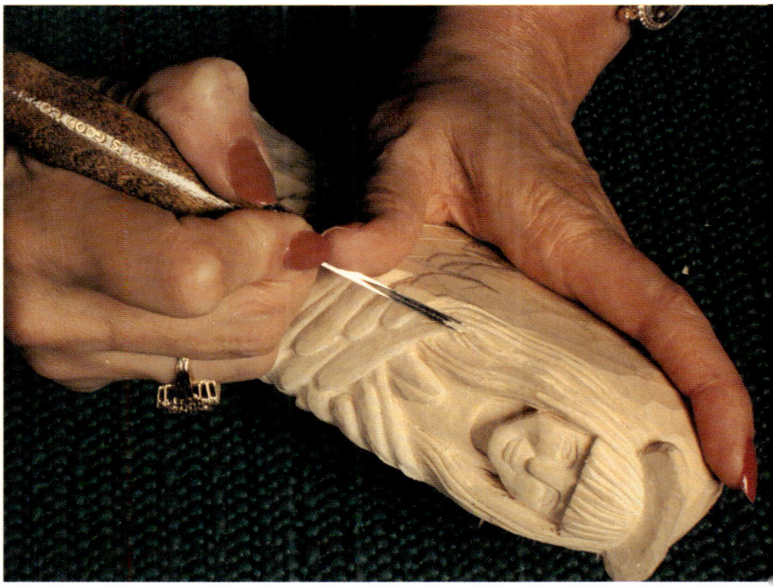

Continue down her long hair.

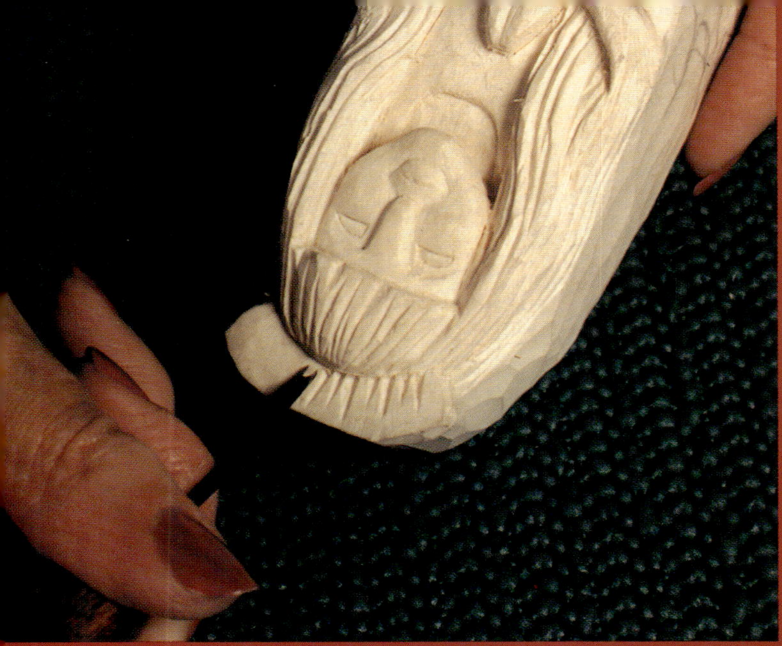

Cut in her halo marks.

Move on around the back texturing the rest of her hair at random.

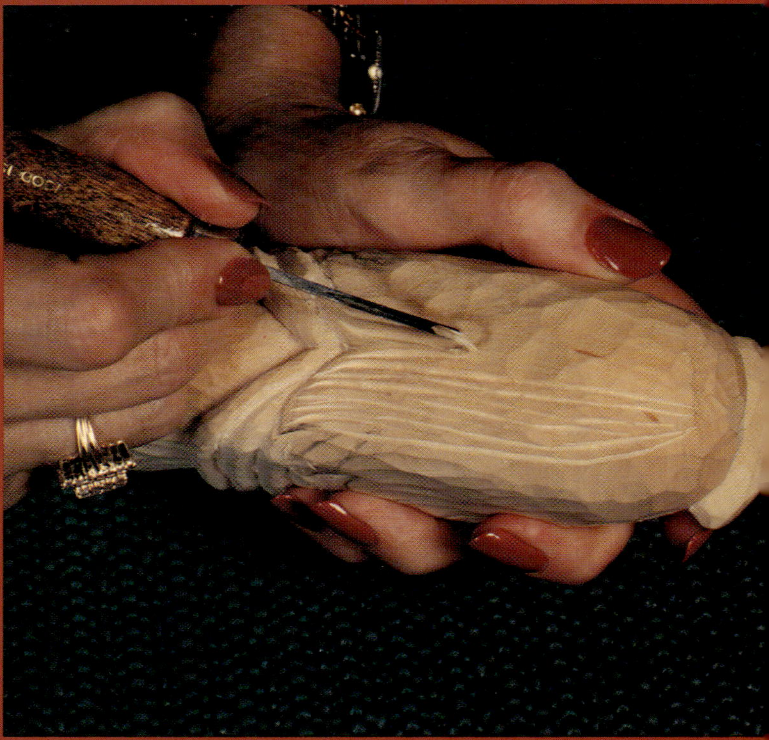

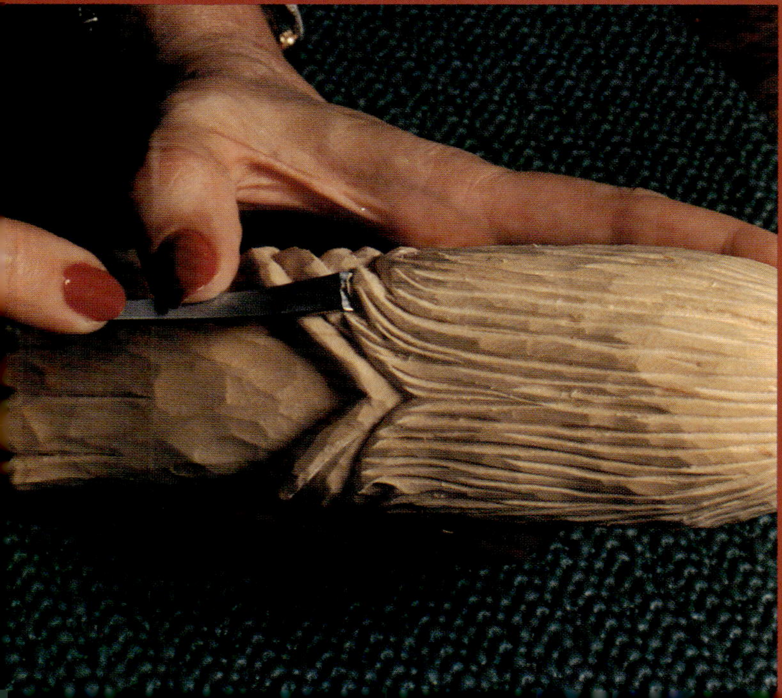

Score the bottom of her hair, then with your chisel, remove enough wood to define and finish.

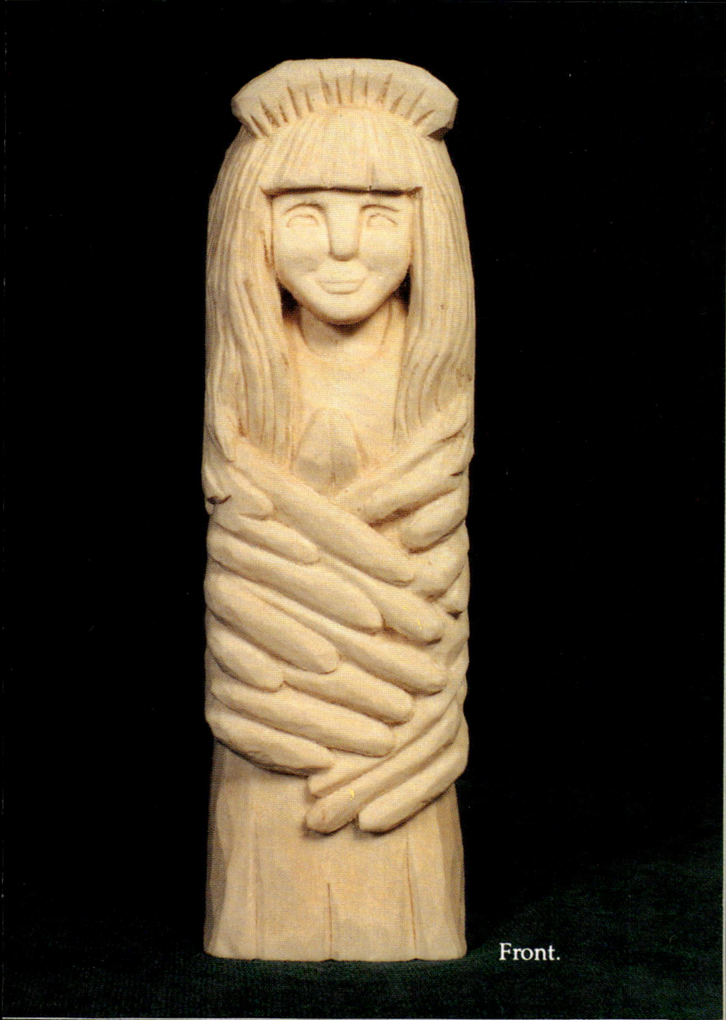
Front.

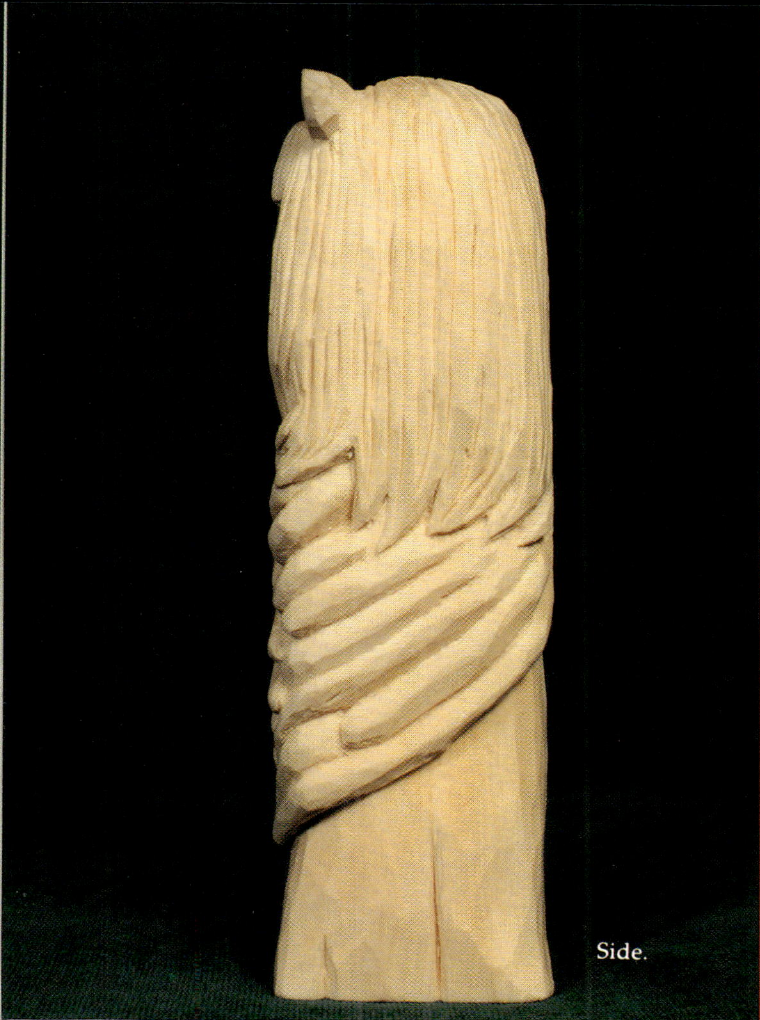
Side.

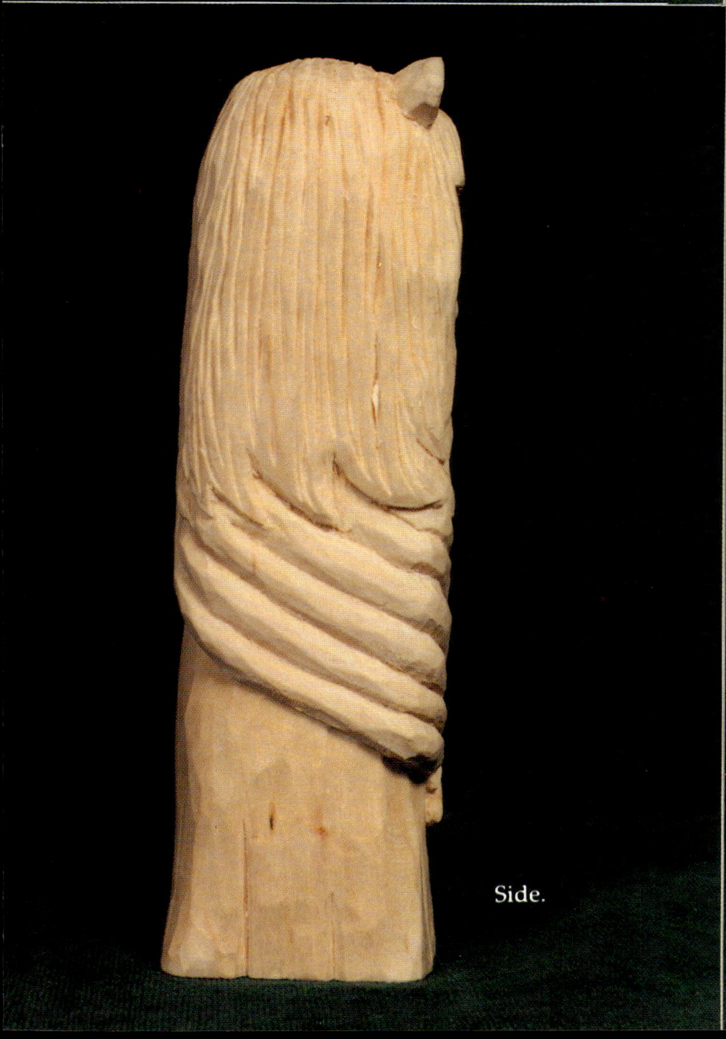
Side.

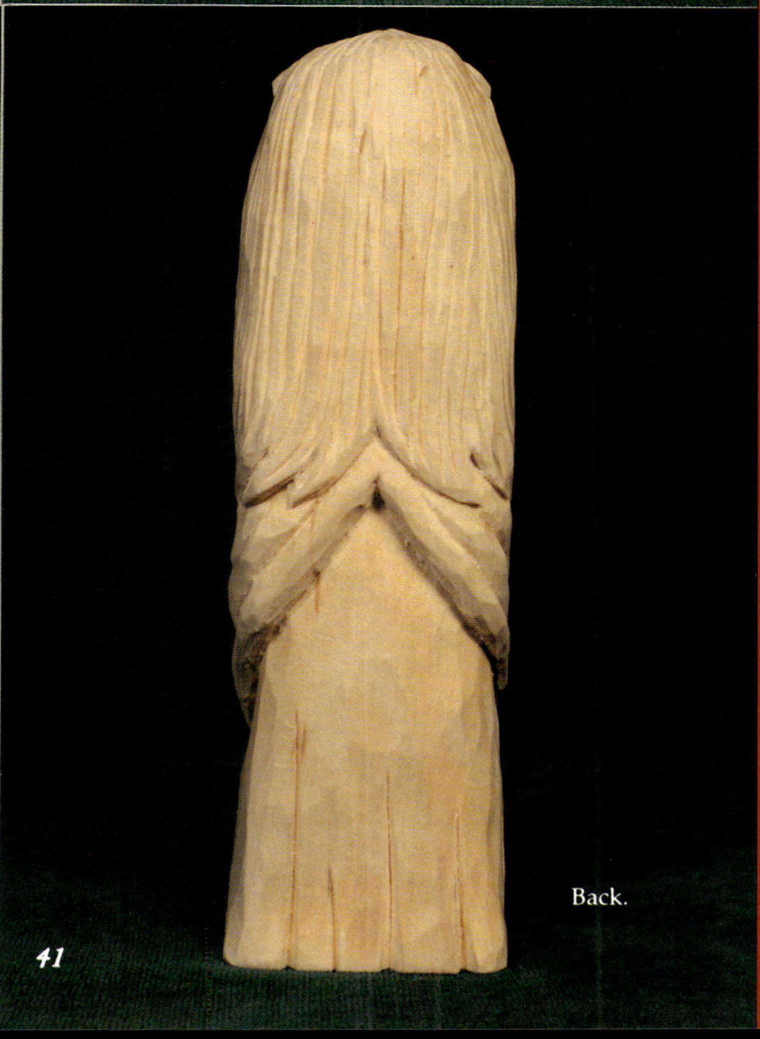
Back.

CARVING BABY JESUS

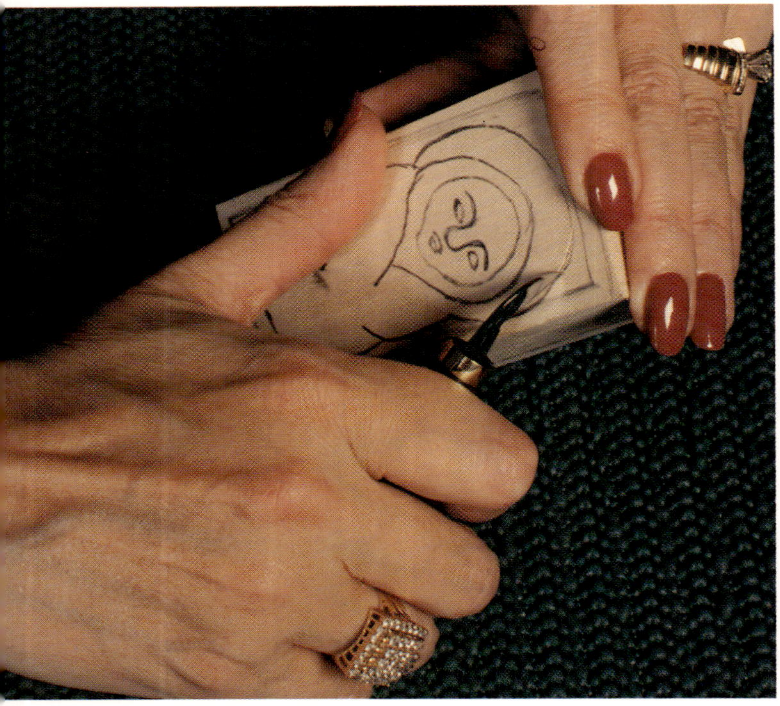

After cutting the wood and transferring the baby Jesus pattern, score all of the lines.

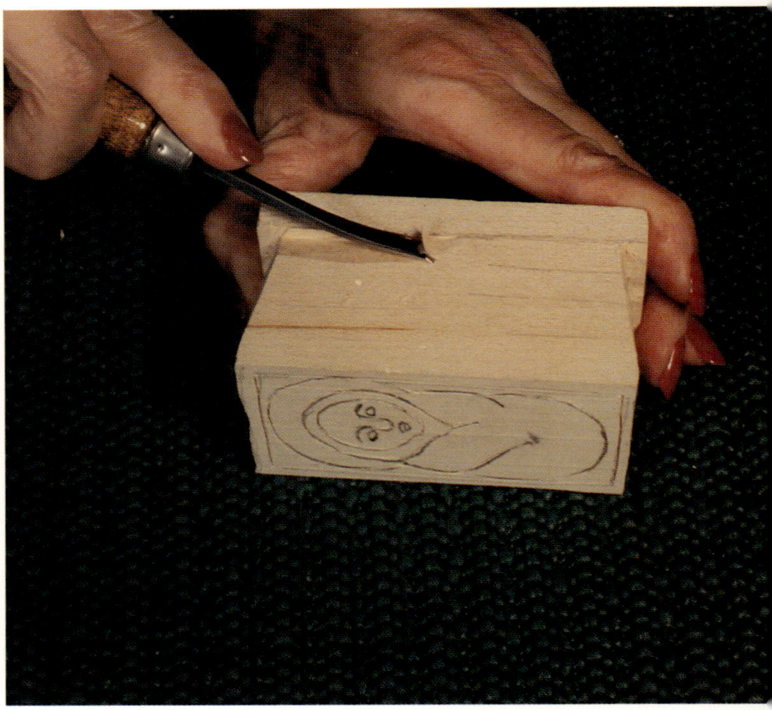

Now with your chisel, remove wood to angle the sides to the base.

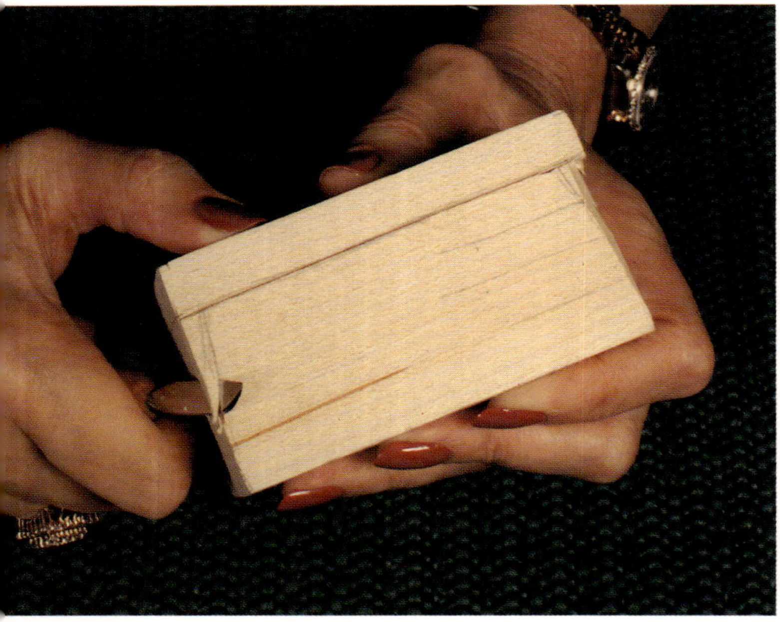

Using your carving knife, start at the ends and cut an angle from the top of the crib to the base. This is all end-cut and tough to get through with a chisel.

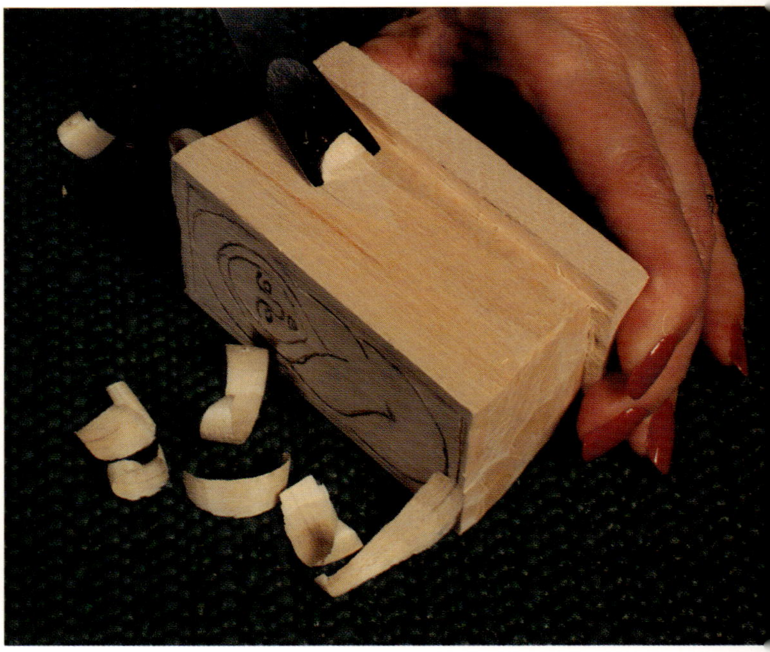

Use the large gouge to create carve marks and shape the sides.

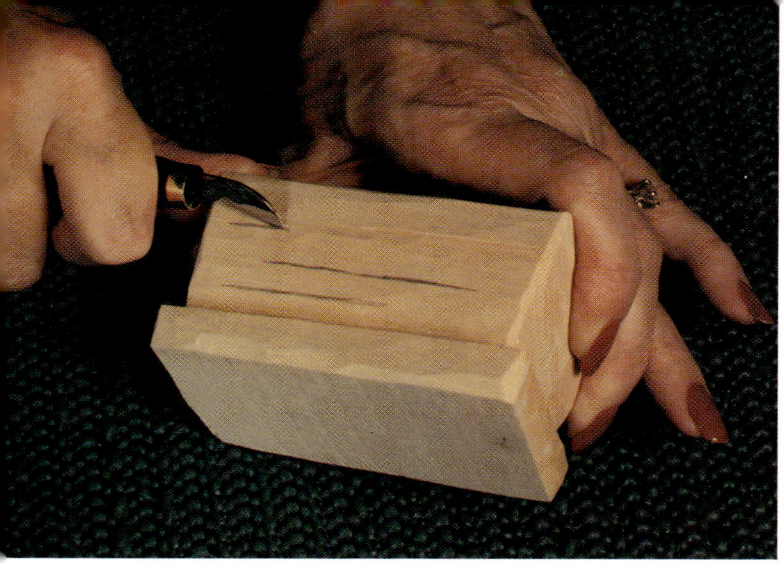

Cut in some lines with angle cuts giving a suggestion of wood slats.

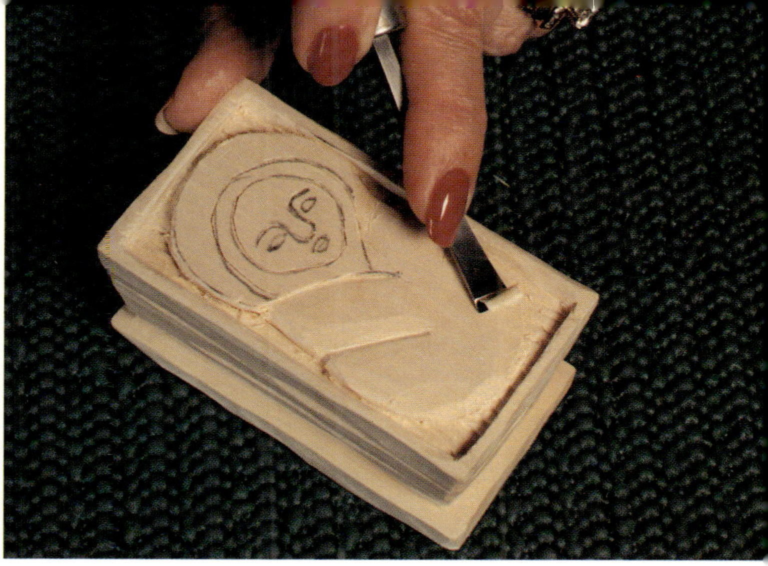

Start rounding off the baby's blanket with your chisel.

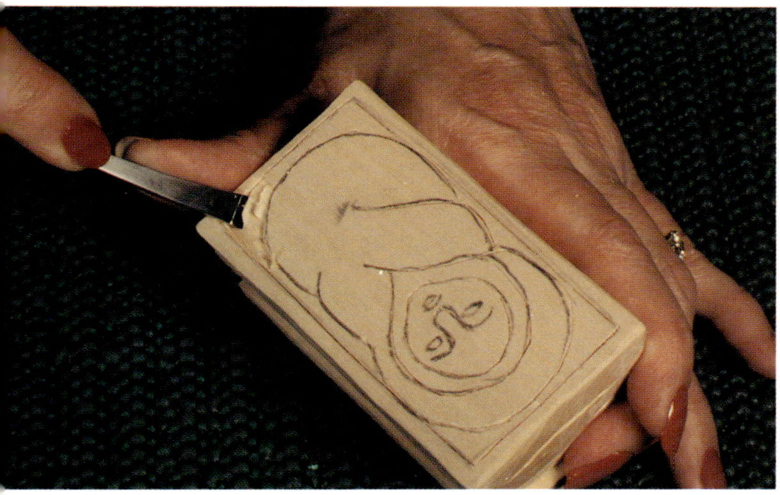

Start removing wood around the baby.

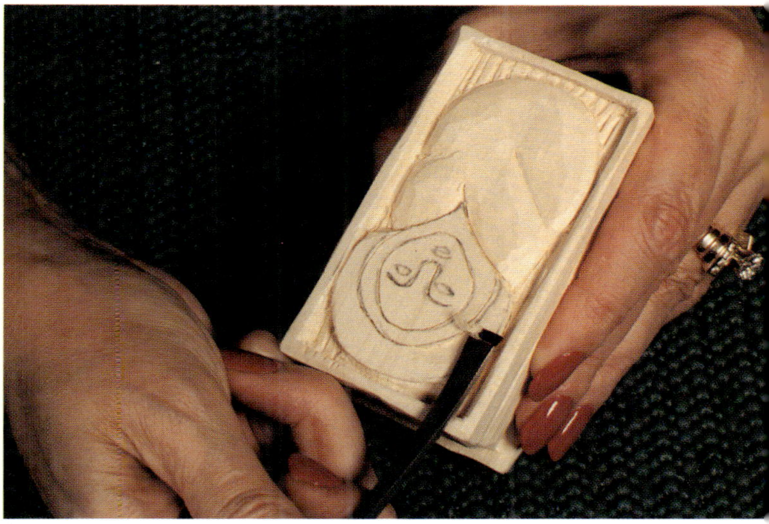

Angle in and remove wood at the base of his halo, then round off the top.

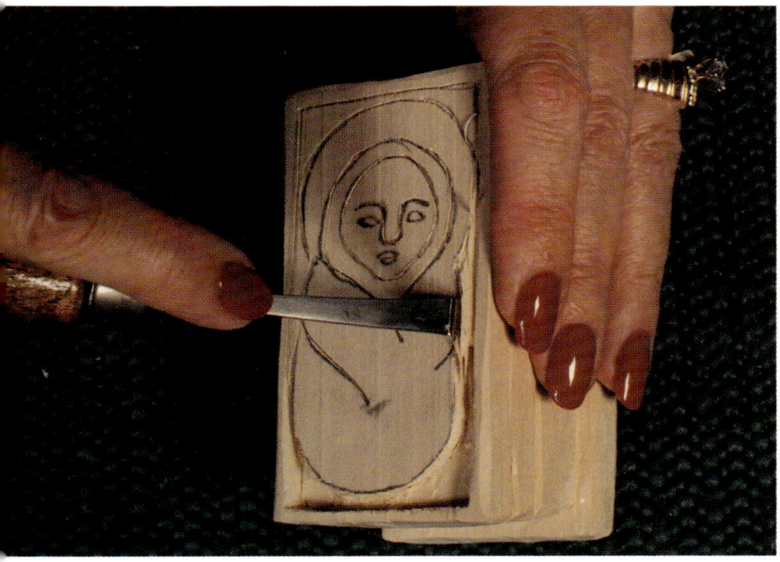

Continue on around very carefully. The sides of the crib are delicate.

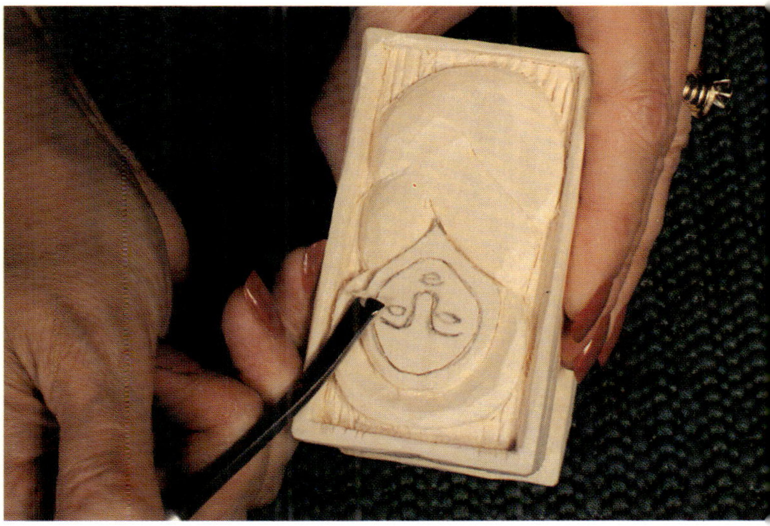

Using the corner of your chisel, round off the top of his head covering.

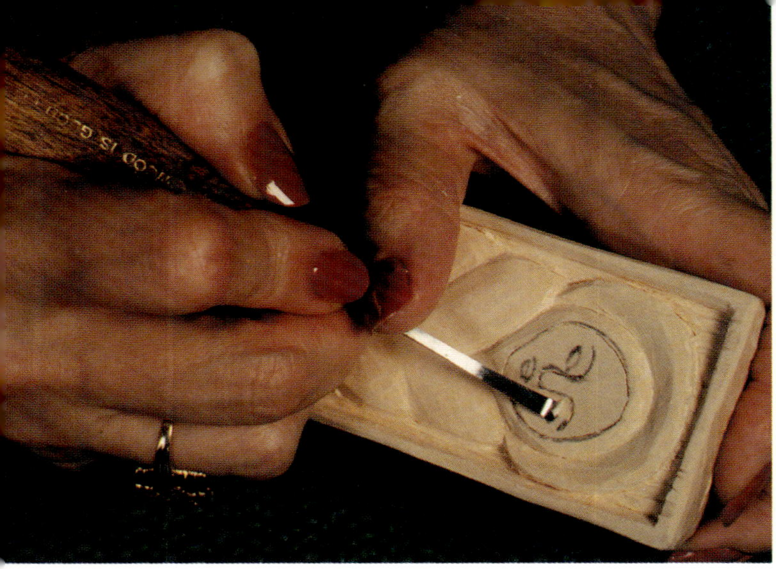

Carve down his little face going up the side of his nose to the eye socket.

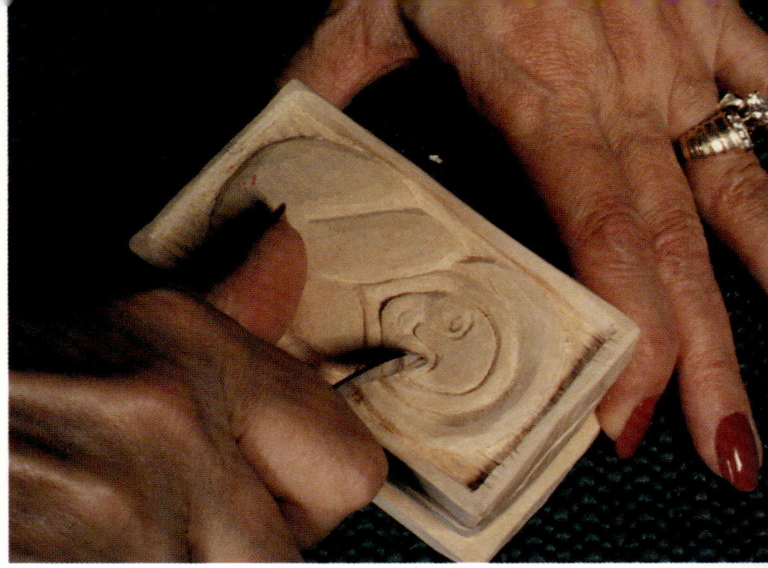

Score in the eyes.

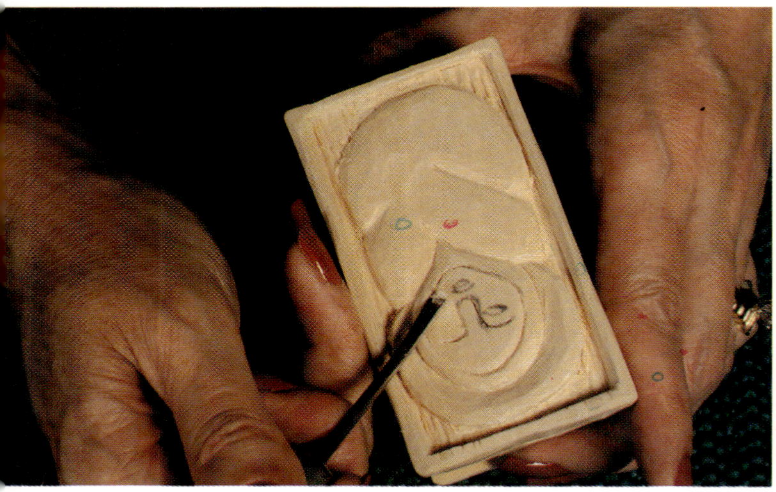

Round off the edges of his nose and face.

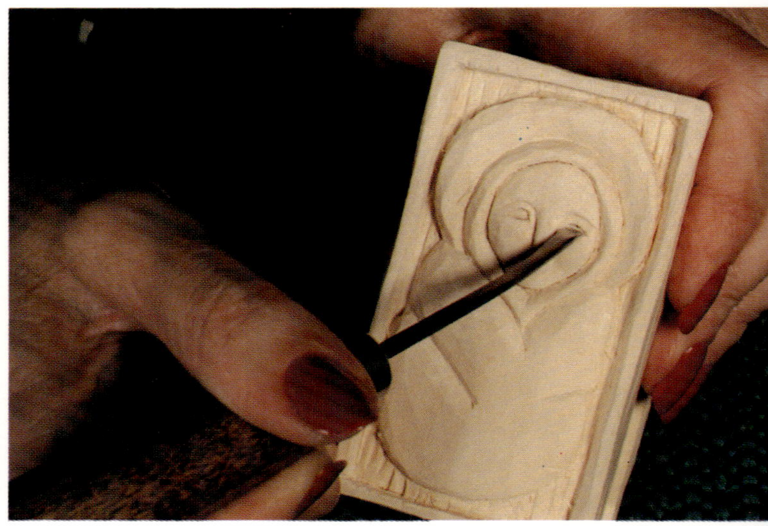

Remove enough wood to create a flat surface for painting.

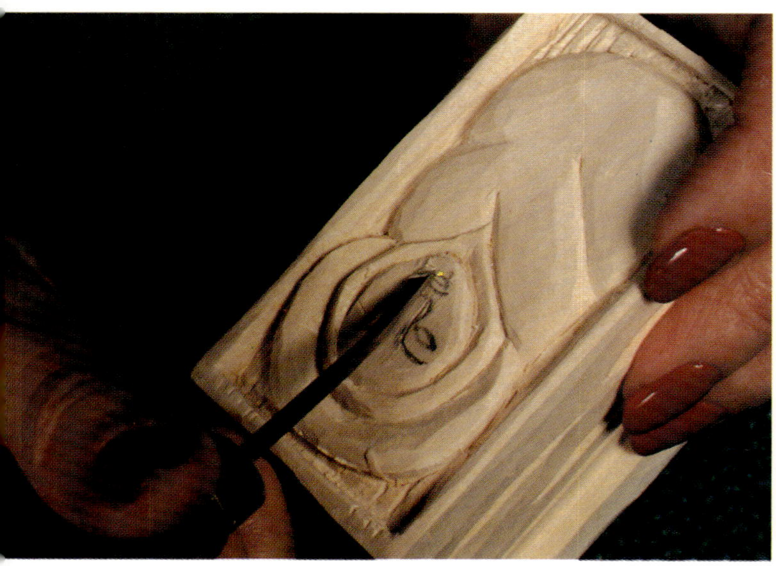

Very carefully start removing the wood from around the mouth, creating his chin and cheeks.

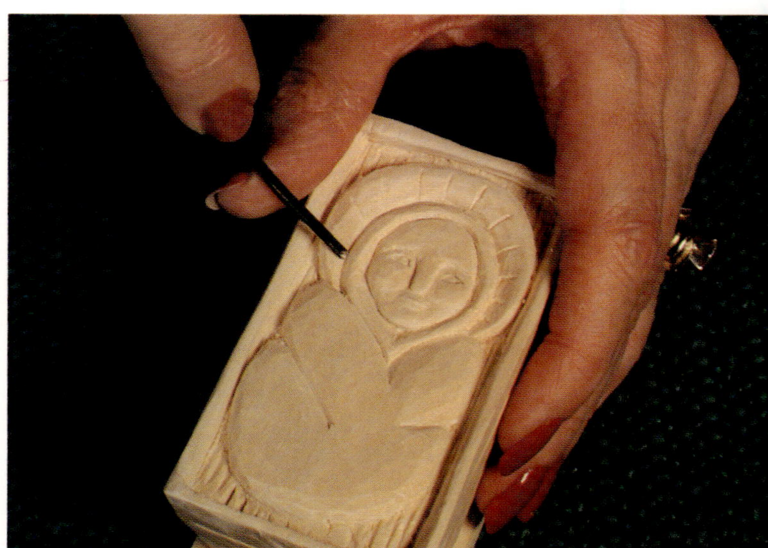

To finish, with your V-parting tool, cut in halo marks and straw bedding.

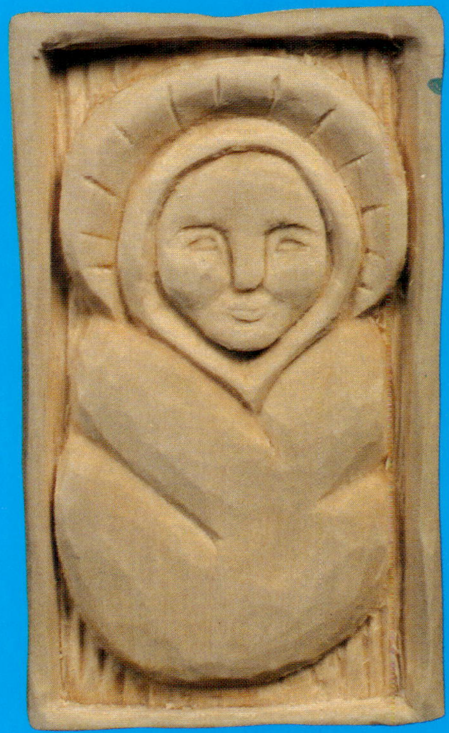

Top.

Side.

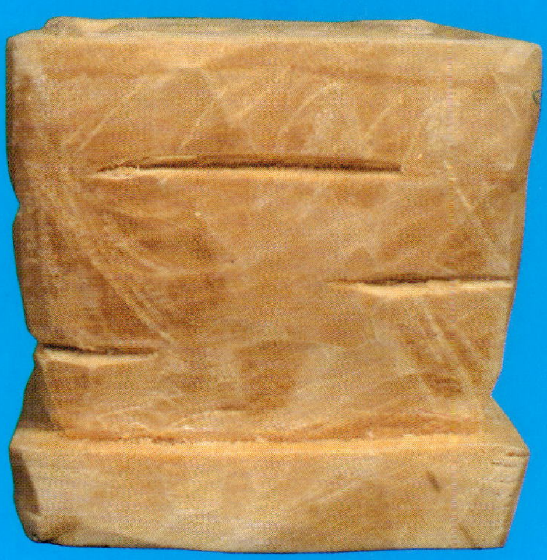

End.

THE PAINTING PROCESS

The paints I used are Ceramcoat craft acrylics manufactured by Delta, except for raw umber by Country Colors and Glorious Gold by Deco Art. Because paint names vary, a color palette is below.

Color Palette

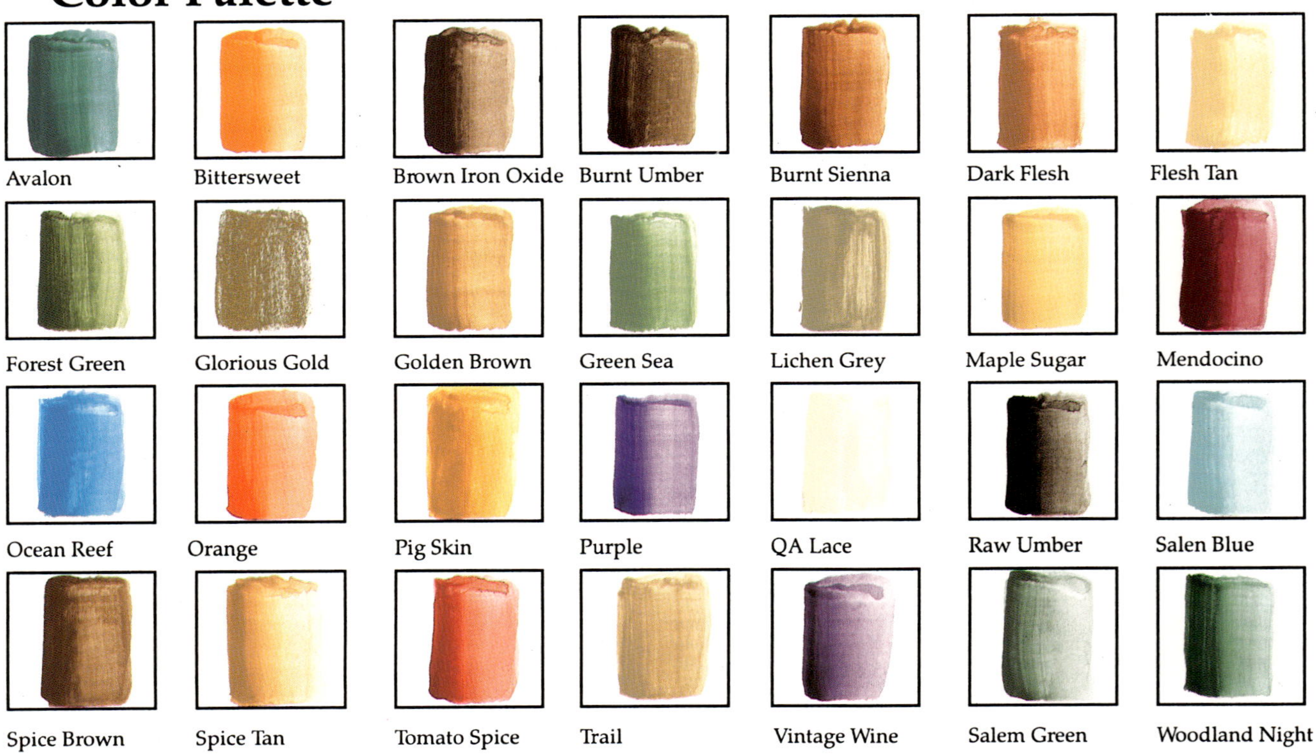

King I: 6.5″

Face: Dark Flesh, Tomato Spice, shade with Dark Flesh
Eyes: Bonnie Blue, Raw Umber, QA Lace
Hair: Raw Umber
Robe: Forest Green
Gown: Tomato Spice, Pig Skin
Crown: Pig Skin rubbed with Glorious Gold, Tomato Spice

King II: 5.5″

Face: Dark Flesh, Tomato Spice, shade with Dark Flesh
Eyes: Salem Green, Raw Umber, QA Lace
Hair: Burnt Sienna
Robe: QA Lace, Glorious Gold
Gown: Woodland Night with a touch of white
Shoes: Glorious Gold
Crown: QA Lace rubbed with Glorious Gold, Woodland Night

King III: 6.75″

Face: Dark Flesh, Tomato Spice, shade with Dark Flesh
Eyes: Burnt Sienna, Raw Umber, QA Lace
Hair: QA Lace shaded with Lichen Grey
Robe: Orange, Glorious Gold shaded with Raw Umber
Gown: Vintage Wine, Orange
Turban: Vintage Wine, Glorious Gold-Feather

Mary: 5.75″ and Jesus: 3.5″

Face: Dark Flesh, Tomato Spice, shade with Dark Flesh
Eyes: Ocean Reef, Raw Umber, QA Lace
Hair: Maple Sugar shaded with Golden Brown
Robe: Ocean Reef, Glorious Gold
Gown: QA Lace
Crib: Brown Iron Oxide shaded with Raw Umber
Straw: Pigskin
Hood: QA Lace
Blanket: Ocean Reef
Halo: Glorious Gold, shaded with Raw Umber

Joseph: 6.75″

Face: Dark Flesh, Tomato Spice, shade with Dark Flesh
Eyes: Burnt Sienna, Raw Umber, QA Lace
Hair: Burnt Umber
Robe: Purple
Gown: Pigskin, Glorious Gold

Angel: 6.75″

Face: Dark Flesh, Tomato Spice, shade with Dark Flesh
Eyes: Raw Umber, QA Lace, Salen Blue
Hair: Flesh Tan, Spice Tan
Brows: Spice Brown
Crown: Pigskin shaded with Tomato Spice
Dress: Salen Blue shaded with Avalon
Accent: Glorious Gold, Tomato Spice, Woodland Night

Shepherd: 6″

Face: Dark Flesh, Tomato Spice, shade with Dark Flesh
Eyes: QA Lace, Green Sea, Raw Umber
Brows: Spice Brown
Hat: Green Sea shaded with Woodland Night
Gown: Vintage Wine
Rope: Vintage Wine, Glorious Gold
Staff: Spice Brown

Animals: Donkey: 7″; Sheep: 3″; Hen: 1.75″

Hen:
Feathers: Bittersweet, Tomato Spice, Pigskin, shaded with Mendocino
Eyes: Raw Umber

Donkey:
Body: Trail
Highlight: QA Lace
Shade: Brown Iron Oxide
Define: Raw Umber
Eyes: Burnt Sienna, Raw Umber

Sheep:
Body: QA Lace shade with Trail
Legs & Face: Trail Shaded with Burnt Umber
Eyes: Burnt Umber, QA Lace highlight

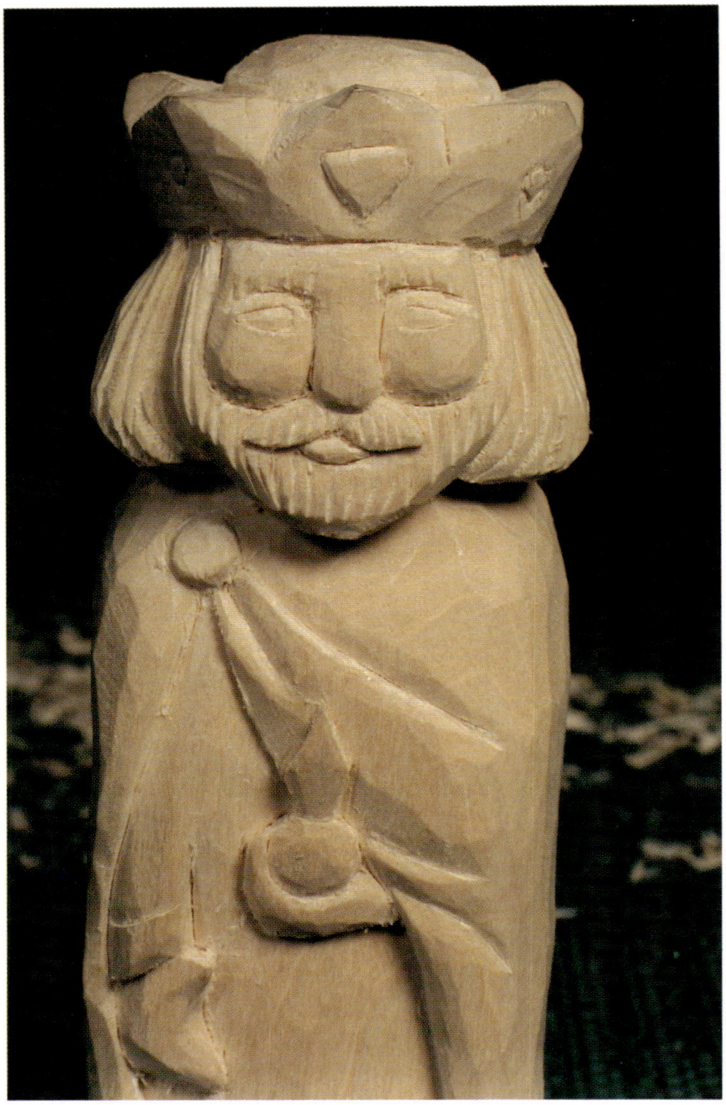

Time to paint.

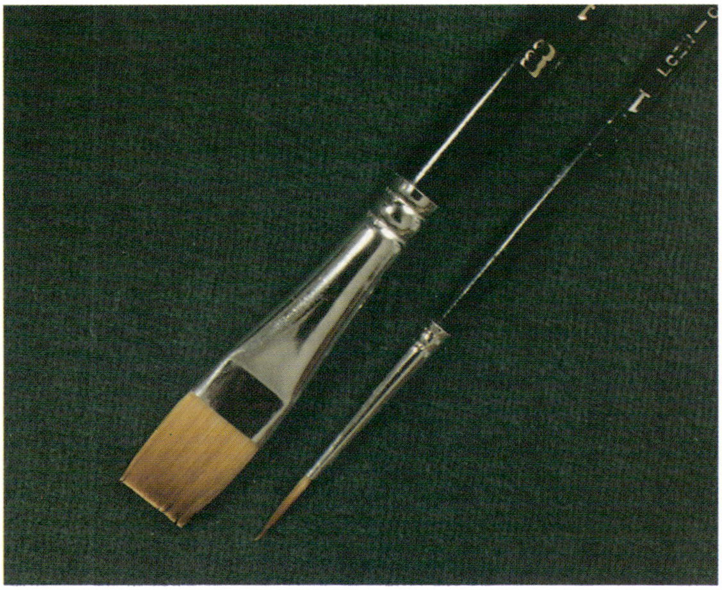

My favorite brushes are a 1/2″ flat and a #1 liner.

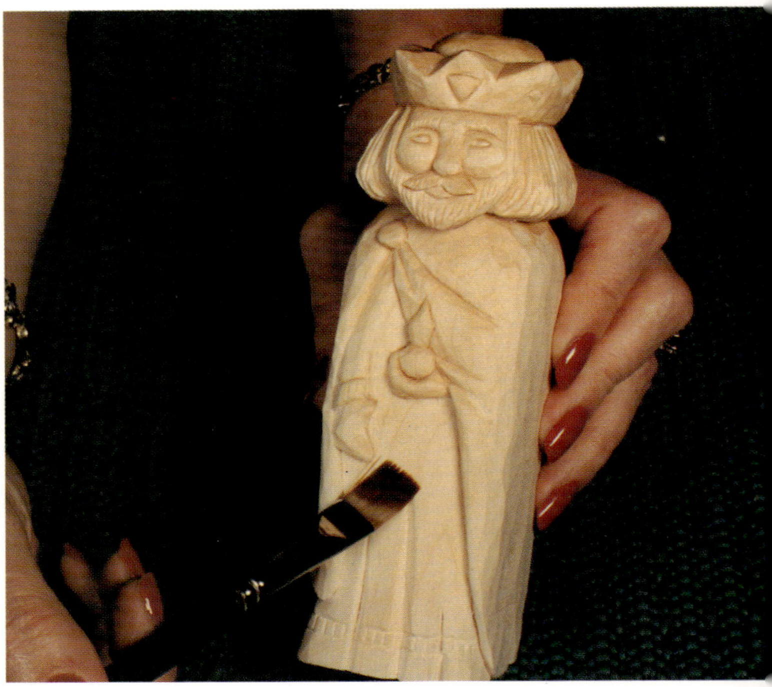

In the painting process the first step is to seal the wood with wood sealer. This will insure a quality finish.

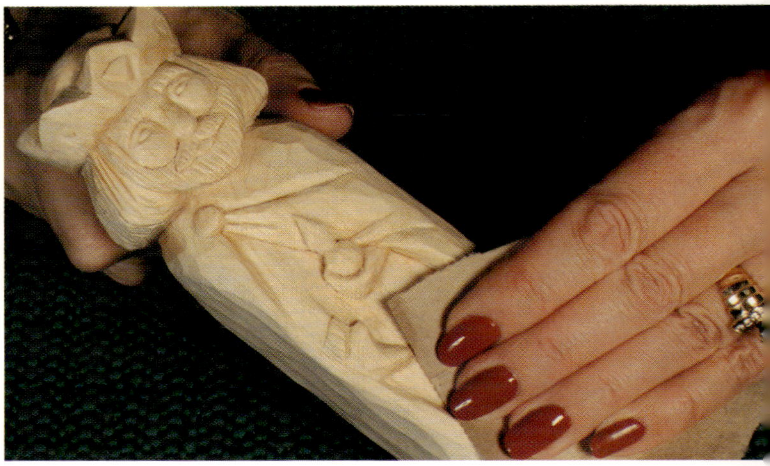

After the sealer is dry, rub the carving down with a piece of brown paper bag. This will smooth out any little bumps. You are now ready to paint.

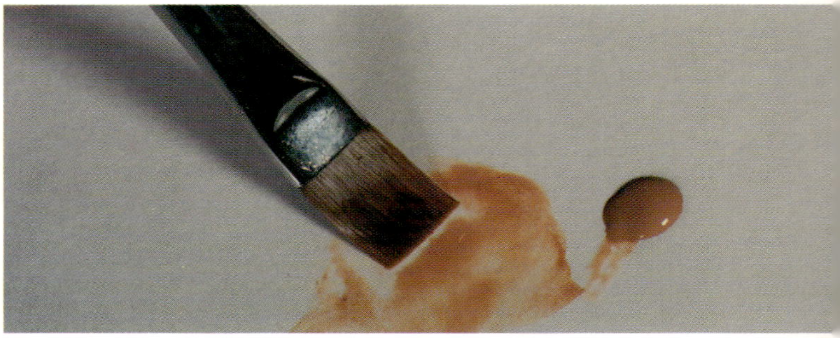

Mix the paint five-to-one: five parts water to one part color, give or take. Because the paint will be sheer, you can still see the wood. I prefer this look to opaque.

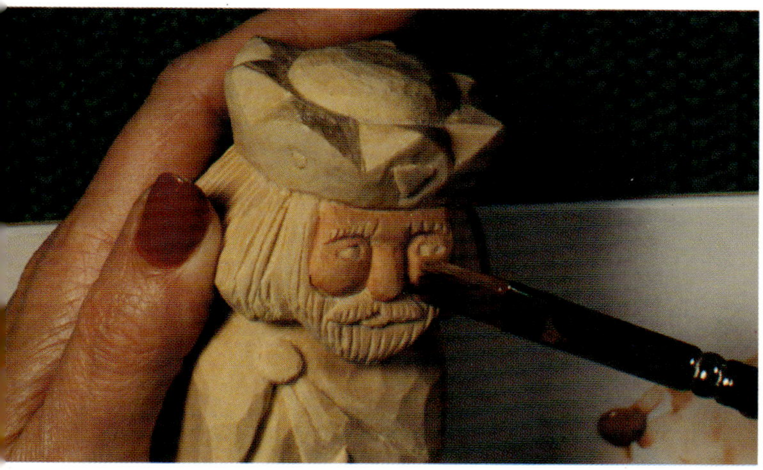

Start with the face, using the 1/2" flat brush. Though the face is small, this brush is easy to handle and gives you an overall even application. Base with the flesh color.

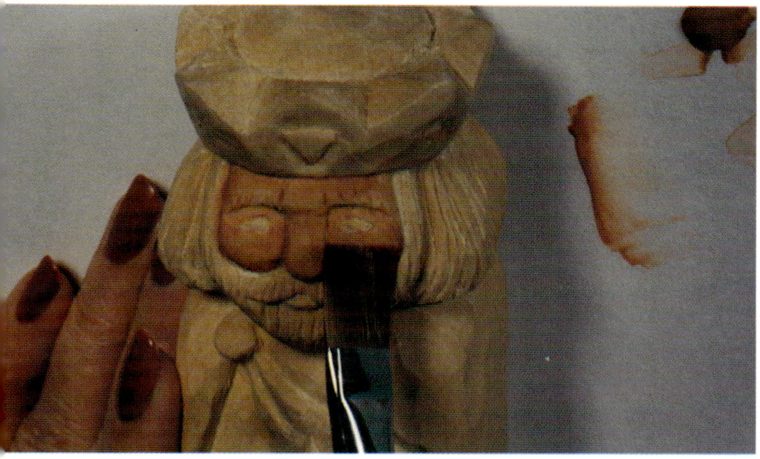

Now you need to side load and shade. Rinse the brush leaving it fairly wet, dip the corner in the shade color, make several strokes on the pallet paper so that the color starts to bleed and fade into the rest of the brush. The corner should still have plenty of color. With one stroke around the face and sides of the nose, the process should be complete.

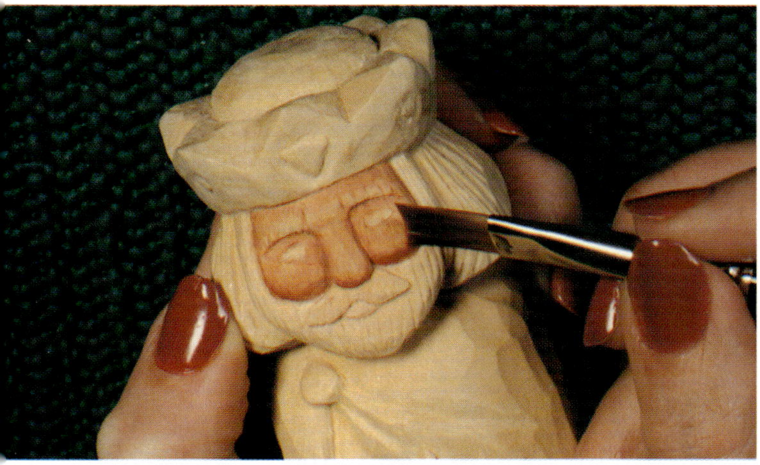

Again side load with the blush color and just go beneath the cheeks and nose, bringing the color up slightly.

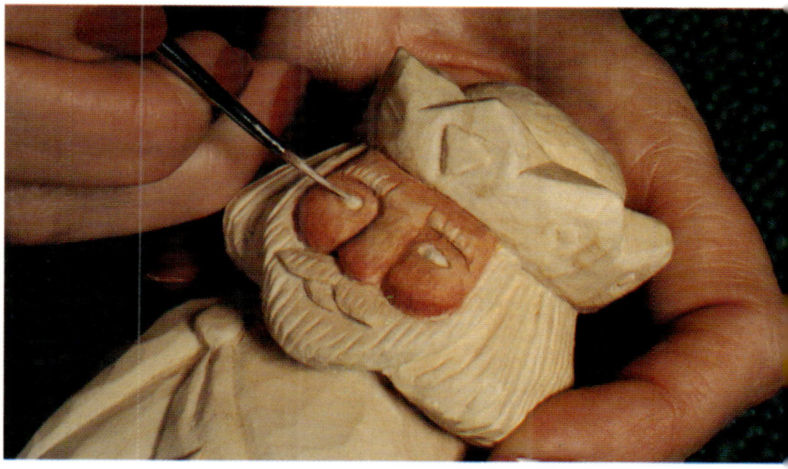

With your liner brush, base the light color in the eye area.

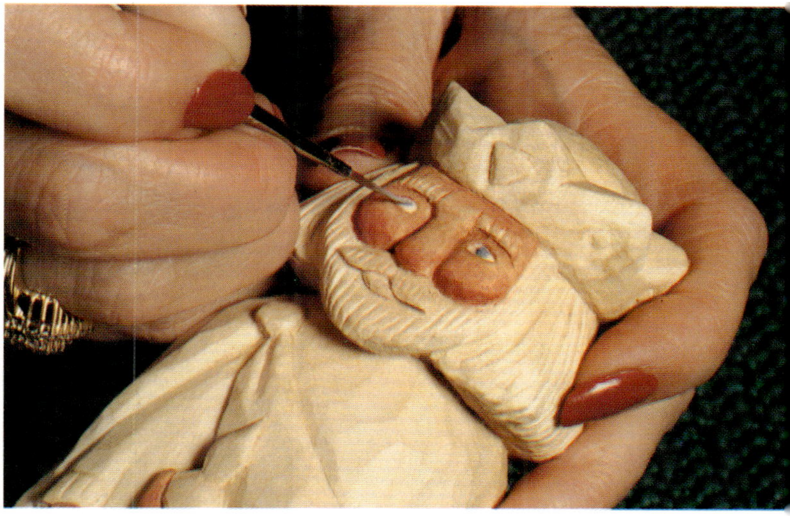

Place a dot of the eye color in the center making sure to touch the top and bottom of the lids to "anchor" the iris. If you don't do this, your little guy will look either angry or very scared.

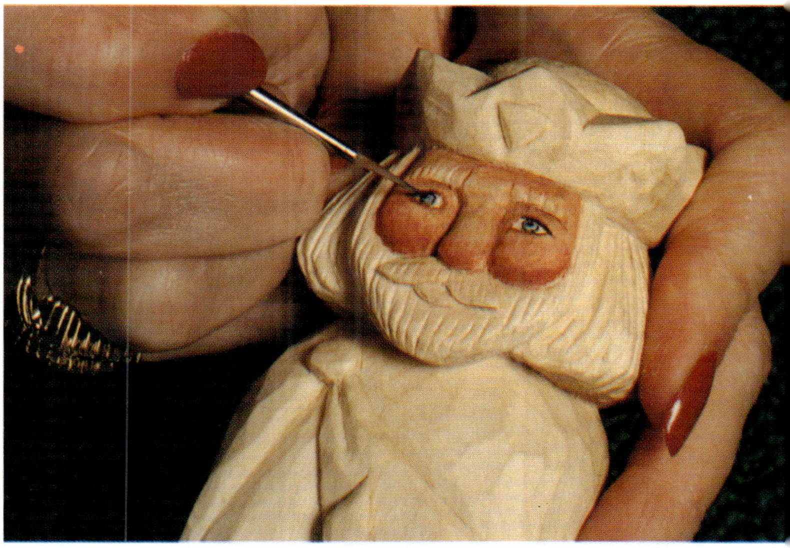

With the darkest color, add a pupil and lines.

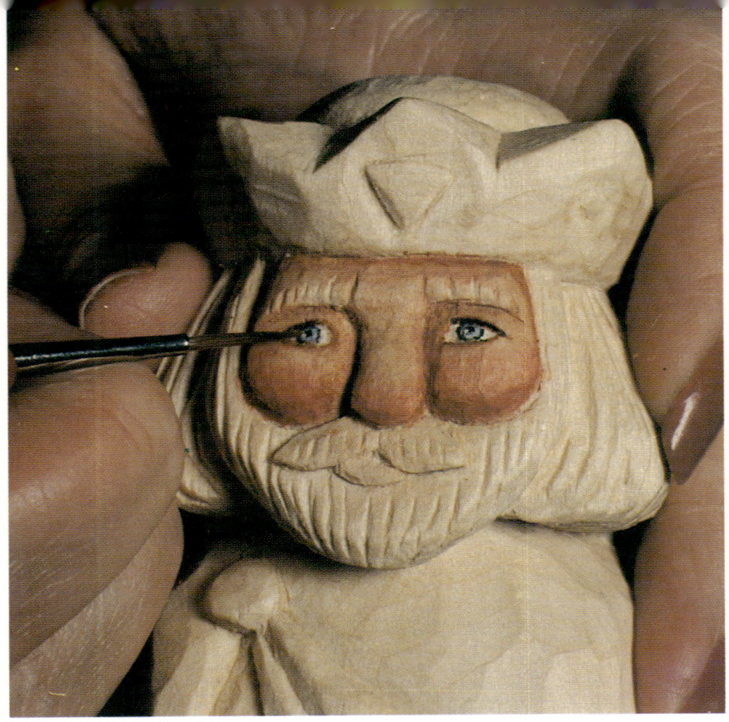

With the light color, add a highlight on the iris.

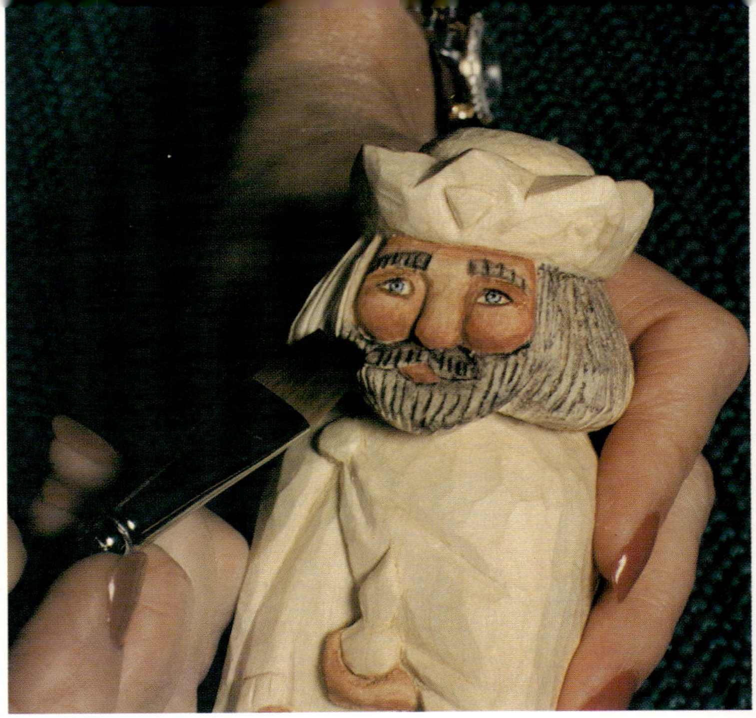

Use your 1/2″ brush for the beard and hair. If the color is too deep, rub with a damp cloth. Keep it soft.

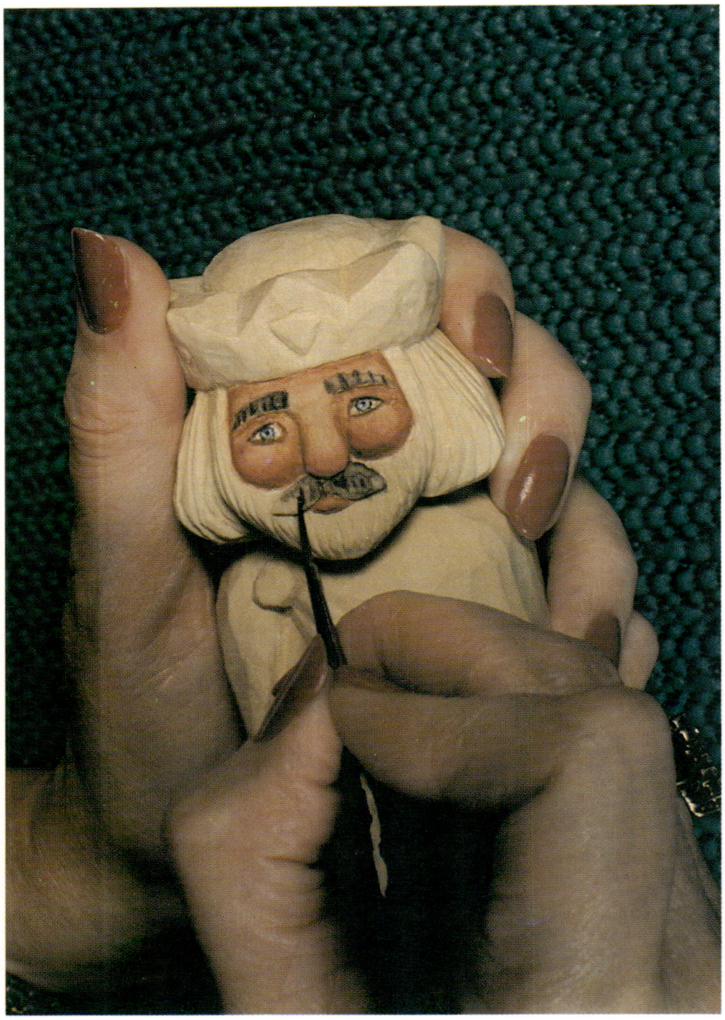

Continue with your liner brush, making sure the color is diluted enough, paint the brows and the mustache.

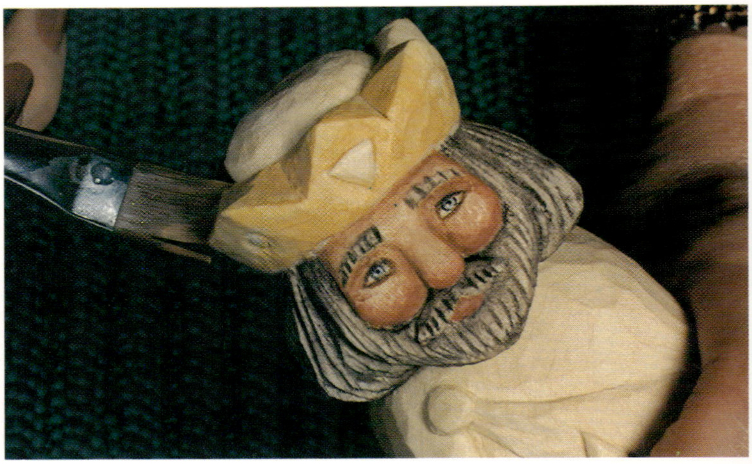

Paint the crown, button and trim.

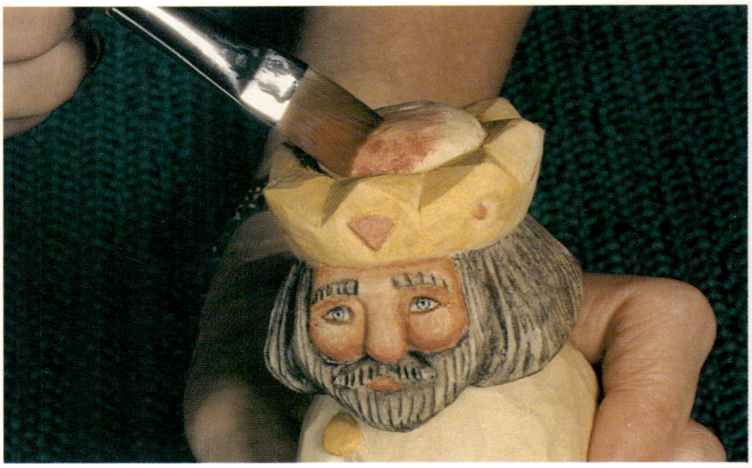

Paint the top of his crown and ornaments with the red.

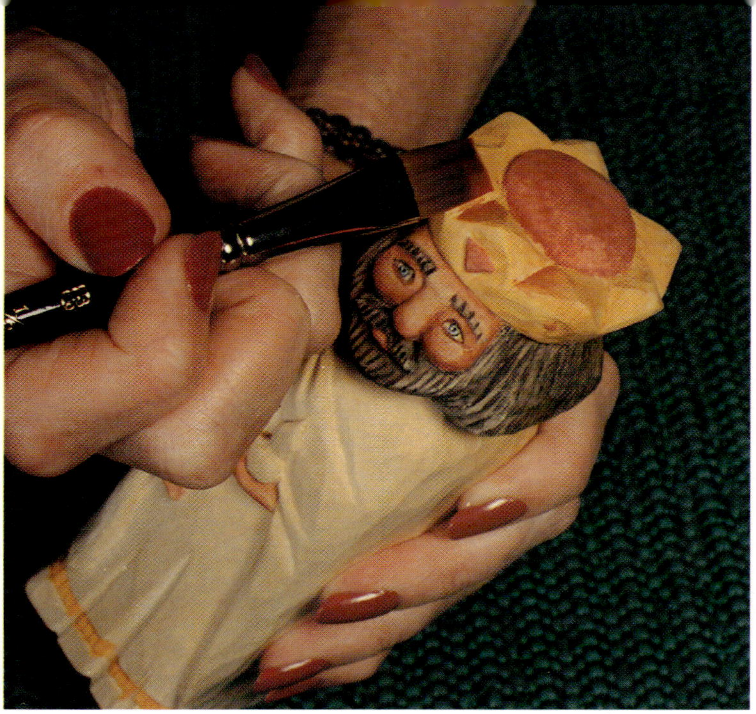

Side-load your brush and shade his crown with the same color.

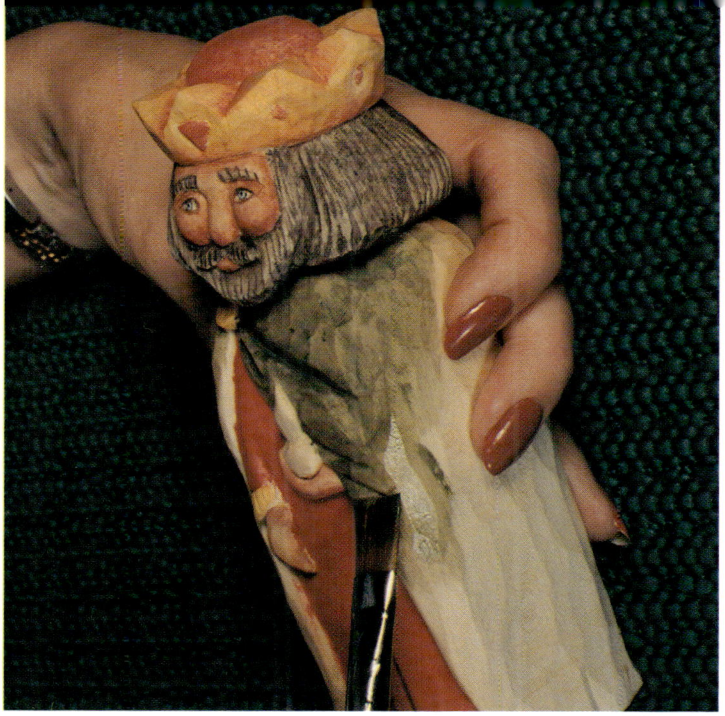

The green is next. Be sure to slowly build the color, so it is not too dark or solid.

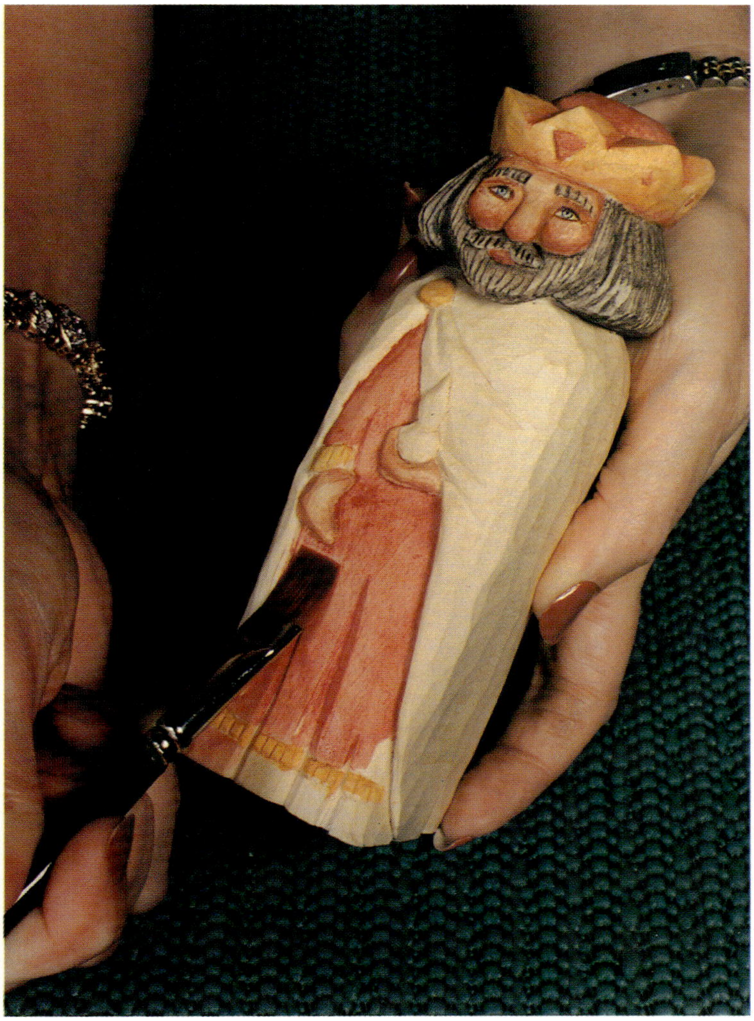

Continue with the red to paint his gown.

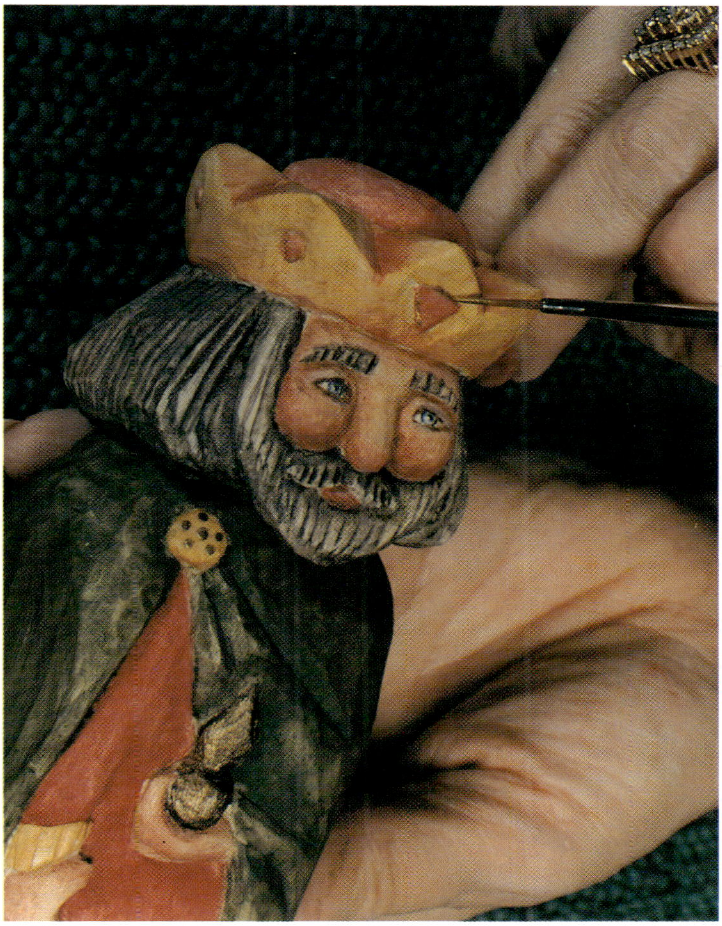

Finally, add gold to his bottle, button and crown ornaments. Next, rub just a little gold paint and water between your fingers, then rub it on the crown peaks. The bottle is shaded with brown. Three coats of matte finish spray and you are done!

THE GALLERY

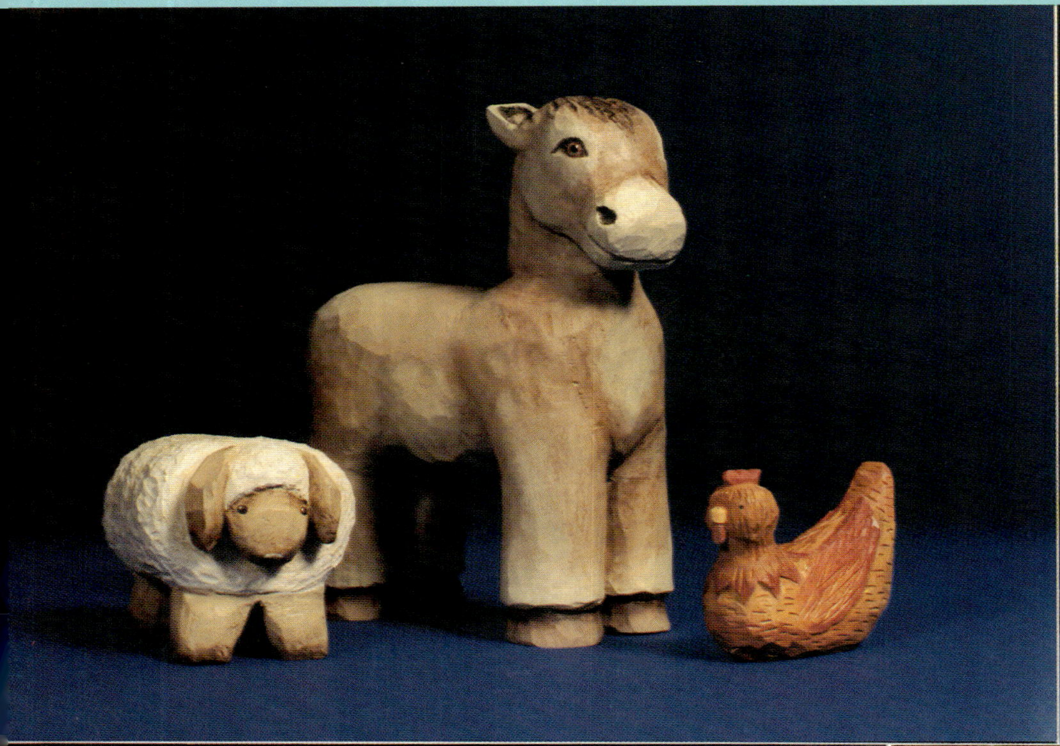

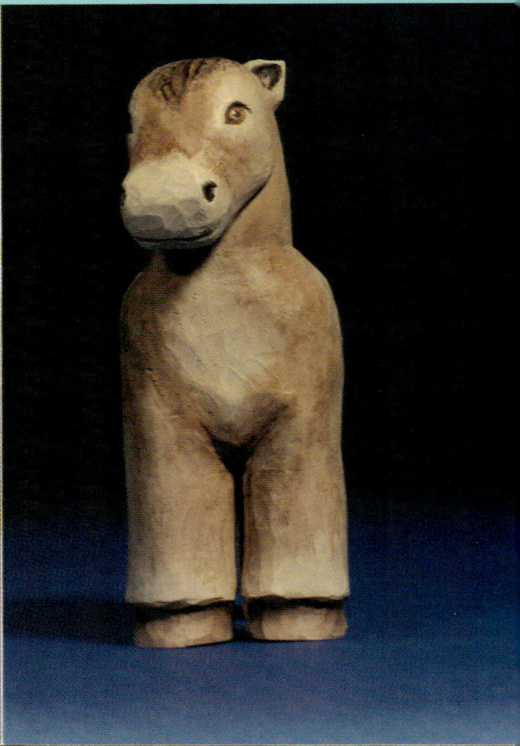

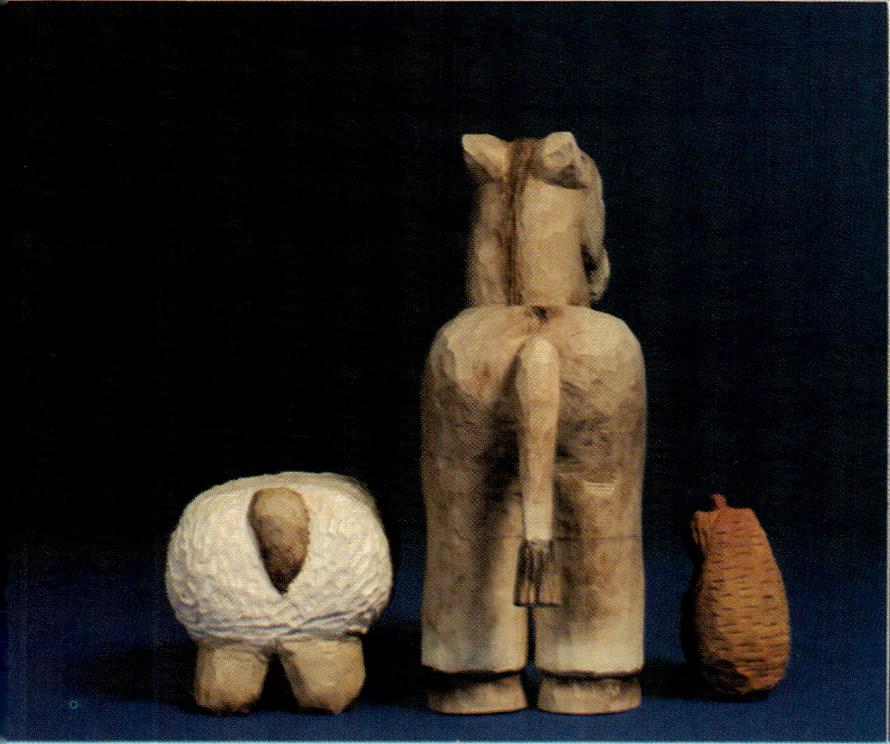

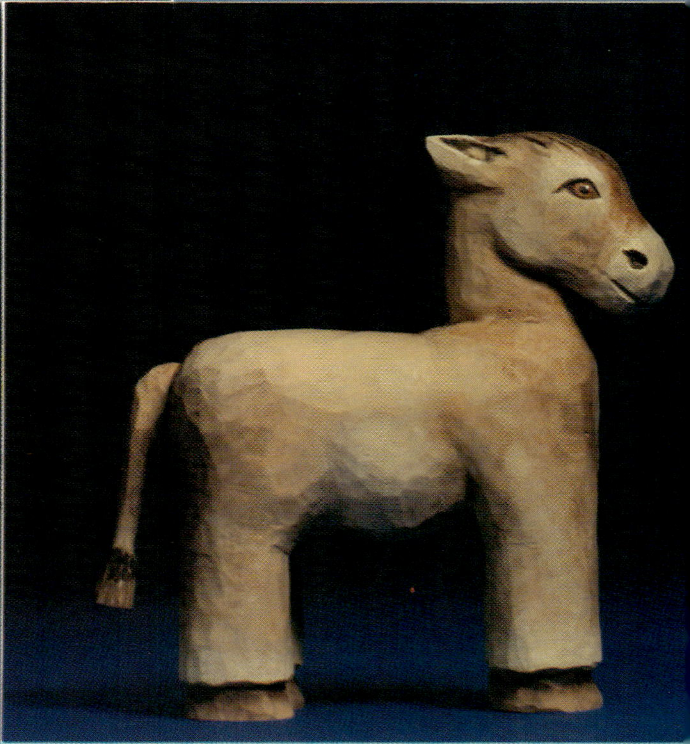

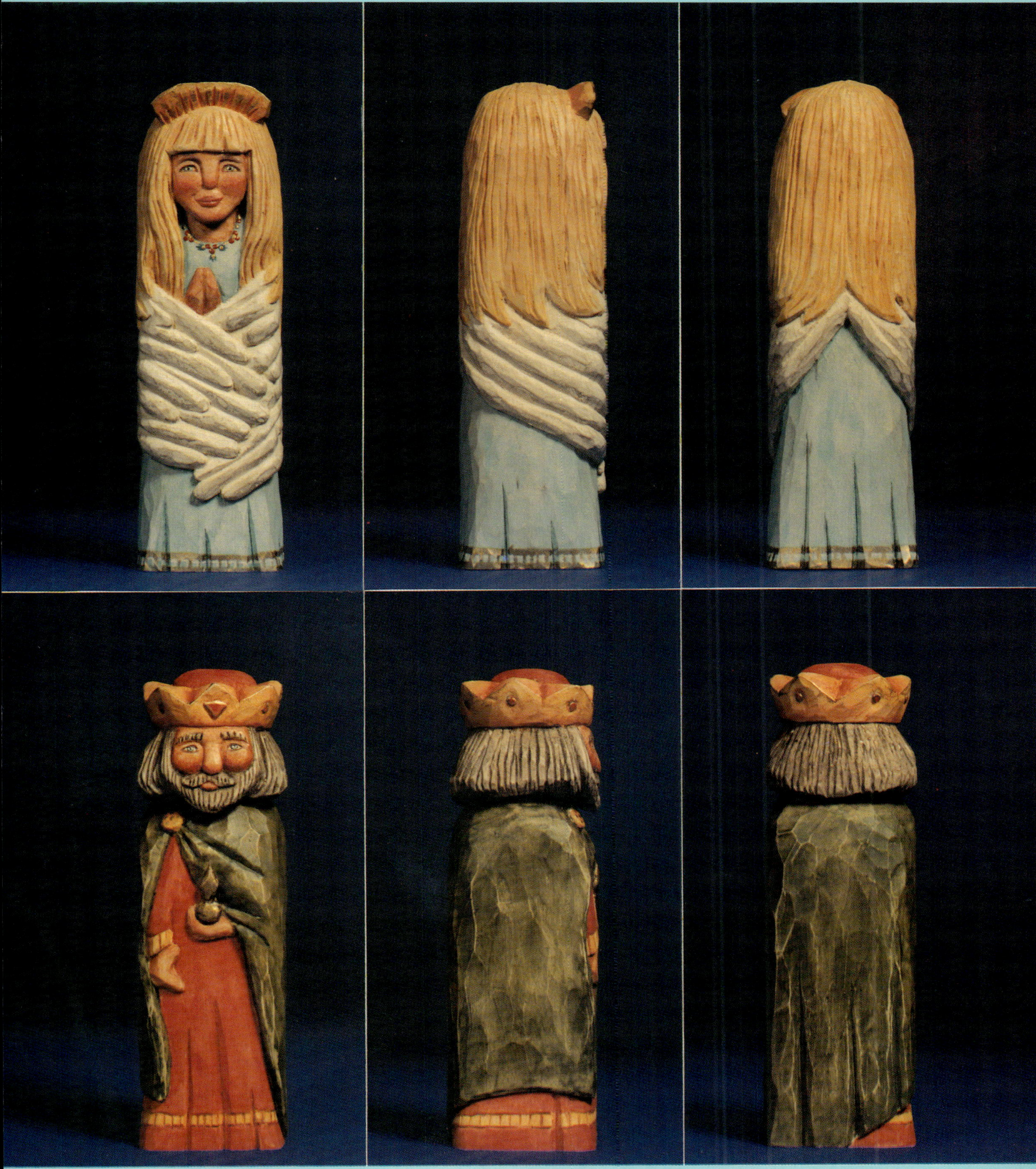

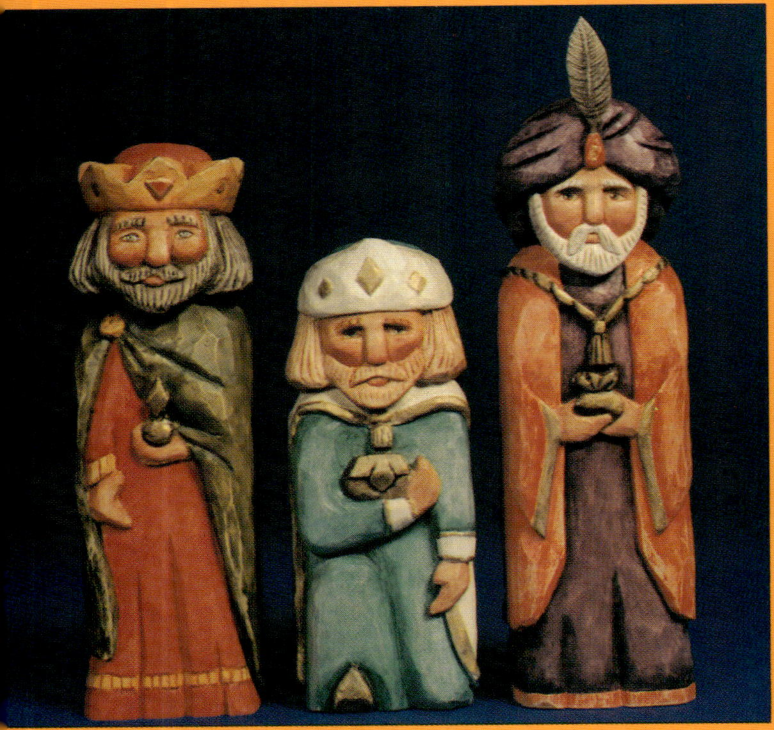

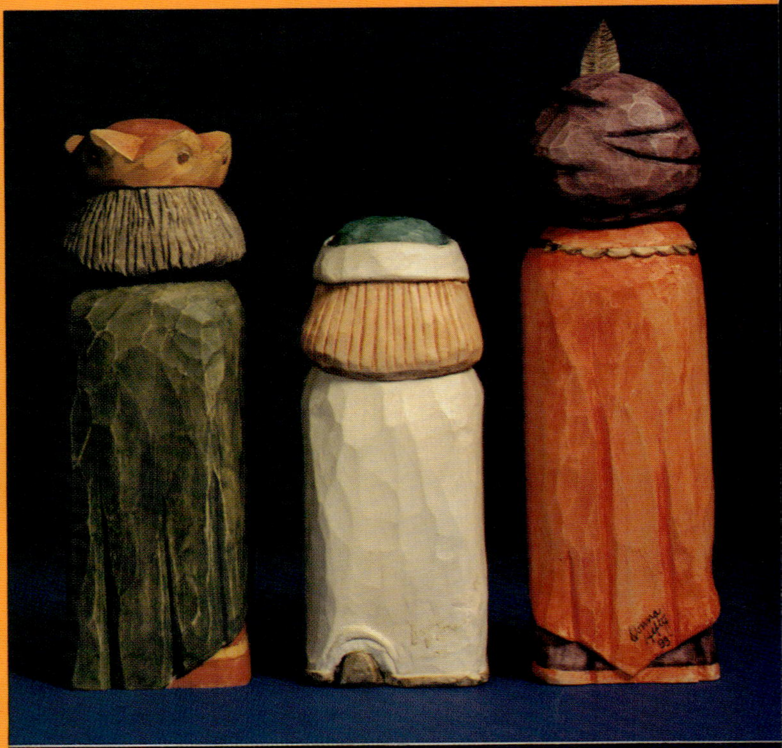

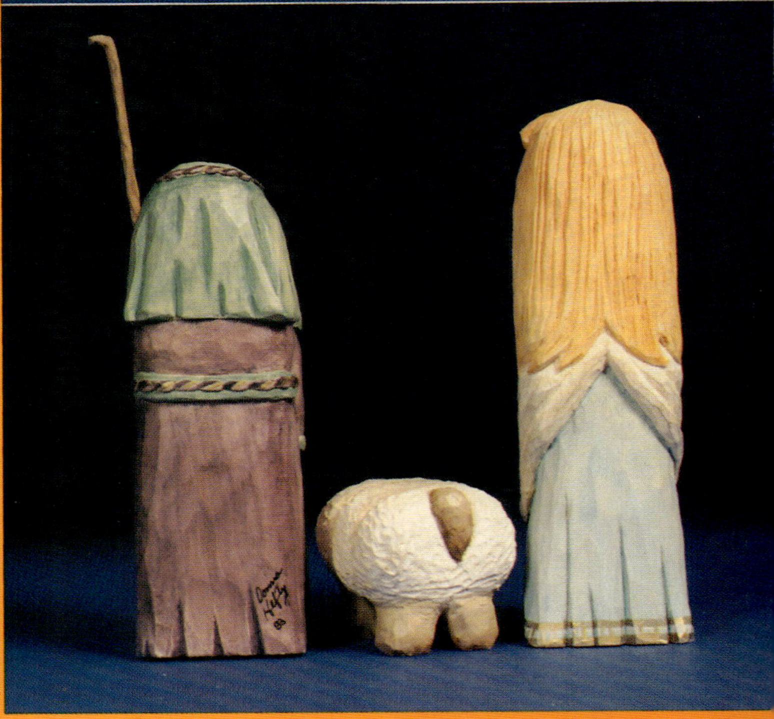

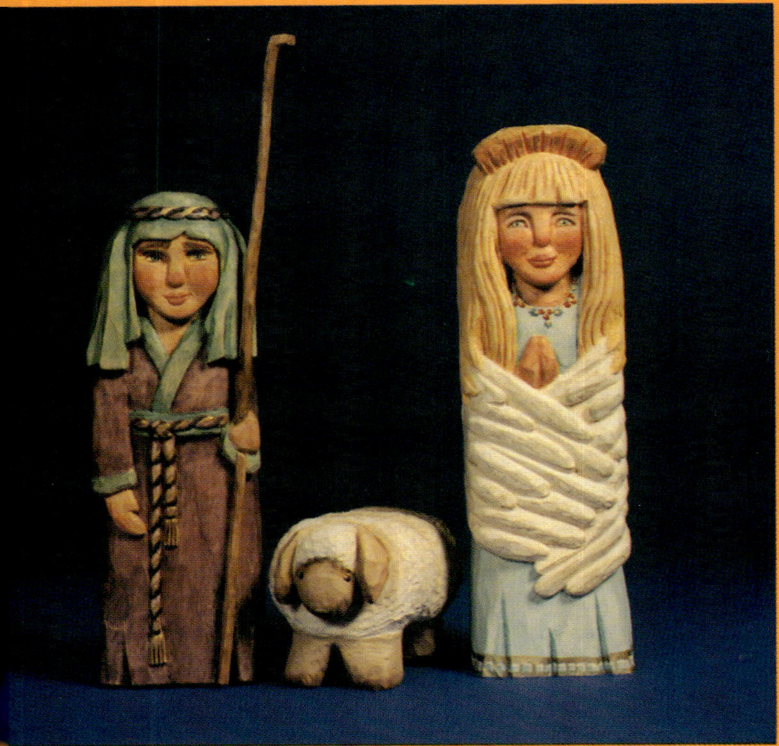

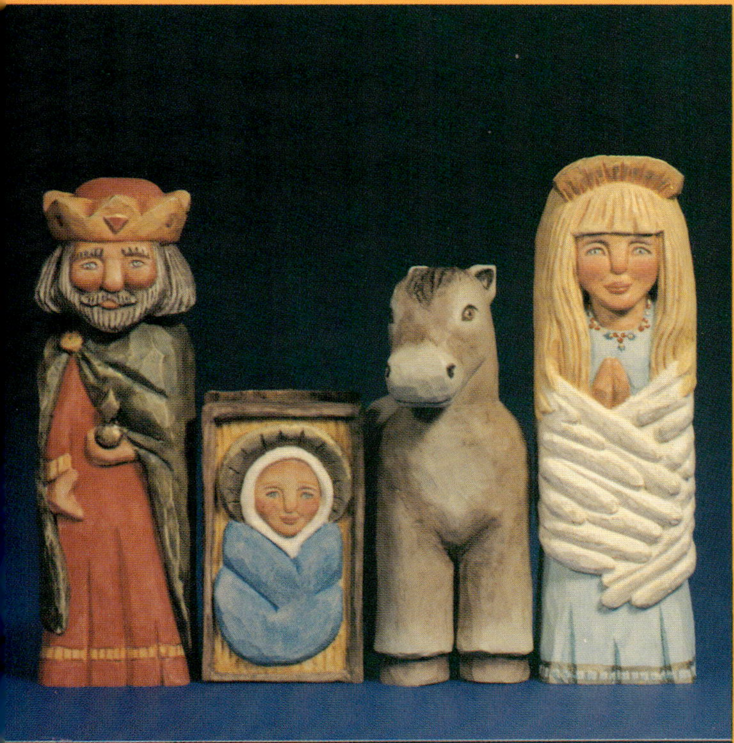
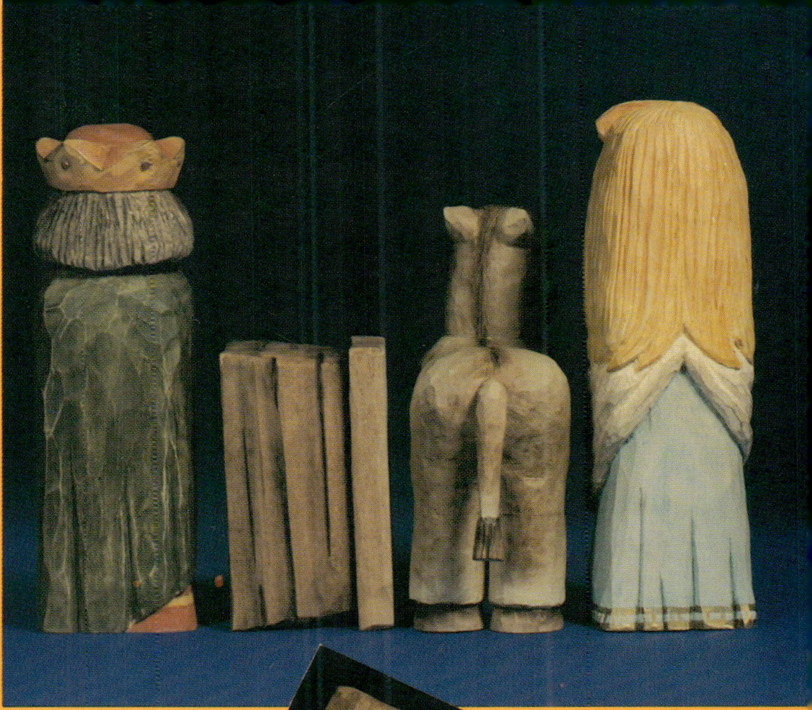
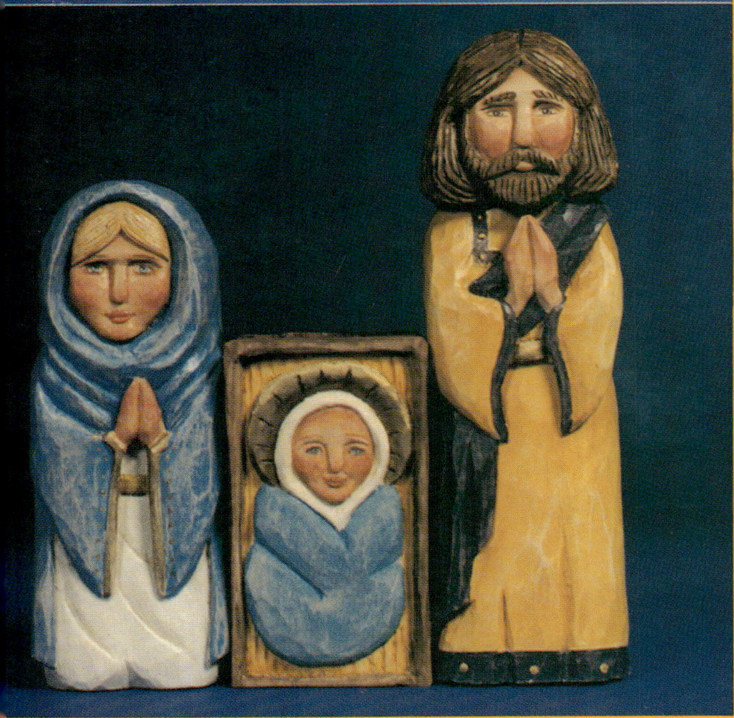
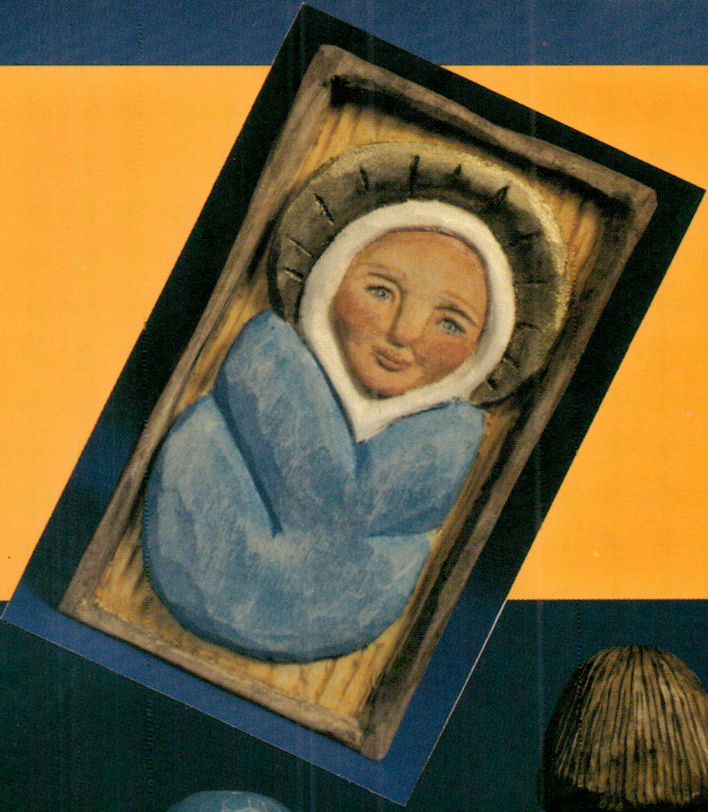
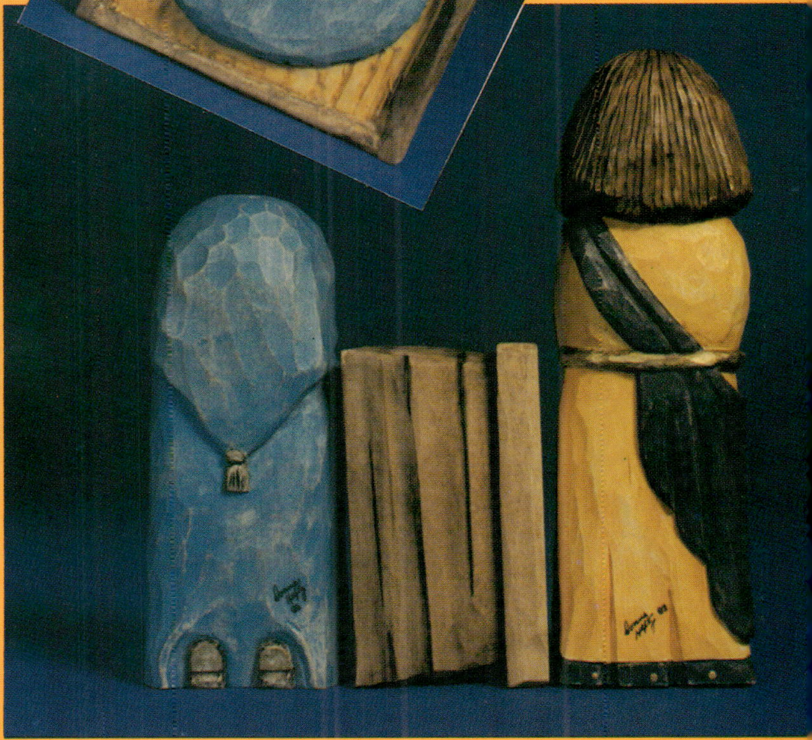

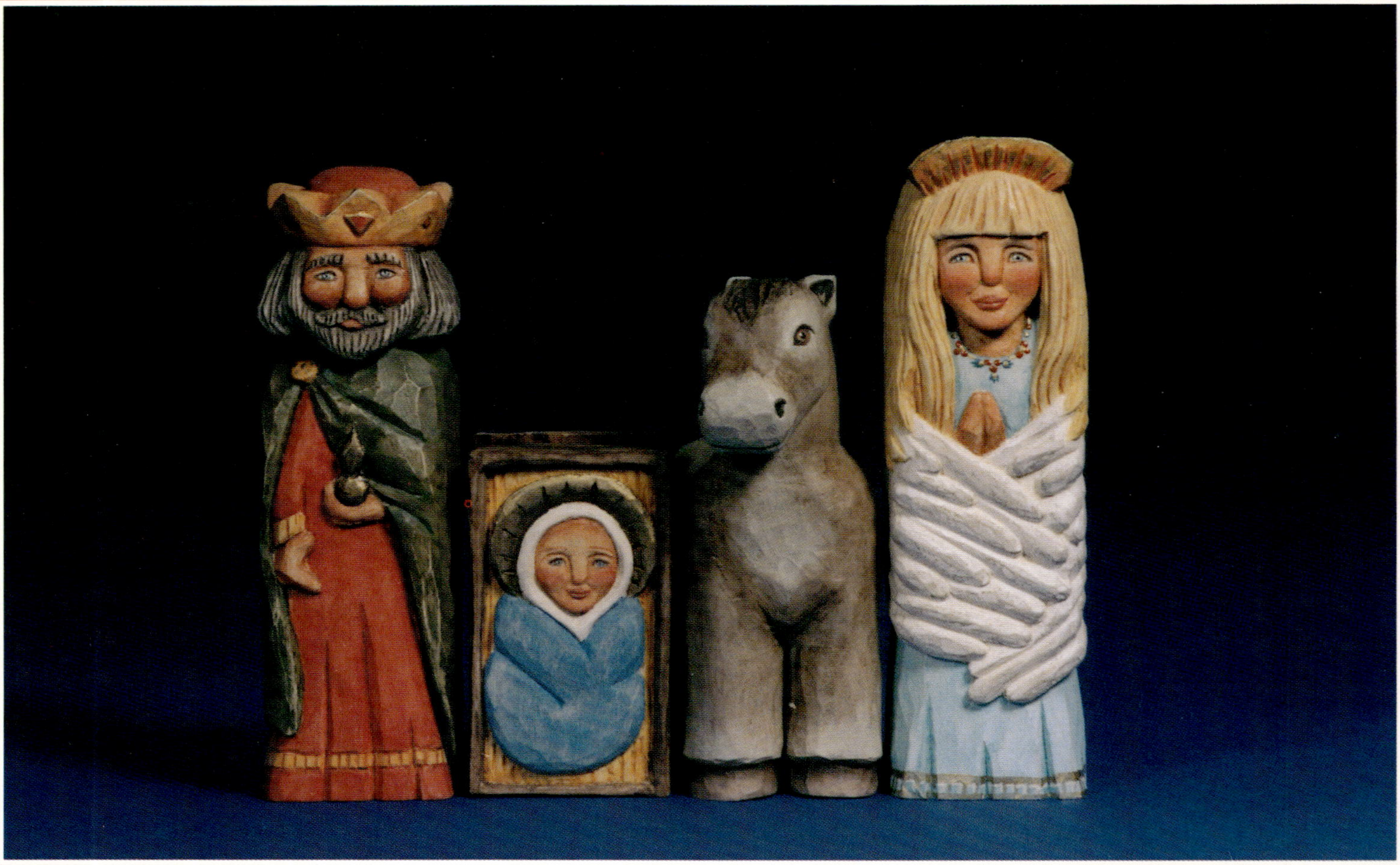

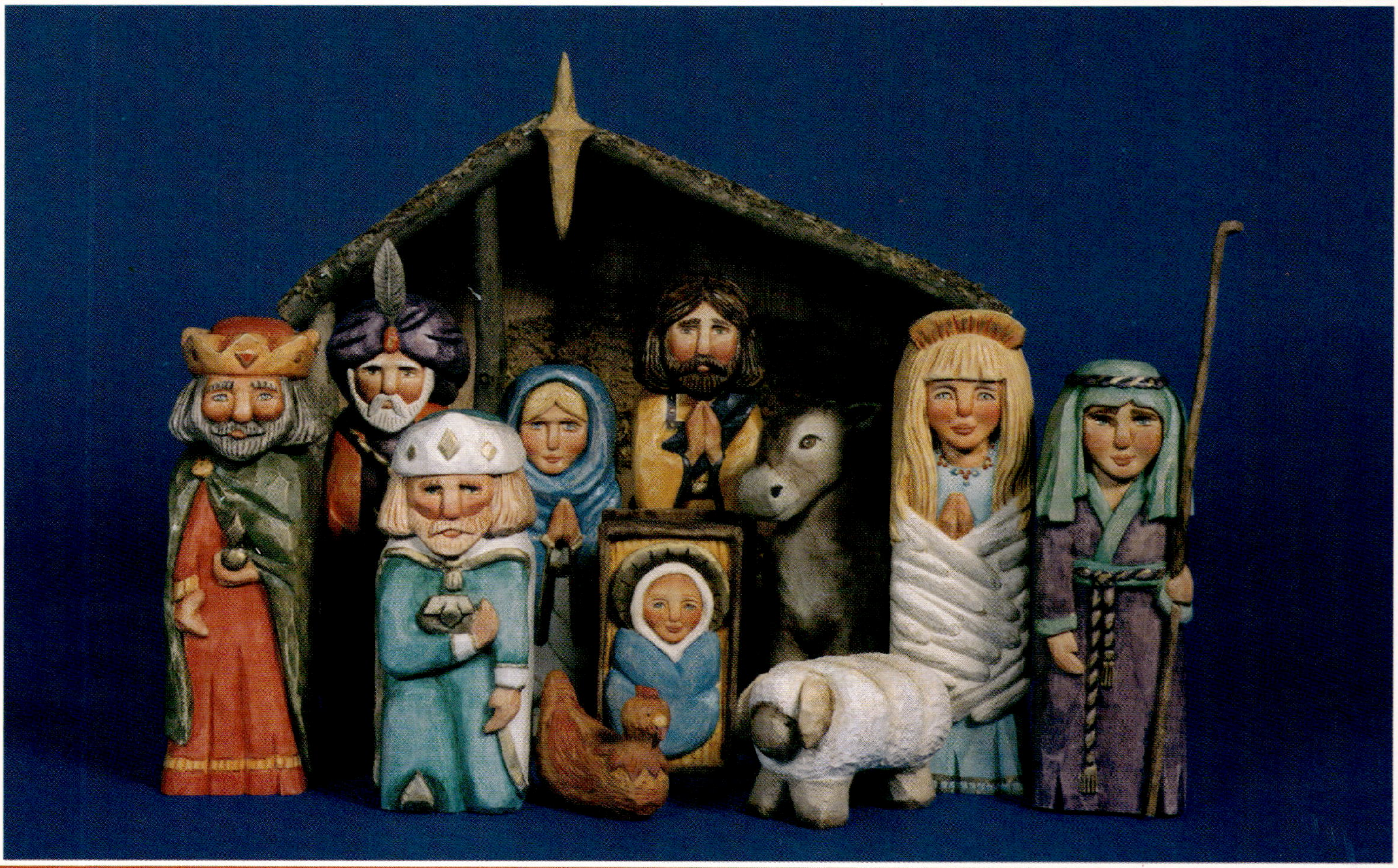

PATTERNS

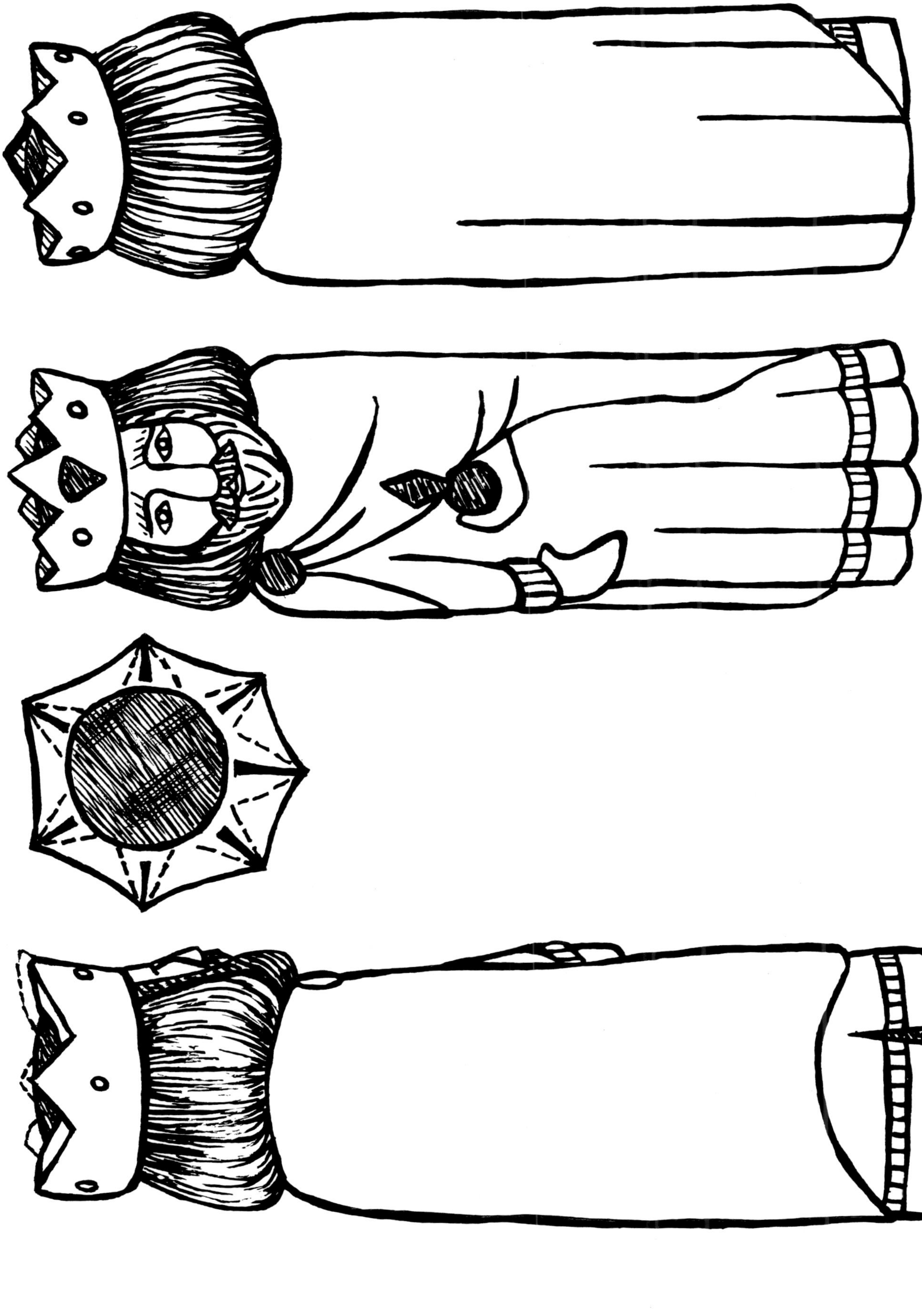

King I

King II

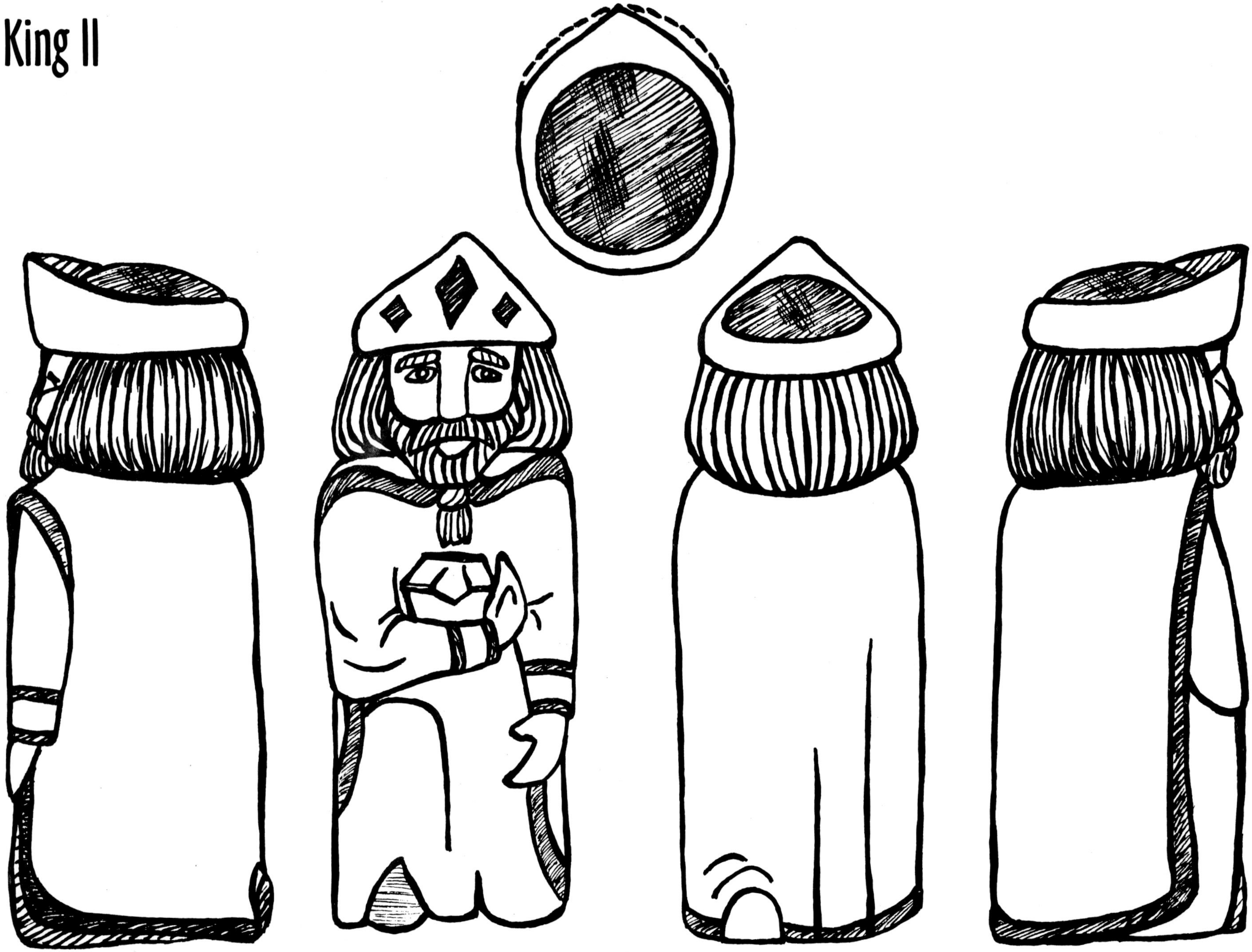

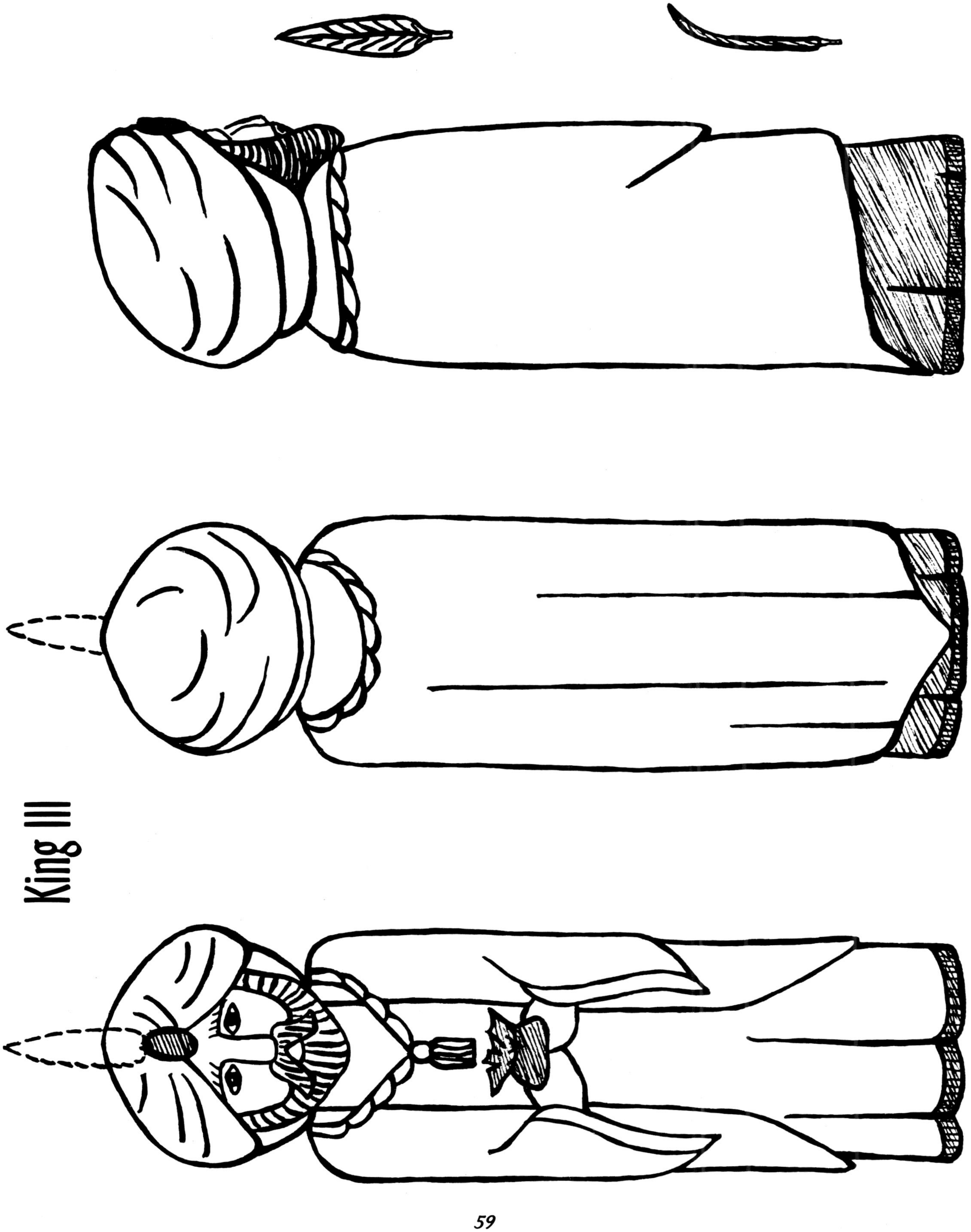

King III

Mary and Jesus

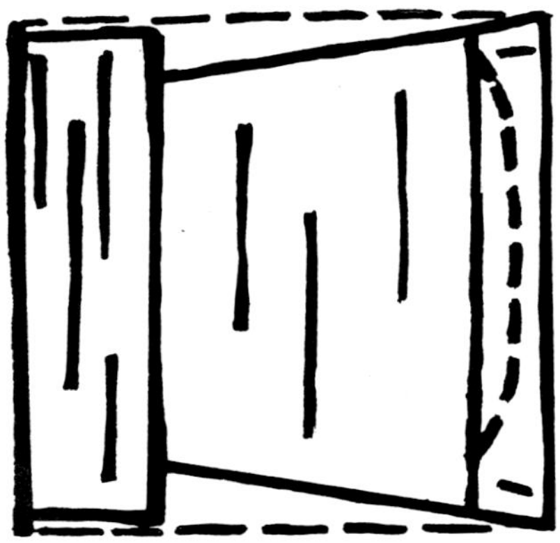

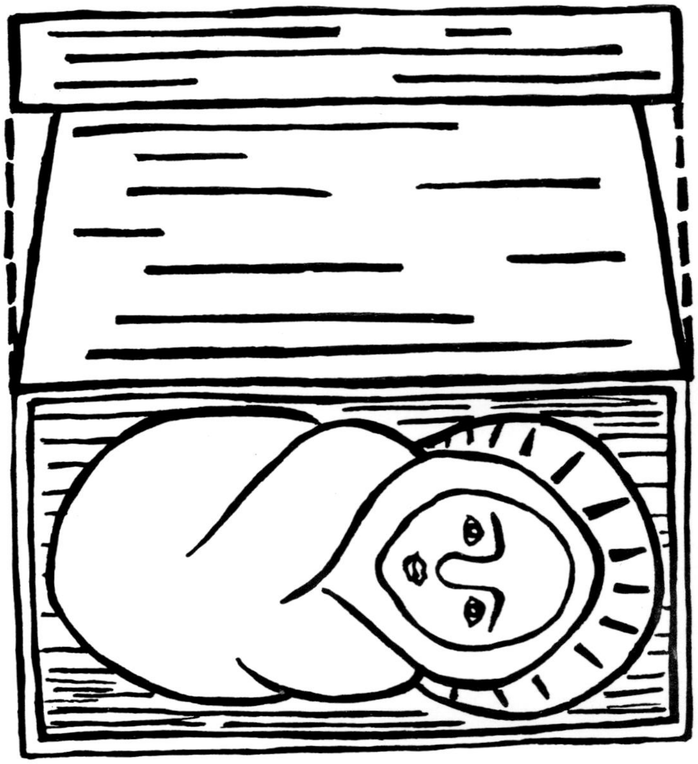

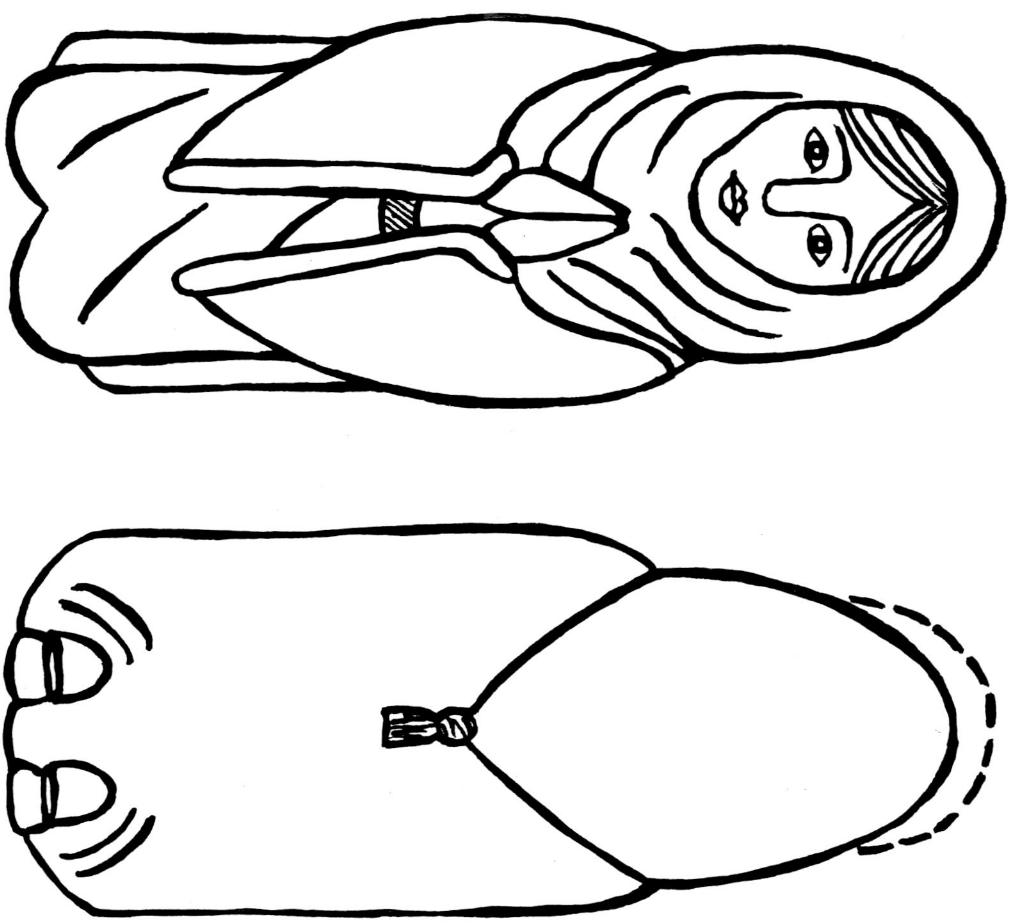

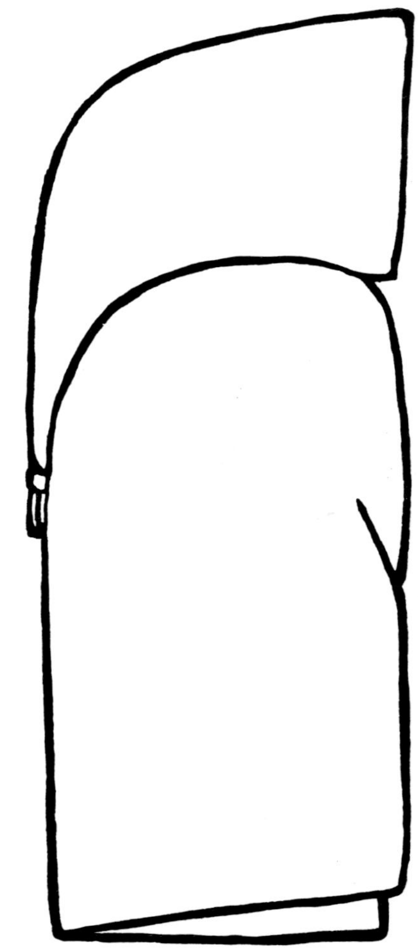

Joseph

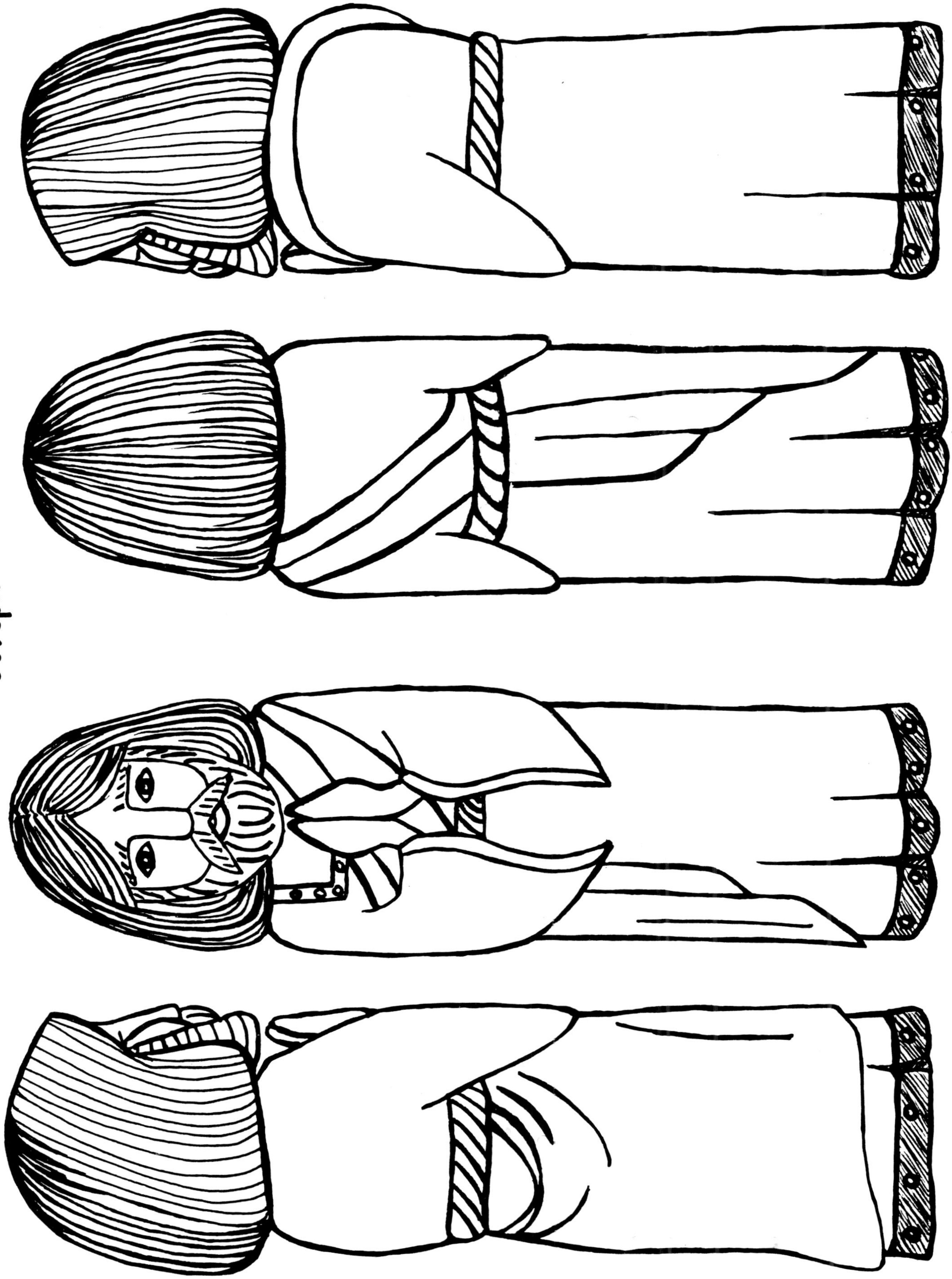

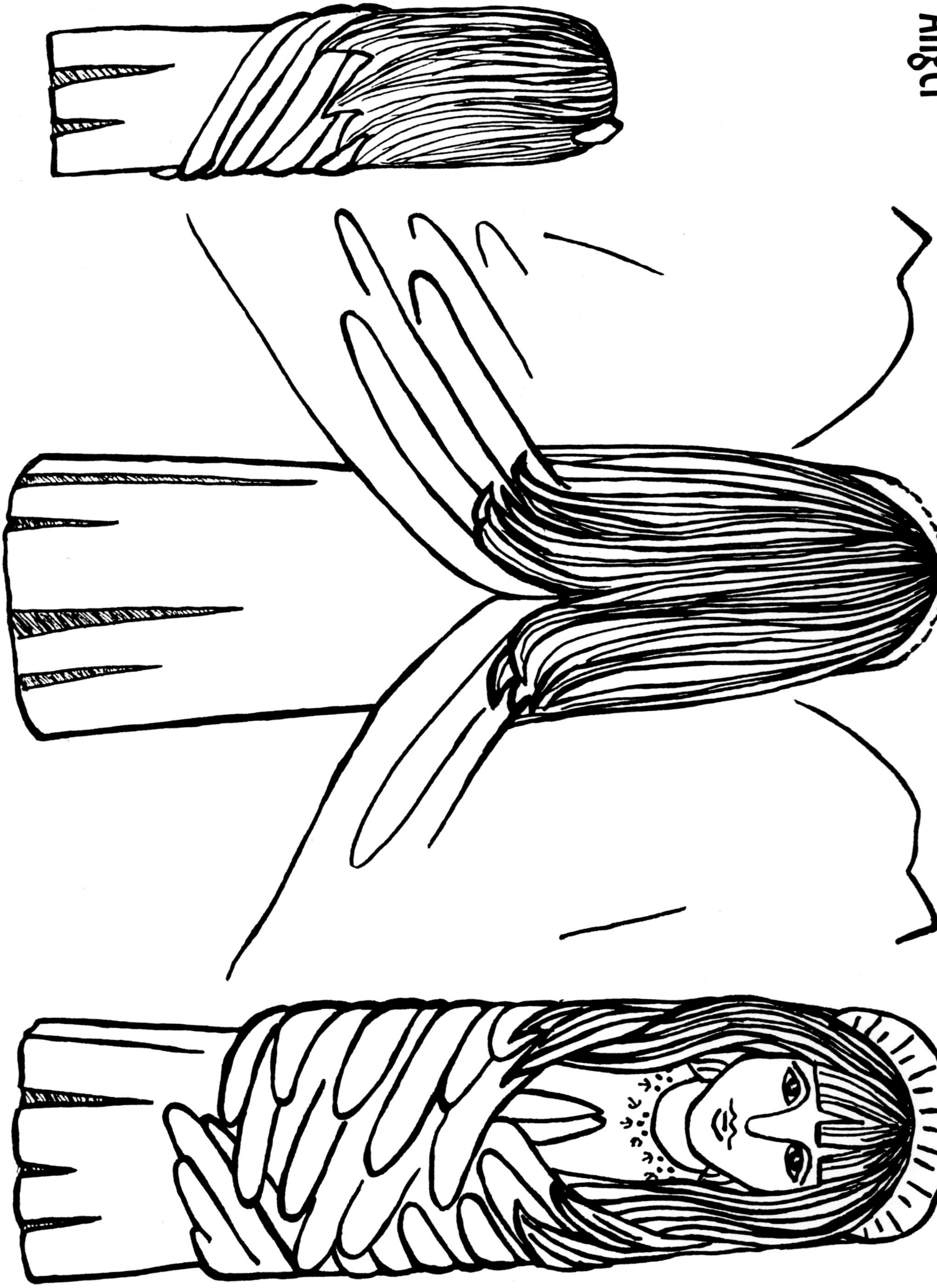

Angel

Shepherd

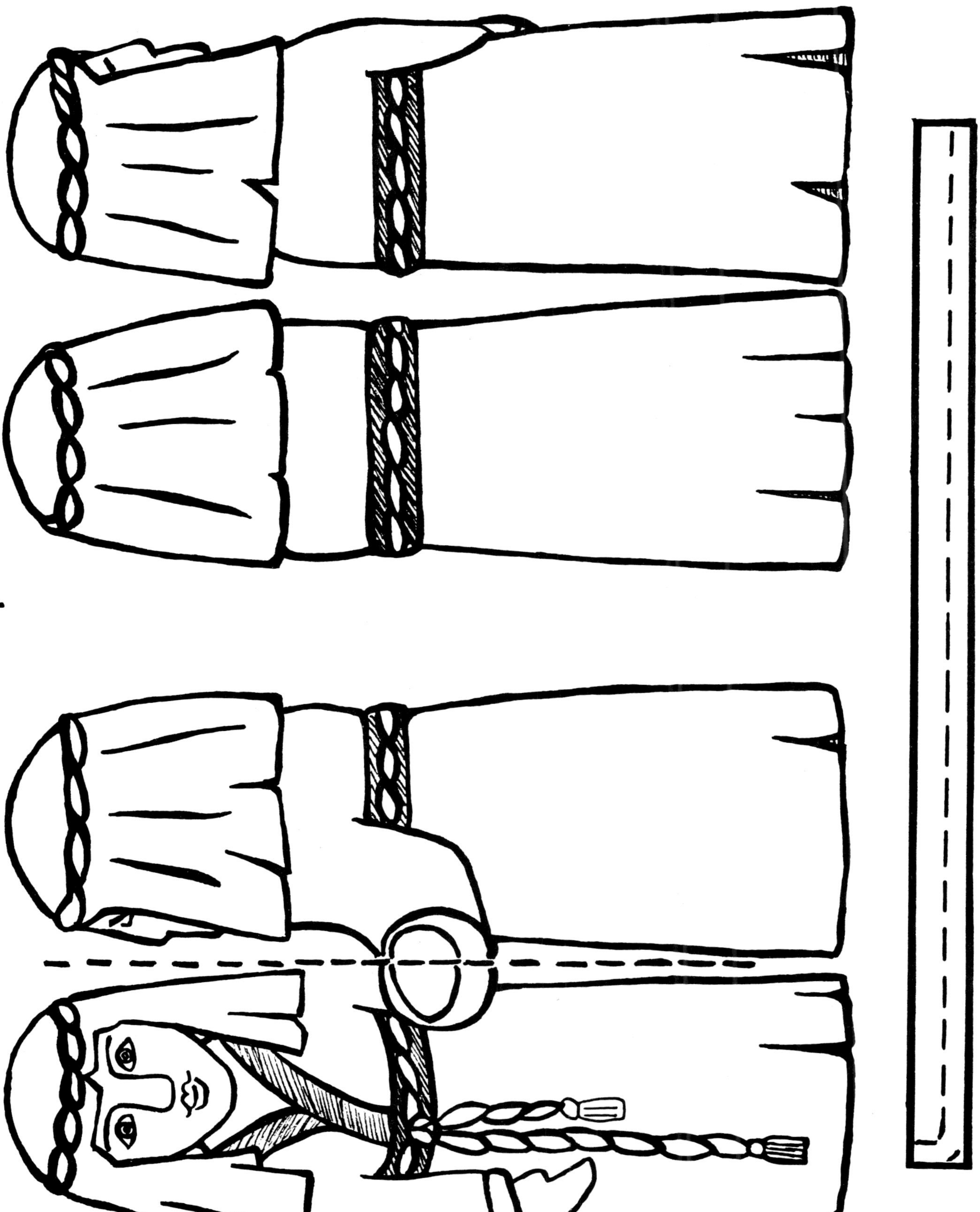

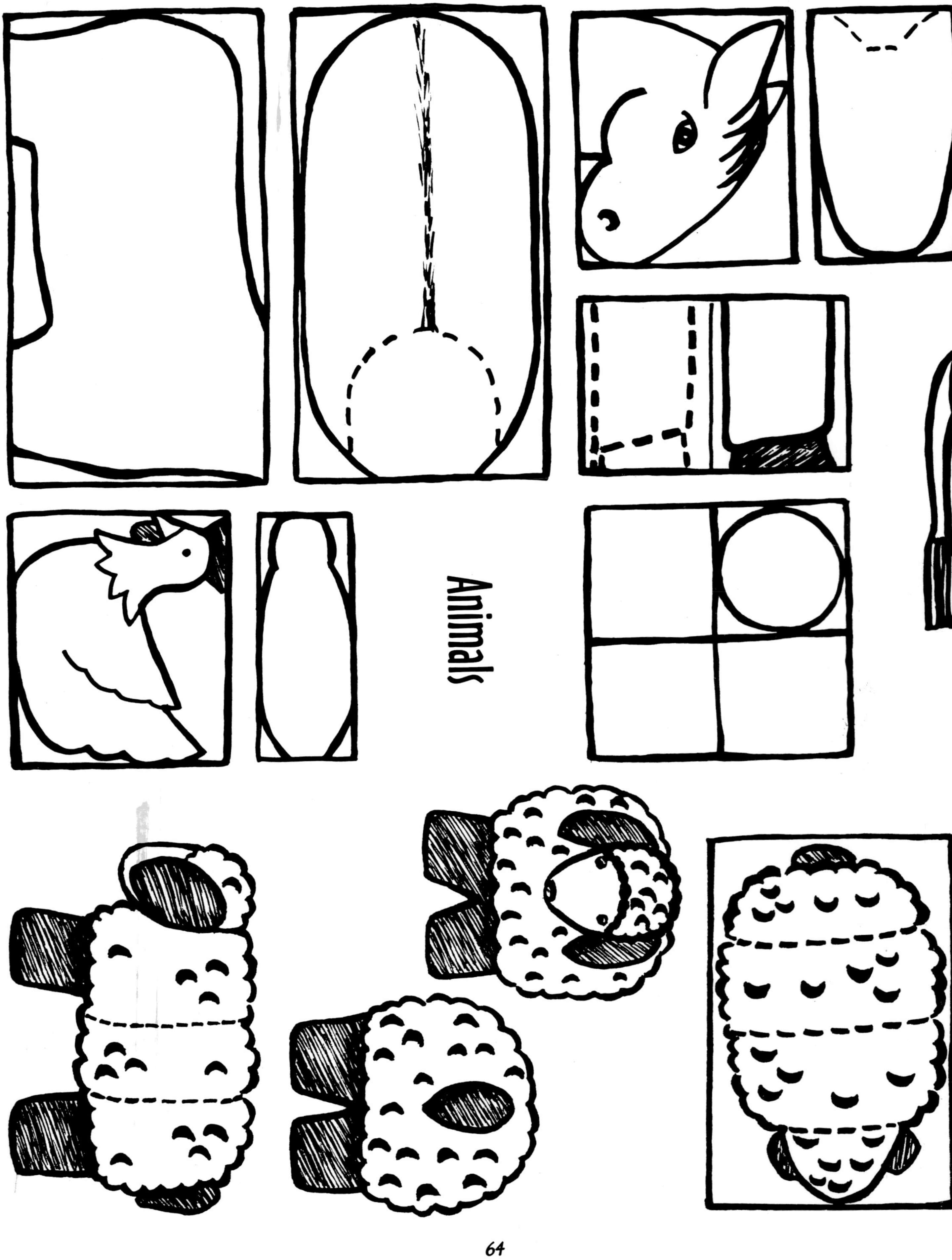
Animals